THERE IS NO ETHAN

THERE IS NO ETHAN

HOW THREE WOMEN CAUGHT AMERICA'S BIGGEST CATFISH

ANNA AKBARI

GRAND
CENTRAL

New York   Boston

Copyright © 2024 by Anna Akbari

Cover design by Caitlin Sacks. Cover photo of face by /Mia Takahara/Plainpicture. Cover photos by Shutterstock. Cover copyright © 2024 by Hachette Book Group, Inc.

Grand Central Publishing
Hachette Book Group
1290 Avenue of the Americas, New York, NY 10104
grandcentralpublishing.com
@grandcentralpub

First Edition: June 2024

Grand Central Publishing is a division of Hachette Book Group, Inc. The Grand Central Publishing name and logo is a registered trademark of Hachette Book Group, Inc.

The publisher is not responsible for websites (or their content) that are not owned by the publisher.

The Hachette Speakers Bureau provides a wide range of authors for speaking events. To find out more, go to hachettespeakersbureau.com or email HachetteSpeakers@hbgusa.com.

Grand Central Publishing books may be purchased in bulk for business, educational, or promotional use. For information, please contact your local bookseller or the Hachette Book Group Special Markets Department at special.markets@hbgusa.com.

Print book interior design by Taylor Navis

Library of Congress Cataloging-in-Publication Data

Names: Akbari, Anna, author.
Title: There is no Ethan : how three women caught America's biggest catfish / Anna Akbari.
Description: New York : Grand Central Publishing, 2024.
Identifiers: LCCN 2023057414 | ISBN 9781538742198 (hardcover) | ISBN 9781538742211 (ebook)
Subjects: LCSH: Swindlers and swindling--United States. | Online dating--United States. |
    Online manipulation--United States. | Akbari, Anna. | Fraud victims--United States--Biography.
Classification: LCC HV6697 .A63 2024 | DDC 306.730285--dc23/eng/20240312
LC record available at https://lccn.loc.gov/2023057414

ISBNs: 9781538742198 (hardcover), 9781538742211 (ebook)

Printed in Canada

MRQ

Printing 1, 2024

For Anna and Gina. Finally.

THERE IS NO ETHAN

THE FINAL DAYS OF ETHAN SCHUMAN

Phone call
December 28, 2010

Anna: *Hey Matt—You seem to know everyone, so I'm wondering if you've ever heard of a guy named Ethan Schuman? He also went to Stuyvesant and Columbia and would've overlapped with your years. I'm emailing you some photos.*
Matt: *I don't know the name, and he doesn't look familiar.*
Anna: *Hmmm...OK, thanks.*

*   *   *

Facebook
March 3, 2011, 3:17 p.m. EST

To: Matt
Gina Dallago wants to send you a message

Hi Matt,

I came across your profile on the Stuy 1993 Reunion page. I was hoping you could take one second to help me out with something.

I met someone online who claimed to be named Ethan Schuman. He said he was 35 years old, from NY, went to Stuy, then Columbia. After a couple weeks, I realized he was playing me, and I couldn't believe much of anything he told me. He admitted that he had given me a false name, but said everything else was true. I'm trying to figure out who he is so I can know with whom I was corresponding and to whom I told private information.

So in the chance that this guy really is a Stuy/Columbia grad, can you identify him based on this photo?

Thanks so much in advance!

Best,
Gina

* * *

Email
March 4, 2011, 4:20 p.m. EST

From: Anna Akbari
To: Gina Dallago

Hi Gina,

I'm a friend of Matt's. Funnily enough, I came to him with the same question you did about "Ethan Schuman." I'd love to talk to you about this. Please email or call me.

Best,
Anna

* * *

Email
March 4, 2011, 5:52 p.m. EST

From: Gina Dallago
To: Anna Akbari

Hi Anna,

Wow, how very, very strange to hear from you, but I'm so glad you contacted me. I've had a confusing week dealing with so-called Ethan. I bet we can help each other shed some light on what was probably a frustrating experience for both of us.

I'm going to give you a call when I leave the office.

Sincerely,
Gina

*   *   *

Email
March 4, 2011, 10:24 p.m. EST

From: Anna Akbari
To: Gina Dallago

So great speaking with you earlier! "Ethan" is not exactly deny-ing that he lied about his name, but I think those are real photos of him. He does however "want to meet up this month." I told him to forgive me if i highly doubt that he will actually materialize.

I'm going to contact the woman he said was his ex-girlfriend— the other "Anna"—and see if she can answer any questions.

Tonight I went on a date with a real live human and we ate real food and drank real wine!! Good, real people do exist!

Going to continue to keep you posted, of course—but also want to say that I would love to meet you in person if you ever find yourself in NYC! We have an eternal bond!

*   *   *

Email
March 4, 2011, 11:03 p.m. EST

From: Gina Dallago
To: Anna Akbari

oh I would love to meet! I'm in ny all the time; maybe if you and ethan got along so well, and Ethan and I got along so well, we will, too!

let's hear it for real men, real experiences, and real love!

I need time to stew this over. do you really think he would meet? I don't know what to believe still.

*   *   *

Email
March 4, 2011, 11:10 p.m. EST

From: Anna Akbari
To: Gina Dallago

I don't think he will. But if I threaten to make the photos and email address very public, he may concede.

You are like my sister now—it's great to have another woman who was equally affected and understands! As a sociologist, this is beyond fascinating to me...

*   *   *

Facebook
March 5, 2011, 2:47 a.m. EST

To: Anna Akbari
Anna B. wants to send you a message
Subject: hello

hi anna

you sent me a friend request—i'm curious as to what it's about; did you want to get in touch with me? is it to do with somebody we both know?

best,
anna

*   *   *

Facebook
March 5, 2011, 2:47 a.m. EST

From: Anna Akbari
To: Anna B.

Hi Anna,

Thanks for responding. Yes, it is to do with someone we both know. You need not accept the friend request—I just wanted to find a way to reach you. I think you're in England, so Skype is probably best. I'd love to talk to you sometime this weekend, if you're open to it.

Kind regards,
Anna

*   *   *

Email
March 5, 2011, 3:01 a.m. EST

From: Gina Dallago
To: Anna Akbari

strange! almost like she expected it? like it's happened before?

did you see that part of my email correspondence with Ethan where I mentioned her by first and last name? he seemed very unfazed.

maybe he has warned her? do keep me posted!

*   *   *

Email
March 5, 2011, 3:08 a.m. EST

From: Anna Akbari
To: Gina Dallago

Agreed, definitely seems like she was not at all surprised by the correspondence.

The only question is: did she actually meet him or was she another victim?? Impossible to predict. I look forward to connecting with her...

I replied to his texts and emails tonight. I told him to come clean if he is truly sorry. If he does not disclose the truth by tomorrow, I will tell him he has 24 hours, after which time I will forward his photos, email address, and identifying details to media outlets. Much of what he told us is true, I'm certain. we ARE making progress!

*   *   *

Email
March 5, 2011, 3:14 a.m. EST

> **From: Anna B.**
> **To: Anna Akbari**
>
> how on earth did you find me on facebook—i don't think i come up in searches! i'm impressed!

*   *   *

Email
March 5, 2011, 3:15 a.m. EST

> **From: Anna Akbari**
> **To: Anna B.**
>
> i did some stealth searching that impressed even myself!! I'll explain shortly...

*   *   *

Email
March 5, 2011, 3:16 a.m. EST

> **From: Anna Akbari**
> **To: Gina Dallago**
>
> sending Skype request now—we can all connect on a call...!

*   *   *

Email
March 5, 2011, 3:17 a.m. EST

> **From Gina Dallago**
> **To: Anna Akbari**
>
> Omg!

*   *   *

Skype
March 5, 2011, 3:20 a.m. EST

> **Participants: Anna Akbari, Gina Dallago, Anna B.**

In the middle of the night, across three cities and two continents, Gina, Anna, and I talked at length on Skype. From my tiny railroad apartment in an old tenement in Hell's Kitchen, I'd navigated the whirlwind that was Ethan Schuman alone for more than two months. He was an emotional wrecking ball, occupying my mind and inbox 24/7. My life was already bursting with activity, between teaching at New York University and all my side hustles, but Ethan was all-consuming: All hours of the day and night, regardless of what else I was doing, I was either communicating with Ethan or thinking about him. British Anna and Gina felt similarly overwhelmed by the chaos Ethan introduced into our lives, so we felt both relief in knowing we weren't alone in being duped and an instant bond from our shared experiences. None of us had actually talked on the phone with Ethan or met him in person, and yet we all felt a deep, intimate connection with him.

He had been communicating with the three of us incessantly, but was very selective regarding what he told us about one another. British Anna and Gina knew about me, but I knew about only the other Anna, not Gina. A lot of the details he supplied were correct, but many were fictional, manufactured to make us jealous of each other—and perhaps to prevent us from trying to connect.

We'd sleuthed our way into finding one another, but the big question remained: Who was Ethan Schuman? How had he manipulated the three of us so profoundly? Whoever he was, we knew he must be exposed and stopped before he did this to anyone else.

PART 1:

THE COURTSHIP

CHAPTER 1

What's in a Name?

December 26, 2010

Welcome to the real world." This was the first email I received from Ethan Schuman.

At this point, I'd been online-dating for years. I dabbled in Nerve.com, the edgier alternative to more conservative sites like Match.com, then eventually migrated over to OkCupid, intrigued by its datacentric approach to predicting compatibility. Much like real-world dating, the online experience was hit or miss—some weirdos, some players, some nice-but-boring guys, and the occasional gem—so I didn't think of meeting online as any better or worse. It was merely another outlet for connecting with a potential partner.

I took a numbers approach to it, willing to try out lots of different connections, most of which didn't materialize into anything. There were the polyamorous Burning Man devotees, all eager to convert me; the antiscience guys who hadn't been to a doctor in the better part of a decade, rivaled only by the antihygiene men ("There is no toothbrush in the animal kingdom," one less-than-fresh man informed me); or the alpha guys, who, while initially attracted to an ambitious woman with a career, quickly revealed their true desire, best articulated by one man: "I'm searching for an Executive Vice President of my household." Thanks to these and countless other nonstarters, I knew what I did and didn't want in a partner. But rather than a checklist of dealbreakers, I had one big ask: I wanted an equal. Someone who matched my energy and curiosity. It's an intangible quality that isn't easily communicated on a dating profile, but I knew it when I encountered it.

Out of the gate, I had a feeling it might be Ethan.

His user handle was "BeyondSleeping," because he was "just too excited about life to waste time sleeping." Ethan was thirty-five, six feet tall, approachably attractive, and came with a PhD and a job he described as "stealing from the rich." He advertised himself as someone who preferred women between the ages of thirty and forty-five and "knew how to make a woman feel loved." He drove a BMW, had a dog named Harvey, loved elbow patches, pickles, and fountain pens, and preferred boxers to boxer briefs. He was both an atheist and "Jewish and somewhat serious about it," and thought everything one needed to know about romance was summed up in *When Harry Met Sally*.

Ethan was born in New York, the youngest son of Russian Jewish immigrants. His sister was married and lived in NYC, and his brother—the "rebel"—had married and moved to Santa Monica. His mother was a music teacher and his father a lawyer; they lived in New Jersey.

He told me he owned a three-bedroom apartment (because "I think of you and your ovaries") on the Upper West Side, as well as another apartment in DC. He graduated from Stuyvesant High School in NYC, then majored in physics at Columbia. He completed a PhD in applied math at MIT and now split his time working for Morgan Stanley and the U.S. government, which left him living and working between DC, Ireland, and NYC.

Ethan was impressive—there was no denying that. But we felt well matched. I'd finished my PhD in sociology two years earlier and moved from teaching at Parsons School of Design to teaching in the Media, Culture, and Communication department at NYU. The pay was crap, but it was a prized position that allowed me to develop a curriculum based on my dissertation, an exploration of identity and self-presentation—and I really loved teaching.

But it wasn't Ethan's résumé that captured my attention. It was his cleverness, his openness, and perhaps most of all, his eagerness to keep the conversation going that swept me off my digital feet.

*   *   *

It was the day after Christmas 2010 and the eve of yet another epic New York snowstorm when I found Ethan on OkCupid.

OkCupid encouraged the abundant exchange of words with its users: There was even an IM chat feature built into the platform! Users rarely met after a couple of brief messages—instead, there was often a lengthy back-and-forth before a date was set. The profiles lent themselves to novel-length self-descriptions, and many users took advantage of the generous word limits permitted for each question prompt. Some user profiles read more like philosophy essays than modern-day dating profiles, but such was the trend of that era. Typing long-form prose came more easily back then, in part because users were accessing the dating sites almost exclusively via a computer, rather than a phone. If apps like Bumble and Hinge are a human catalog (imagecentric and glossy), old-school OkCupid was the Saturday night bar experience in virtual form (clever openers, witty banter, and long-game verbal rapport-building).

After an hour of exchanging messages and chatting via IM on OkCupid, Ethan and I moved over to Gmail and Google Chat: Ethan.Schuman@gmail .com, complete with a photo of himself and G-chat status updates that were irrelevant to me. Everything seemed perfectly normal—and rather exciting.

The quick pace of our conversation signaled to me that Ethan loved wordplay and verbal sparring as much as I did. During some early flirtatious banter, I told him I had a thing for vowel names. "You're vowel-y, which I appreciate," I teased. "For the sake of orgasms, you mean," he quipped, never missing a beat. There was a celebratory, nerdy joy that leaped off the screen as we frantically typed back and forth. After hundreds of banal exchanges with guys who struggled to move a conversation beyond "How's your weekend?" Ethan felt like an oasis, and I just wanted to drink him in.

Ethan: *I like the name anna.*
Me: *really? is it because of its hebrew roots and connection to "grace"*
Ethan: *nah*
Ethan: *more oedipal*
Ethan: *oedipusal?*
Me: *oh no. please tell me it's not your mother's name*
Ethan: *oedipus-istic*
Ethan: *it's my mother's name*
Me: *greeeeat*
Ethan: *and my ex-gf's name*
Ethan: *i thought i'd marry her just because her name was anna*

That was the first of many references to his ex, another Anna. I appreciated that we'd both lived full lives prior to this moment, and my own experiences with my ex-boyfriends were a huge part of my history, so his mention of her didn't immediately bother me. "We didn't work out because of circumstances/distance/life's a bitch type of stuff," he glossed over. Then casually dropped that she was "as hot as I'd want an Anna to be."

An interesting characterization, I noted. Did he have higher hotness expectations for other names? "No, lower. If you carry my mom's name, you better earn it."

Wondering if I'd measure up, he sweetly reassured me: "You're ahead of the game. You start from a good place. The name already warms my heart."

I knew it might just sound like a thing a guy says to woo a woman, but there is something to it. Studies have shown that we are partial to certain names based on our own personal associations, and those influences shape how we see and connect with a person. Ethan didn't need to be aware of this to feel a subconscious connection with me. I put our names in the "win" column of those early courtship hours.

"Have you googled me yet?" I asked. "I've resisted the urge—for the few minutes I've known your full name."

By this point, I'd become a master googler of guys I met online. With little more information than is given to a Starbucks barista, I was able to find everything from a professional résumé to someone's dating history to their political persuasion—in under sixty seconds. Did it kill the mystery? Maybe. But it also filled in a lot of blanks and prevented me from wasting my time (or theirs). So I couldn't wait to start exercising my detective skills on Ethan Schuman.

Ethan, however, took a different approach.

"I don't believe in googling. I think it's cheap. The things you want to tell me, you should have the right to tell me."

Hard to argue with that. But what of curiosity?

"The curiosity should consist of asking you questions. I'm curious, but I'm curious to get to know you."

"Ok, well that's very idealistic and lovely," I countered. "I can't promise I'll adhere to the same rules. But that's just background noise. In-person connection is the name of the game for me. Not resumes and bios."

Ethan was a private person who took his privacy seriously, something he made clear in our first night of messaging, noting that I'd be sorely disappointed when I eventually gave in and worked my Google magic. (I was.)

"Why will I be disappointed? By the Google results—or the in-person?" I asked, already knowing the answer.

"Ha, hopefully not the in-person," he replied. "The Google results. I don't believe in putting my life on the internet, and I also can't have my life on the internet for some of the work that I do. There are some people who do excellent for themselves by networking and becoming public figures and icons, that's just not me."

So, as the hours ticked by, we continued to peel back the layers the old-fashioned way, as Ethan preferred: by asking questions.

He appreciated that while I came from Iowa, I was anything but bland. "You're a crazy mutt," he marveled. "Never heard of an Iranian marrying an Irish woman from Iowa. How did your parents meet?"

"Looooong story. Best discussed a) in person and b) with an alcoholic beverage. Teaser: sort of a Top Gun type situation."

"At least give me a hint. Which country?"

"They met in Texas—where all great Iranian/Irish-American romances start."

I felt myself swept up in our budding connection, but at the mention of my parents, I started to tread more carefully. I dreaded sharing my origin story in early get-to-know-you dating conversations. My parents' love story was a cross between a romance novel and a political thriller. My father, a pilot and rising star in the Iranian Air Force, met my mother when she worked for the U.S. government on an Air Force base in Texas (back when the U.S. and Iran were on friendlier terms). They are both hopeless romantics, so the political complications of their cross-cultural love affair didn't faze either of them. As the Iranian Revolution heated up, so did their relationship. Oblivious (or at least willfully ignorant) to the growing dangers of a relationship that was not sanctioned by the Iranian state, my mom moved to Iran to make a life with my father. While they are wildly different people in many respects, they both operated from a mindset of "love conquers all," geopolitical realities be damned.

They celebrated when my mother became pregnant and made a plan to return to the United States to settle as a family. Meanwhile, unrest erupted around them in Tehran, so my mom left first, fearing for her safety and mine, eager for my father to join her. They communicated mostly via letters that took weeks to arrive, and after months of delays, my mom received the call that broke her: He wasn't coming. The Revolution, his job, pressure from his family . . . The excuses were plentiful, but never fully clear.

My father was a mysterious foreign phantom my entire life. I never met him, and only had one brief late-night phone exchange with him when I was five. The stories my mother told me painted him as a man who was as cunning as he was charismatic. His temper flared one minute, only to love-bomb you the next. My mother knew the day I was conceived (Valentine's Day), and perhaps in an effort to compensate for his absence, she went to great lengths to remind me every year that I was a product of true love. A messy, complicated, against-all-odds relationship, but true love nonetheless. While the devastating end of that relationship closed my mother off to romantic love, I remained a believer. Their ill-fated love story wasn't mine.

But not all of my dates saw it that way. One guy declined a second date after learning I'd never met my father. I must have daddy issues, he concluded, stating a preference for someone with a more "traditional" family. An absent mystery parent, cultural ties with a country that was hostile toward the United States, and a number of other stranger-than-fiction family details definitely drew some dating intrigue, but more than anything, it was a liability, and I dreaded sharing it.

By the time I met Ethan, I was adept at navigating questions about my family, often deflecting with humor and trying to initially project the picture of something far simpler than reality. But Ethan seemed unfazed—at first.

"Have you ever been to Iran?" Ethan asked.

"Never. Except in utero. Too dangerous for me."

"Me, too," he agreed. "I have a good Iranian friend, we have this running joke: Every 6 months or so, I send her an email and ask her if it's time for me to be shown around Iran yet. And every 6 months she says, 'Not the best idea.' I'm a Jewish American. Can't get worse."

I was raised Catholic and don't subscribe to any particular religion. I'd met more than a few Jewish men in New York who casually dated women from diverse backgrounds, but were clear they only wanted to marry a Jewish woman. So I wondered if the fact that I wasn't Jewish would be an issue. "I don't date Jewish women exclusively. I date women who have that balanced mix of heart and spunk," he told me.

Hmm...OK. But Ethan remained fixated on my half-Persian roots, despite my insistence that I had no active connection to Iran. Maybe I'd categorized him as "different" from the others too soon.

"The country has a rich history, rich culture, really attractive, intelligent people, but they're probably the most dangerous country in the world, certainly the most corrupt," he confidently proclaimed.

"Well…they may have some stiff competition on that front," I countered. I was no Iran apologist, but that struck me as a rather subjective and unqualified assessment.

I was ready to shift to a new topic. How had we covered so much in a single night?

"Hey," he wrote, thankfully changing course. "Isn't it weird that any Anna I date would have the same name after I married her? You have absolutely nothing in common with my British ex named Anna, but if I married either one of you, you'd transform into the same person. Crazzzzzzy."

"Well…see, that's where you're wrong. I'd never change my name. Dealbreaker?"

"Haha. Of course you wouldn't. There go my Anna Schuman fantasies."

CHAPTER 2

About Time

December 27, 2010

Ethan had a past, and he didn't try to hide it. Without hesitation, he admitted in our first lengthy G-chat that he was divorced. She was a nice Jewish girl whom everyone loved—except for him. He thought she was sweet and attractive but "remarkably asexual." They'd met young; he was twenty-five, she was twenty-three and a virgin. They dated for two years, were married for five, and divorced three years prior to when we met.

He admitted that her asexuality led him to cheat, which I didn't love, but I did sympathize with finding yourself with the wrong person and not knowing how to gracefully extricate yourself. It finally ended when she asked if he'd like to have children with her, and his honest answer was no.

Since the divorce, Ethan had been in two other relationships, both of which were much better and reminded him "what it was like to be with someone you actually want to get naked every time you see them. If I can spend two years with a woman and still want to rip her clothing off, I think it's possible to spend fifty years and want the same."

Ethan and I were aligned when it came to dating timelines. Neither of us needed years to determine if we were compatible with someone.

"I think it's the dumbest thing," he went on. "You date for three years waiting to see if someone trips up."

I mentioned that I'd come to know myself and developed my ability to read others well enough that within three months of dating, I had a strong sense of whether it was someone I might want to make a life with. I didn't need three years.

"So all I'd have to do is court you for three months, and you'd be able to tell me if I were a match or not?" he teased. "That's wonderful. I'd time you. My parents were married after three months, actually."

"Let's put it this way," I clarified. "I'd know if I thought I could live with you, wanted to potentially have kids with you, and could honestly see us together for a prolonged period of time after three months. Money back guarantee."

Ethan was great at riffing on ideas, so he took my three-month framework and pushed it a step further: "You should organize it even more: Say, in 3 dates, you decide whether you want 3 months, and in 3 months you decide whether you want a future."

Marriage, divorce, soulmates—we discussed it all, but the conversation never felt too-fast-too-soon. It often felt like Ethan was completing my own thoughts.

We were eager to make a plan to meet up, but our timing was terrible. Ethan was visiting family in New Jersey, I was in Manhattan, and we were presented with several of the worst snowstorms in recent memory, making immediate travel nearly impossible.

"I'm leaving for California on Wednesday for nine days," I said reluctantly, sometime around our third hour of messaging that day.

"So I have to wait nine days for our first date," he replied matter-of-factly. "Then I'd like to make two plans with you."

He was heading to DC for work as soon as the weather cleared, but might be back by Tuesday, before my flight. Assuming he couldn't drive into the city the following day due to weather (still TBD), we made a plan to meet either on Tuesday night, work permitting, or on the day after I returned from California. I could live with that.

Just after 1 a.m., he typed, "Anna, I'm falling asleep—through no fault of yours!"

"Oh my. Yes. It is late." Where had the hours gone? "Time for bed. Plus, if we keep talking, you'll know everything about me before we even meet."

I sent him my number and he promised to keep me posted on his travel plans.

"Great meeting you, Anna," he signed off.

My mind raced. I couldn't stop smiling.

CHAPTER 3

"Do You Believe in a True Identity at All?"

December 28, 2010

Like most New Yorkers, my social life was packed. From roller skating with the Central Park Dance Skaters to singing an embarrassing amount of karaoke, I had lived in New York long enough to often have two or three things scheduled on any given night. Several of my friends were lifelong New Yorkers around Ethan's age, so when he said he was from the area, I suspected we likely knew some people in common.

Ethan mentioned that he went to Stuyvesant High School and Columbia University, and my friend Matt also went to both schools. I estimated that even though they'd graduated in different years, their time would have overlapped. It was a long shot, but I wondered if they knew each other. Both schools were big, but so was Matt's Rolodex. He was one of the most hypersocial, well-connected people I knew. Hell, he was even the alumni representative! So I shared a photo with Matt and asked if he knew someone named Ethan Schuman. He didn't remember that name and the person in the photo didn't look familiar.

Ah. Oh well.

*   *   *

The weather had turned from snow to slush, so I was hopeful Ethan might make it into the city before I left for my trip. After "going to play with [his] car and see what's what," he reported back that while his car would start, the plows hadn't been through. He was still stranded in Jersey at his parents' house, where he'd been for five days. He was eager to leave.

That night, I was all packed for California, with twenty-five minutes before my self-imposed bedtime. If I couldn't see him in person, at least I could get a little digital Ethan time.

Ethan revealed he was high (to survive yet another day at his parents') and said he'd been smoking pot at his parents' place since high school. I drank socially, but other than that, I told him, I was "one of those annoying, vice-free happy people. I don't even drink coffee."

"Oh geez." I could feel his eyes rolling through the chat. "Are you a flaming liberal at least?"

"I suppose I am. Does that somehow substitute as a vice?"

"In my book, yes. That's your one flaw."

Aaaand . . . now we were back to politics—which I'd already realized was one of Ethan's favorite topics.

It was 2010, Barack Obama was two years into his first term, and Donald Trump wouldn't announce his candidacy for another four years. It was a different political climate, to say the least.

Ethan characterized himself as a "New York Republican," which he insisted was "its own breed. We're not of the Sarah Palin variety, and we're not socially conservative—so we can deal with powerful women and all that jazz."

He assured me that his conservatism was rooted in economic and foreign policy and he supported healthcare reform. What about immigration? "My parents are immigrants. I'm first generation," as if that fact told me everything I needed to know about his policy stance. My political views leaned much further in the opposite direction, but he felt confident that as long as I didn't get all "antiIsrael" on him, we'd be fine. Plus, he added, "I have a brain and a heart."

He went on: "I'm a sane Republican. If I had a photo of someone in my home, it would be Kissinger."

"My friend is writing Kissinger's new book with him," I mentioned.

"I want to date your friend."

"I'll let him know."

I didn't love this conversation. I grew up in a very liberal household, with NPR playing in the car and the *PBS NewsHour* as our dinner companion. Throughout my extended family, political opinions were expressed freely and vociferously. My grandparents were die-hard Roosevelt-era Democrats, and my mom took me to a Walter Mondale–Geraldine Ferraro political rally as a kid. And yet I tried to keep an open mind when it came to politics and dating. I didn't need someone to agree with me 100 percent of the time, and I was open to evolving some of my views. That hadn't always worked out, however.

In 2004, during the George W. Bush versus John Kerry presidential campaign, I dated a Wall Street guy. His mother, a Mexican immigrant, had a holiday card from Bush displayed in her home, and he had a Bush credit card (who knew that was even a thing?). In the months leading up to that election, sparked by his family's embrace of unfounded conspiracy theories, politics wedged itself between us. In one particularly heated argument, I broke my $5 deli umbrella and screamed "*That's it! It's him or me!*" in reference to his constant defense of Bush. That relationship eventually ended for reasons beyond politics, but I never wanted to repeat that dynamic in a romantic partnership. Ethan's approach to politics seemed a world apart from that of my ex, so, for the moment, I took him at his word and tried to turn us toward less contentious topics.

"Ok, I can't talk politics anymore," I announced without further explanation.

"Are you going to San Diego with a dude?" he said, unceremoniously pivoting.

Ugh. Discussing politics suddenly grew more appealing. My trip to California wasn't an ideal situation to explain to a guy I'd just met and really liked. Yes, I was going with a guy, but not one who posed any threat to Ethan. We'd dated on and off (but mostly off) over the course of two years. He was a sweet guy with whom I had great sex, but there was never anything deeper than that for me, and I always made that clear. When we were still casually dating, I said he could join me for a home exchange I'd arranged in San Diego over New Year's. He was a surfer and had friends out there, and since I wasn't seeing anyone else, I didn't mind if he tagged along. By November, I realized he had developed strong feelings for me and knew we needed to either cut ties or transition into a purely platonic relationship. He insisted he could handle just being friends, so we agreed he could still join me for the trip. Whatever physical attraction I previously had was completely over at this point, but convincing Ethan of that might prove difficult.

Did I even need to convince him? We'd just met. I was confused.

"Why do you ask?"

"To see if I can contact you while you're there. It's fine if it's a dude. I'm not asking to make a big deal out of it."

"Ok, so here's the deal—"

"No deal, don't tell me. That's cool."

"You can contact me, but listen—I'm going with someone I dated off and on. This Surfer Dude. But we're just friends now and he knows I've moved on."

"Can you tell me whether I can contact you or not?" He was losing patience.

"I'm 100% single. Promise," I assured him. I sounded shady.

"I want you to think about the fact that I'm hooking up with your friend. The one who's working on Kissinger's book," he teased.

"The guy," I clarified.

"Yes."

He playfully suggested we make a bet that I'd sleep with my travel companion. "If I win, you buy me a drink," he declared. And if I won? "How about, I'll buy an Obama pin and wear it whenever I take you out for the next three months," he offered, calling back to our previous conversation. I sent him a link to an I ONLY SLEEP WITH DEMOCRATS shirt; if he also wore that, we had a deal. He countered with an I ♥ REAGAN shirt.

"You know what's funny is that I can't even figure out your facial expressions during all of this," he noted.

"We could've video chatted, but I sort of refuse before I meet you. Video chat distorts you. Not a good first impression," I demurred. Maybe it was my own self-consciousness, but video chats were not the most flattering back then. Not to mention the lighting, the angles—I was years away from figuring out how to favorably position myself in front of a computer camera. And I really liked this guy. I wanted to put my best foot forward when he finally saw me, and I wasn't leaving it to technology.

So, instead, we sent each other more photos—each of us with friends and family, singing karaoke, or in various costumes. Photo by photo, we complimented each other, zeroing in on specific body parts. "Trying to figure out the hair," I said curiously. "Sort of a 50's pompadour?" "Haha my hair has a mind of its own," he acknowledged. He mentioned his affinity for women with curly hair and revealed he preferred women over thirty, because he found it attractive "when a woman has herself figured out." He told me he liked my collarbones, my lips, my arms. I told him I had big feet for my size. "You have good teeth," I observed, as if assessing livestock. It was intimate and flirtatious, without crossing a line.

As the conversation meandered, Ethan reminded me of his intentions and relative conservatism, lest I forget he was a Serious Man with Serious Intentions. "I hope you realize how traditional I am. All I really want is a nice home with a nice wife and three nice kids," he admitted, not really joking.

"How good are you at weeding out when I'm serious from when I'm rambling?" he asked.

"I'm a very good judge of character and of bullshit," I assured him.

He dared me to say something honest. "I want an honest feeling."

"Well, as much as someone can like someone they've never met—and whose pheromones they haven't experienced (I'm all about pheromones)—I am more intrigued by and attracted to you than I have been by anyone in a while.

"That said," I continued, "I'm waiting to find out what's wrong—BESIDES the fact that you're a Republican divorcee, and I think that, at the end of the day, you'll choose to be with a Jewish girl."

"Good job," he replied. "Students, she hit it out of the park."

Pleased with myself, I asked for his honest statement about me. Unsurprisingly, he started with my appearance, but assured me he found me to be "more than hot": "You're really sexy, you're smart, which adds to your sexiness all the more, but I don't think you'll keep me after the potential 3 months."

I was taken aback.

"Let's talk in high school terms," he suggested, then went on to explain that he'd be the funny kid in the back row, making obnoxious comments. I'd find him funny and we'd be friends, but I'd be attracted to someone else.

"You're selling yourself short," I assured him.

"I think it's the fact that I'm finding it hard to read you. Although I'm reading a lot of you," he joked.

"What's hard to read?" Wasn't I being wildly transparent?

"I just don't get you."

I was confused. "Well, you haven't met me, so...that could be part of the problem?"

"Yeah, but it's not that," he insisted.

"Then what?"

"I mean, even on G-chat, you can usually tell what someone is thinking beyond just the words they're typing. I have no idea with you. I'm finding it hard to categorize you."

What was happening? We'd been chatting playfully for hours over several nights. What could he possibly misunderstand? I felt defensiveness mixed with childlike sadness. Just when I thought it was safe to bare it all to this guy, he informed me that everything I'd exposed was...misleading. Where had I gone wrong? I scrolled back through our chats, looking for a clue as to what might have caused the confusion. I desperately wanted him to know me, to feel comfortable with me, to trust me. How could he doubt me? Growing up in an environment where I constantly felt misunderstood and ostracized left its mark, and Ethan was triggering those old wounds. My anxiety spiked.

"Do you not trust the things I've said?" It felt horrible that he seemed to doubt me.

"Every man caters himself to the woman he's trying to impress."

"And vice versa," I concurred, trying to suppress the insecurity racing through me. "One thing I love about getting involved with new people is to see how I evolve through that unique combination."

"So can you become Jewish for me?" Ethan never missed an opportunity to try to convert me.

"I know which parts of me can bend," I replied, ignoring his previous remark.

Since I'm a sociologist, human behavior is my occupational preoccupation, and the search for identity has always been a personal quest of mine: Who am I? How am I perceived? And how can the choices I make change that perceived identity? At the time, Ethan didn't know this, but this was the focus of my academic research.

Changing how and what we present can alter the reality of our lives and our connections. So when Ethan mentioned wrestling with and changing up which version of himself he would present to a woman to impress her, it didn't strike me as odd, but rather as accurate. It's something we all do, to varying extents. I just don't often hear someone outside of my field talk about it as he did.

"I really have no idea how to play the first date with you," he admitted, as if to sum up all the doubts he'd been casting.

"What are your options?"

"I mean...I can be refined Ethan..."

"Or Reformed Ethan, or Orthodox Ethan, or Conservative Ethan..."

"Haha. At least you know your denominations. You showed off well," he assured me.

"Damn straight. NYU prize in Religious Studies—not for nothin'!"

"I think developing feelings for you would result in a heart attack for me," he said, seemingly half joking, half serious.

"Ha. Possibly. But might be worth it."

"I just want dating to be over already."

Ethan believed that you learn more about life, love, and yourself through a lifelong commitment to one person, rather than endless dating.

"It's the way I work," he explained. "I'm good at math because I can stare at one problem for a month and never get bored of it. I get angry when someone tries to distract me with something else."

I understood his point. I had a habit of focusing my attention intently on the object of my affection in a way that also served my academic work. I liked to go all-in.

"Well your PhD is more about observing. It's more about detachment," he said with an air of authority about my work.

I could feel my defenses rise. I was used to guys misunderstanding my work. But his comments felt dismissive. I committed to sharing more of it with him in an effort to earn his admiration.

I told him about the various identities I tested out for my dissertation by changing my appearance in public, trying on everything from an overzealous tourist to a preppy Upper East Sider.

"That's pretty cool," he said admiringly. "There was that woman who became a man for the sake of dating and wrote a book, right?"

It didn't ring a bell.

"It is WAAAAAYYYY past my bedtime. I have to get up in THREE hours!" I cringed at the thought of my rapidly approaching flight.

"I'm not ready for you to go to bed," he admitted.

* * *

I emailed Surfer Dude, who was already in San Diego, with the address of our apartment. "It's next to the Vons shopping center on Carmel Creek Road. I told the owner noon. Will let you know if that changes."

"Ok, sounds cool."

Indifference. After some heated exchanges around unrequited feelings, indifference was the overwhelming sentiment between us. Or so I hoped. I wanted a drama-free week.

"Ethan—" I said, shifting my attention away from emailing Surfer Dude and back to G-chatting with the guy I was anything but indifferent toward.

"That's the first time you've used my name," he said approvingly.

"I know. Did it excite you?"

"Yes."

What was that Dale Carnegie quote? *"A person's name is, to that person, the sweetest, most important sound in any language."* That certainly seemed to apply to Ethan.

The film *Catfish* had premiered that fall, and the series wouldn't come out for another two years. I sent Ethan a link to the trailer.

"Do you know this movie?"

"Nope," he replied.

"Watch this. THAT COULD BE US/YOU?!" I joked. "Am I in the sequel to Catfish right now??"

"That's hilarious," he said after watching the trailer.

"It's also really sad."

"That's totally a movie we should go to together," he suggested.

"Why is that?"

"The irony."

"Because we're chatting as if we ACTUALLY KNOW EACH OTHER??" I asked.

"Yup," he said.

"So what are you not telling me? Any other big deal-breakers I should know about? You already told me you're Oedipal, so I know that much. Divorced? Check. Heartbroken? Check. Pothead? Check. Republican? Double check. That pretty much completes my scorecard."

"Haha. See, I'm fallible," he teased. "How about you? Well, I don't have to ask that. You're a handful. Period."

"It's just a matter of whether or not you're up for the challenge."

"And whether I have the right pheromones."

"TRUE," I said, laughing.

I was still hours away from boarding my flight, but we set the details of our first date, ten days in advance. January 7, the Friday after I returned. Dinner at eight. He would pick me up.

"You really think you're adaptable without sacrificing your true identity?" he asked again, circling back to our previous topic. "Or do you believe in a true identity at all?"

"Good question," I said admiringly. "The true identity is constantly unveiling itself, but it's also constantly creating itself."

"So not only will you give me heart attacks, you'll also give me headaches."

"It's like Durkheim's concept of the self (yes, I'm going there). He believes we are first social beings, and that is where we build the self—not vice versa. That social self doesn't stop accumulating once we can talk or once we graduate high school. It's a work-in-progress."

"How do I know this isn't just one of your 'identities'?" Granted, it was 4:30 a.m., but he seemed serious.

"Which part?"

"This whole 'professor on OkCupid' role."

"You don't think I really teach at NYU? That's easily remedied if you google me."

"No, I mean, maybe you are—but what if that's also just part of your thesis? Wouldn't that be crazy."

"You mean if I'm using OkCupid as an experiment?"

"I really hate online dating," he admitted.

"You realize that you are not an experiment, correct?"

"Fine. I think I scared myself with my own vivid imagination. I'm like a dog who frightens himself with his own shadow."

"You were really thinking this was all some sort of sociological experiment?" I was somewhat shocked.

"Who knowsssssss."

"CATFISH!!" I teased.

"I'm safe. Worst thing that can happen here is I have stinky phero-mones," he concluded.

I told him about a woman I lived with briefly in Brooklyn. She was in her late forties, single, and never married. Through friends, she met a guy who was divorced and really liked her. He wanted to date her, but she was very closed to the idea. When he asked how he could get to know her, she said that if he really wanted to date her, he could write an essay explaining why he was interested in her. So he did. Their first date was spent walking in the woods, discussing the essay. They walked for so long that he passed out from hunger. And then they fell madly in love.

"She was 6′4 and he was 6′7," I added. Their mutual extraordinary height somehow made the story even more absurd.

"Haha a man in love will even starve. I can see myself doing that for a woman I was crazy about," Ethan considered.

"Oh good, because that leads me to your assignment," I joked. "It should be 1500 words, double spaced, Times New Roman, MLA formatting."

"I'll do it," he said without hesitation.

Was he serious? He was. I certainly hadn't shared that story in the hope he would reciprocate, but admittedly, his eagerness to do it excited me. We renegotiated the length down to 750 words and agreed that he would send it to me on January 6, when I flew back to New York.

"You have the right to make me complete an assignment of your choos-ing after this one is done," I offered.

"Nope," he replied. "Chivalry. I'm courting."

"Aw. Points," I said, finishing off some oatmeal. "I just ate breakfast. You kept me up so late, I need f-ing breakfast." It was 5 a.m.

"I'm starving, too. I can't eat," he said.

"Are you fasting until our date?"

"I have this stupid biopsy thing to do in a few hours," he said, noting that he was heading to NYU to investigate some medical issues. "It's a boring story, there's a narrowing/compression going on in my esophagus, and they need to find the cause of it."

"What could that mean?" I was concerned.

"I'm dying," he replied, making a joke of a very serious topic.

"So my essay will be your goodbye letter?" I played along, wanting to lighten the mood.

"Yes. But I'll have time for a pity fuck. I'm dying on the 8th."

By 6:15 a.m., I was running late for the airport, and it was time for his dad to drive his massive SUV through the unplowed streets of Jersey to get Ethan to the hospital on time.

"Hablamos pronto, Schumanito. Si dios quiere."

"Keep in touch, Bigfoot."

CHAPTER 4

Worth Fighting For

December 29, 2010

My flight to California was brutal. I was operating on no sleep, going to meet a guy I didn't want to be with, while traveling across the country from the guy I increasingly wanted. I was absolutely dreading the next ten days. But Surfer was a good guy, and it was too late to back out, especially for someone I'd known for only a few days. Plus, I was desperate for a little sunshine and above-freezing temperatures. I told myself it would be a sort of meditative retreat with a friend. It was only one week.

As eager as I was to meet Ethan, a little long distance didn't scare me. This was an area in which I excelled. Due to moving around a lot, most of my long-term relationships endured significant stretches of long-distance communication. My college boyfriend and I met in the summer on Nantucket, only to be ripped apart when I left for Ireland for the school year and he headed back to Stanford. We didn't have cell phones or Skype, only expensive long-distance calls, email access via twice-daily treks to the university computer center, and the postal service. He was my first love, and it was so all-encompassing that I sobbed uncontrollably when we parted. Existing without him physiologically devastated me. I ached for him. I wasn't sure I could breathe without him. The distance took its toll, and after a couple of months, we hit pause, only to resume dating (still long distance) later that winter. I joined him in California in May and we headed to

Hawaii together to work for the summer. Then he returned to California and I returned to school in New York—more long distance. After we broke up at the end of that year, I met another guy as I prepared to leave for the Peace Corps. It wasn't the same sort of soul-rocking love, but I adored him. We weren't exclusive during the Peace Corps, but we emailed regularly and spoke on the phone, and we got back together when I returned. Later, in grad school, I met a British guy at the consulting firm where I worked part-time. We were kindred spirits. I never knew relationships could be so fun before him. When he moved to France for business school, and I stayed in New York to finish my PhD, breaking up wasn't an option. We tried to make it work with hours-long Skype sessions, but I was too broke to afford more than one trip to Europe, and communication gradually broke down. So while I hadn't married any of those guys, those relationships all withstood months and even years of long distance. I never sought out long-distance relationships—they were difficult and often painful—but as a result of staying open to love, even when moving around globally, I'd learned how to stay connected to someone who was not physically present. A week was nothing. I'd trained for this.

While waiting for my flight, I emailed Ethan: "Holy crap I'm tired. What did you do to me?? Cruel."

"Hope you're getting your rest. Just not on Surfer Dude's shoulder."

I was focused on his trip to the hospital.

"I think I may have deferred death once more. I made a deal with the devil. It's just there's this girl I have to see about," he teased.

I had a few hours' layover in Dallas. As I wandered the airport like a zombie, I replayed the last few days in my extremely fuzzy brain. Hadn't he mentioned that his birthday was January 7? The day we'd set for our first date? That couldn't be right. Maybe he hadn't realized? I wanted to give him an out, just in case.

"You want to spend your birthday with me? Are you sure? I mean...I'm flattered and it works for me, but I don't want you to miss out on some sort of birthday revelry on my account. Though I'm sure we can properly celebrate." I was rambling.

"I was kidding. Thought the birthday gimmick would get you to sleep with me. My birthday is July 10th, and yours?"

"Funny—sleeping with you wasn't my natural reaction. But good try. The essay is your meal ticket, I'm telling you..."

We emailed sporadically as I made my way from New York to California, but I never got a clear answer about the doctor's appointment, so in between discussions of cell phones (he was using an Irish number as he straddled jobs and countries), I asked again. "How was your doctor's appointment? What's wrong with your stomach?"

"Appointment was dandy. They said that I qualified for the Olympics. They even said that these Olympics were special," he replied, once again deflecting.

My mind lingered on the cell phone issue. I was starting to feel annoyed by the fact that we were limited either to email and IM or to texting on his expensive international phone (we still hadn't talked on the phone). Technology was a different animal back then. FaceTime wouldn't hit the Apple store until the following month, and iMessage didn't launch until later that fall. WhatsApp existed, but it was not well-known in the United States (I hadn't even heard of it yet), so unless you were using Skype on your computer, traditional phone calls and texts were the default for international communication at the time. That also meant that when he was away from his computer, we relied on texting with his Irish phone for our correspondence. And it was not cheap.

"You realize that you probably annoy people by forcing them to text and call your international phone, right?"

And by "people," I meant me. Finances weighed heavily on me my entire life, and money was particularly tight at this moment. Perpetual poverty, despite my advanced degrees and job at NYU, was the dirty secret I always tried to hide. Ethan's phone was outing me.

"So, seriously, I'm curious about your condition. What's the deal?" I asked again, trying to change topics and slightly annoyed that he wouldn't give any sort of direct answer.

"Well, you know, some women think I'm worth 20 cents," he said in an attempt to shame me for shying away from texting with his international number. "You want my diagnosis? For what purpose? How are your periods? Consistent? Painful? How long do they last? Because those questions are pretty much the same thing as you interrogating my diagnosis."

Whoa. Clearly I'd triggered him.

"Jeez. I was just expressing interest. Ok, I'll refrain from asking. I don't go to the hospital due to my menstrual cycle—so, no, not at all the same thing. And it's 50 cents. For the record."

That was the first taste I'd gotten of Ethan's expert ability to cut with words. It was unexpected and ruthlessly executed, and he shifted back to "normal" as quickly as he went in for the kill. It reminded me of the Wall Street guy, the first and only emotionally abusive boyfriend I'd had. His cruelty was crippling, and yet I felt irrationally connected to him. Agonizing over that relationship pushed me into therapy, and even then it took far too long to extricate myself from him.

"I have kind of a scroll of diagnoses to choose from," he replied, as if to appease me.

"I'll not ask about them. Clearly you get offended if people take interest." I was still hurt from his response.

"Well I apologize then." But his next email suggested he wasn't too sorry: "I don't usually get offended by people who are consistent."

"I'm consistent!" Where was this coming from?

"Yes, consistently judgmental."

"What did I judge?? Observant and judgmental are not the same."

What was he referring to? I once again replayed our correspondence in my mind. Was he angry that I'd asked him about the dates his photos were taken? In his profile photos and the photos he'd emailed me during one of our G-chats, it appeared that several years had passed, and his body had evolved a bit. Did he think I was judging his appearance for noting the difference? Or was he emotionally distraught about the medical stuff? He was sleep-deprived, and that appointment had to be unsettling, so I wanted to give him the benefit of the doubt.

"You're just bad with your words then. Because your statements don't differentiate between the two."

"I'm excellent with my words, for the record. And once again, I'm confused. Lots of confusion." Maybe he was high? Yes! I was hoping he was high.

"I was high earlier today," he confirmed. "Anesthetics are sweeeet."

"I'm just confused why you suddenly turned unpleasant. I was asking about your doctor's appointment because it sounded serious. Wasn't trying to pry. But you certainly don't have to share anything with me."

"Okay, sorry, you're just difficult to penetrate in some ways."

I was often accused of being too direct, but hard-to-read was a new one for me.

He continued, "It's not a big deal. Just have swallowing issues (I hope you don't share them) and they're trying to rule out esophageal cancer."

A blowjob joke and a casual mention of potential cancer—all in a single sentence. How very Ethan.

"Well, that's really serious. And scary," I said, trying to find the right words.

I wanted to be supportive but not overly smothering so as to scare him away before we met—and yet, after four days and dozens of hours of communication, we already felt so close, so connected. Striking that balance was tricky.

I also wanted to get to the bottom of these recurring insinuations that I was somehow sending hard-to-read mixed messages. "How am I difficult to penetrate? I'm an open book."

"Ehhhh. A book opened to the wrong page just to confuse me."

I tried not to take the bait. "Ok, these are some crazy riddles you're talkin' in."

"Fine, fine, fine. I'll be nicer. What are you doing tonight?"

Huh? And just like that, Ethan was over it. Whatever was bothering him suddenly seemed to disappear. It was like it never existed in the first place.

The same could not be said for me.

"I mean, why wouldn't you want to be nice to me? YOU HAVEN'T EVEN MET ME. Usually, people like to be nice until they meet someone."

But Ethan had already moved on to marveling at the fact that I was doing a home exchange. "Normal people actually do that?"

I assured him I'd completed many of them in the last several years, trading for some truly amazing places.

"That's really fantastic. And even more fantastic to be the kind of person who pulls that off successfully."

He sent me an email on a separate thread with the subject: "PSA."

Dear Anna,

I apologize for being defensive, and consequently offensive, with you. I'm over it.

Yours truly,
Ethan

It was technically an apology, and yet the language and tone were decidedly dickish. Nonetheless, I thanked him and told him he seemed like someone who always tries to correct a situation.

"Comes from a lifetime of consistently fucking up," he confessed. "I have lots of experience in janitorial work in my relationships."

Ethan asked me to take some photos of the week and send them to him. I didn't have a camera with me, and my 2010 iPhone camera wasn't great. I didn't take a lot of photos back then—I preferred to be in the moment. Plus, I hated having my own picture taken. There are entire years of my life in the early 2000s with hardly any photos memorializing them.

"It's interesting how important it is for you to be as encapsulated and ensconced in an experience as possible," he observed. "That's admirable. You must experience life in a very different way than most other people."

Sitting there in the chaotic airport, my exhausted body melted, and I felt overwhelmed with emotion. That was exactly the kind of response that kept me coming back to Ethan again and again. Had he annoyed me with his irrational meanness? Absolutely. Was his defensiveness around his medical issues a minefield to navigate? Definitely. But had any other man ever "seen" me the way he seemed to? So effortlessly, so fully, and in such a brief amount of time? He understood—or wanted to understand—why I made the choices I did, what motivated me, what made me tick. He was peeling back the layers, not just validating the surface. Without ever meeting him in the flesh, I felt more naked before him than perhaps any man I'd ever known. If he understood me this much now, I could only imagine the depths we could go to together over time. We recognized our mutual intensity. Ethan said he craved it in women, and the absence of it in his ex-wife led him to seek it elsewhere. My usual fear of being "too much" didn't surface with him.

"You know, even if our pheromones don't hit it off, we're obviously extremely complementary in lots of significant ways. That's pretty swell," I noted with intentional innocence.

"My pheromones have been training, using lots of mouthwash and getting spray tans. We'll be fine."

He told me he'd spent much of his morning ("before being conked out") thinking about me: everything from his interest in my sociological experiments to how my body would fit against his. His words made me shy. Never grotesque, just sweetly disarming.

"When I make you blush for the first time, I'll know I can die a happy man," he promised.

CHAPTER 5

Relationship Fast Track

December 30, 2010

Five days into my nightly chats with Ethan and two days into my trip to California, I had two main observations:

1. Ethan did not sleep.
2. Vacationing with your ex is not a good idea.

"Lab rats die from more sleep than we're getting," I warned him. "If I were to date you, would that mean I'd never be allowed to sleep again?" I was somewhat serious.

When I asked him if he ever slept like a normal person, he informed me that he only needed four hours of sleep to be functional.

"Studies show that people who get seven-to-nine hours of sleep are the highest functioning people. So just think how sharp you'd be if you slept an adequate number of hours?"

The weather in San Diego was rainy and cold; no one was working due to the holidays, making it impossible for me to make any progress on my work projects, and I was stuck in an apartment with a guy I desperately wanted to avoid—which left *lots* of time for chatting with Ethan.

"I think it's interesting that neither of us has suggested that we just talk on the phone," I noted. We were avoiding video chat until we met, but at this point, the phone would make sense.

"I'd suggest it. I'm just taken off-guard with the whole ex-boyfriend situation."

He had a point—it would be awkward to chat on the phone with him while Surfer was home. He was out at that moment, but I needed to sleep soon. Perhaps another night.

So our digital conversation lingered a bit longer. At one point, while talking about our grandparents, I shared that I'd recently lost my grandfather to lung cancer. We were quite close.

"I've had this stupid esophageal thing going on, and let me tell you, there's no worse feeling in the world than having difficulty breathing," he responded. Turning the conversation back to himself immediately after I'd just shared something so personal felt a bit abrupt, but perhaps it was to commiserate with the pain of my loss—and I was just happy he was finally opening up about what had prompted his recent medical tests. He was hospitalized from it about a year ago, and it had caused problems ever since. One GI doctor was unable to diagnose anything, but he'd thankfully found a competent one who saw a mass, which was what had been biopsied the other day. He would have the results in a few days. The mass needed to be removed, regardless of the results, as it was creating difficulty with eating and breathing. He'd choked several times already. I had no idea why the floodgates suddenly opened on this topic, a sharp contrast to the hostility that greeted me when I tried to bring it up earlier. Maybe something I said put him at ease, or maybe he had gotten some emotional distance from it by then. Regardless, it was all very concerning to me.

"I do find myself particularly defensive with you," he admitted. When pressed, he explained that it was a result of my being "more experimental, more open-minded," whereas he was "a traditional guy who dates traditional women."

"I'm floored by you in good ways." Then he got to the meat of it—the thing he wouldn't come out and say at first, instead acting a bit cranky and irritable, but that made sense once he finally revealed where it was all coming from: "I'm defensive because I'm anxious about our first date. I don't know what to expect from it, but I find myself really wanting it to go well."

He wasn't alone on that one. There was, indeed, mounting pressure building up to our date. Oh, how I wished we could accelerate a week and just meet. But that wasn't a possibility, and neither of us seemed likely to issue a communication moratorium until that time. Besides—what else did I have to do for the next week?

A recurring theme in our correspondence centered on "Is this really happening? This is so weird!" (usually initiated by me). But I knew quite a few people who had connected under less-than-conventional circumstances. I shared several of them with him:

I lived with a woman in Hawaii one summer, and she met a guy online—not a dating site, more like a chat room. She was instantly obsessed with him. He lived in California, and they IM'd endlessly, not unlike what Ethan and I were doing. This was well before online dating was popular, and at the time, I thought it all sounded crazy. They later went on a cross-country motorcycle trip for their first date.

Another woman I was friends with in New York—eccentric and very endearing—was single and in her late forties. One night, she logged on to Craigslist (yes, *Craigslist*) thinking, *I am not eating dinner alone tonight!* She spotted an ad posted by a guy looking for a dinner date and messaged him: "This is very scary for me, but I'd like to meet you for dinner tonight." After a mishap meeting at the restaurant (she was late and without a cell phone, and he had already left), she apologetically rescheduled for the following night, and he—miraculously—agreed. Oh, and did I mention that *neither of them posted or exchanged photographs?* The man who turned up was a very sweet finance tech guy who was in town from LA for business. They went to Europe for their third date and were engaged and living together within four months—and were still together. When she told me this, I was stunned. All of it sounded improbable and a little insane. What an incredible leap of faith! And yet, it worked and they were happy. So who was I to judge?

"Craigslist?!" Ethan exclaimed, appropriately, when I shared the story. "That's super sketchy."

"I know. But they were both naive enough not to understand how sketchy everyone else on that site probably was."

"It's nice to know we're not alone," Ethan summarized.

Despite these personal anecdotes, I always thought the extended online correspondence thing seemed weird; it was the stuff of other people, not me. In my Media and Identity class at NYU, I asked my students to spend time on Second Life, a multiplayer online virtual world and the original metaverse, where users create avatars and interact with other avatars within the user-generated content. My students thought it was a strange place for strange people, but in their time there, they realized that the people who connected in those virtual spaces had very intimate, very real relationships without ever meeting in person. I started to realize Ethan and I were becoming those people. Even when I studied them, I didn't think that type of deep, virtual-only connection could happen to me. Ethan was definitely not a social experiment, as he feared, but he was making me rethink my personal stance on these topics. Was the body irrelevant when it came to human bonding? Had I been doing it all wrong? Were we operating as Second Life avatars?

"We could be," he considered. "But I think we're holding out hope that it translates to the offline world. And if it does, then it's fucking awesome."

"And I will use it as an example in my classes," I promised.

"Immortalized forever," he replied. "I mean, if you think about it, any level of connection in person will be awesome. If it's just a friendship, then you've proven something as well. I already decided for myself that you're insane enough to keep around in my life. I figure that even if you're not interested in me, you're interesting enough to base one of the characters in my future book on," he added, as if to offset any pressure.

Ah, *the pressure*. We agreed that while that was a fine alternative, we both really wanted to be interested in each other romantically upon meeting. But how could we minimize the pressure? We both agreed we couldn't.

He asked me if I liked opera (I don't, particularly), and told me his parents gave him their tickets to *Carmen* at the Metropolitan Opera on January 8.

"So, wait... You'd see me two nights in a row?" I clarified, noting our first date was set for January 7.

"My parents offered me the tickets today, I only wanted to take you, so I'm asking," he said without hesitation. "How about, you have the option of attending an opera Saturday night with me, and you can tell me Friday evening if you're interested."

"That sounds like a fair plan," I agreed. "And you can tell me Friday if you want to take me."

"I want to take you."

"You might change your mind!" I was almost trying to convince him.

"Why? If we don't hit it off, we don't hit it off. I still think you're a pretty fascinating person."

And so, quite naturally, we progressed from one planned date to possibly two.

December 31, 2010

New Year's Eve. A night I generally dreaded, but even more so given the current situation. Ethan, on the other hand, was a huge fan. He told me that it's a big deal in Russian culture, so he was heading back from working in DC to New Jersey to spend the night with family.

He insisted New Year's was poetic, a time of growth and self-improvement, of taking stock of loved ones who have shared the time with you or passed—he went on about this at length. "You can think back to every other NYE before today and recall where you were, what you wanted, what you had hoped for. It's a measurable way to define the path you've followed and to assess the decisions you've made. You've contended with time and made the best of it. Perhaps cliche, but only because the human experience is one big cliche."

"So, on this, you're all poetry and zen, and on everything else, you're cynical? Very confusing. But a lovely sentiment," I conceded.

"I'm an outward cynic, but try to be a poet about most things in life," he informed me.

He took it upon himself to brighten my spirit by sending a series of emails while we were both counting down the minutes until midnight— me, out with Surfer Dude and his friends at a dive bar in San Diego; and Ethan, first at his family dinner in Jersey, then being dragged by friends to the Meatpacking District, a New York neighborhood bursting with annoy- ing bottle-service clubs and a predominantly "bridge and tunnel" crowd. (**Me:** "I loathe the Meatpacking District." **Ethan:** "I wouldn't be interested in a woman who didn't.")

In an email with the subject "Email 1 of the Evening," Ethan told me he hoped that the Republican Party got its act together and that we "hit it off" in 2011.

I replied, sharing our family tradition of banging pots and pans at midnight. I also told him, "My mom sent me yellow thong underwear for Christmas and said I had to wear it on NYE for good luck in the coming year (where she found that particular tradition, I have no idea)."

At the stroke of midnight on the West Coast, Ethan sent me two more emails:

"Wooooooooo! Happy NEW YEAR, Gorgeous!!!!!"

"Smile for the sake of poetry everywhere. Happy New Year's AGAIN. ON THE DOT! According to my watch at least…"

I might have been physically with Surfer Dude, but Ethan was my New Year's date. Our first holiday, in the books.

January 1, 2011

The next day, we texted (as much as it pained me to pay for it), and I sent him a *New York Times* article called "The Happy Marriage Is the 'Me' Marriage." It reflected on the difference between a lasting marriage and a happy marriage, with the latter resulting from a partnership that makes each person's life richer and more interesting by sparking growth. Many of the points reminded me of his observations around why his own marriage had failed, and, by contrast, our conversations around why our budding relationship held such promise.

"Going for a run. Will read the article as soon as I return and continue the conversation about how much you embody everything sexy and desirable for me," he replied playfully. Man, he was cheesy. But I didn't hate it.

And, true to his word, he read the article, and it sparked a lengthy digital conversation about what humans seek in relationships and the role they can play in our individual expansion. Ultimately, we reached a sort of existential stopping point with no clear philosophical path to romantic bliss in sight. "Each variable makes it infinitely more difficult to optimize. Let's get married when we're both single at 80," he suggested half-heartedly in defeat.

*   *   *

While out with Surfer Dude on New Year's Eve, I bonded with his friend's girlfriend. She was the first person I'd told about Ethan. I was convinced my friends wouldn't support me communicating so extensively with him (who could possibly understand this?), so I wanted to wait until after we'd met to tell them anything.

The girlfriend and I connected instantly. Despite the fact that we were both there with dates, our conversation mostly revolved around online dating and my budding relationship with Ethan. We immediately ditched the guys and disappeared into our own little bubble in the San Diego dive bar. I have no idea what the guys thought we were talking about, deep in private conversation for hours, but letting her in on my secret was a huge relief.

She had also met her boyfriend online, but they were quite shy about telling people this, while Ethan and I had no such hesitation.

That night, I suggested to Ethan that we talk on the phone when Surfer Dude was out—while also acknowledging that maybe waiting until we met in five days would feel better. I was sending mixed messages. I was torn. We were in such a great communication flow, I didn't know how the introduction of new variables before we met in person would affect things. Ethan shared my confusion.

"I'm feeling pretty odd about the whole situation—you being in San Diego with your ex, me being here, us flirting like we know each other, spending nights together, but not at all. I've been thinking about the right way to play this hand, and I'm left confused. I'd love to hear your voice. I'd love to see you. I don't know what is the 'right' progression."

There was an assumption that we were both dating other people, or at least open to the prospect of it, given that we both still had active dating profiles. But we agreed we would be mutually focused on each other until we were able to meet in person. A sort of exclusive waiting period.

Ethan proposed picking me up at the airport, a gesture I found to be incredibly sweet and thoughtful. But I had two reservations: (1) I wanted to look attractive when we (finally) met, and there are few times when I feel less desirable than when I get off a cross-country flight; and (2) I anticipated being really, really nervous.

I started to play through the likely chain of events in my head, imagining him helping me get my luggage inside my apartment, not knowing what state the home-exchange tenants would have left it in. But those thoughts were interrupted by Surfer Dude, who had come home and was supremely irritated that I was, yet again, on my computer. At this point, he was no longer buying the excuse that my technology addiction was work-related. The platonic cohabitation thing was not working for him. It was clear he had agreed to those terms with the expectation that I would change course at some point in the trip, and we would rekindle our romance. When that didn't pan out, he got pissed. His ego was bruised.

I logged off with Ethan, soothed the immediate situation, then found my way back online after Surfer went to sleep. It was only 11 p.m. PST (albeit 2 a.m. EST where he was), so I asked Ethan if he wanted to finish our conversation.

"If you pick me up, my nervousness will be multi-layered," I explained.

"Layer 1," he prompted, playing along.

"*I feel like I look like crap!*" I said, anticipating my inner dialogue.

"Layer 2," he continued.

"*This is such an intimate act with someone I've never met!*" Lest he misinterpret what I meant, I clarified, "—when I load my luggage into your car (that is not a euphemism for a sex act, btw)."

"Well, I'd love to pick you up. Think about it. Or maybe a coffee?" he offered as a less daunting alternative.

"Layer 3 = what is the protocol for this opening discussion? How's the weather been? Traffic? Do we talk the whole ride? Silence?"

I was just typing out all my thoughts at this point. Our comfort level was high after nearly a week of nonstop communication. I didn't have much of a filter left.

"I won't be wearing my cute date outfit, my hair will be a mess, I'll be greasy from stale plane air. Are you sure you want to meet me like that?? But…I would really appreciate the ride. And would love to hang out with you," I said, warming to the idea. "Airport pickup has to be the most hilarious first date ever, no? I'm willing to bet it'd quite possibly be an OkCupid first."

"I would love to meet you like that. We'll have a do-over the next day anyway if we feel like we need it. Then I'll check out your greaseless pores," he quipped. "It could be an airport pickup with a drink/coffee. So we're not entirely psycho."

Ethan asked if it would make me feel more comfortable to video-chat the day before we met.

"No, I'm very against it, I think. What do you think?" I was not at all sure of my response—I really wanted to see him, but I still felt self-conscious about the awkwardness of video-chatting with a stranger. I could wait a day.

"I just want you happy," he said. "(Good answer, right?)"

"Yes, well done. You're good at giving the right answers," I noted.

*   *   *

As we continued to unpack New Year's Eve, he casually mentioned that he hooked up with a girl. The previous night. On New Year's Eve. While he emailed me repeatedly. It was someone he met through friends and was part of his group, but he assured me he wasn't into her.

"I'm confused about how I should feel about this," I admitted.

"I feel guilty for it. I was out and could totally see you making out with Surfer Dude at midnight. I was getting jealous and then telling myself that I was an idiot getting jealous, so I thought if I hooked up with her, then the score would be leveled if you did the same."

"Well, sorry to disappoint you."

We each paused, confused by the strange place in which we found ourselves: getting jealous and negotiating exclusivity before ever meeting.

"Do you want this to matter to me?" I asked. "On one level, you don't (so you don't have to feel guilty); on another, you do (because it means I care). This is so weird. How is it possible to feel cheated on by someone you've never met?" I said this to him but mostly to myself.

It was after midnight, but my mind was in full analytical mode. "Do you think we are sabotaging any chance we might have of truly hitting it off by going through several stages of a relationship before meeting?" I asked as both an academic exercise and a real fear.

"I don't know, you're the social scientist. Wake me up when you've weighed all the pros and cons."

So I attempted to do just that—at length.

"I'm sorry if you're hiding some hurt under your social commentary," he said, reading the subtext of my messages.

He said he had a history of subconsciously testing women, but that they never called him out on it. Their emotions clouded their reactions, and there was no space for analysis. I considered that, unlike other women from his past, perhaps I was operating more from logic than emotion. Maybe the physical distance gave me that edge. He apologized again, admitting that he did want me to care, in exactly the way I predicted.

"But I honestly didn't plan to tell you until we got to the point where you needed to know."

"What point would that be?" I asked.

"Because you deserve to know."

"Strangely," I continued.

"Yeah, strangely, but I'm devoting quite a bit of energy to you, and you're returning quite a bit of energy."

"Yes," I agreed. "It's rare to extend that kind of energy, so intensely, so early."

"I didn't want you to be my first time since my ex. It would be a bit pathetic. Too much built into it for me, and it's not what I want to be thinking about."

The previous day, he'd told me that his British ex had just emailed him an "excessively long" email about all the issues he'd helped her with. It upset him; he felt cataloged into her "past relationship dossier." (I knew she was fresh on his mind.) "I think if we slept together, I'd be split between two trains of thought: One, oh wow, I'm sleeping with her, and two, oh wow, I'm sleeping with a woman I like, post-Anna."

I had to remind myself his British ex was also an Anna. "Are you sure you're over your ex?" I was a bit concerned. "I know you want to be, but I'm not sure you are."

"Yes, but I felt weird seeing someone else naked. I know you can't relate."

"What is that supposed to mean? And why do you repeatedly attempt to justify your actions by taking shots at me?"

He retracted his claws. "I miss being crazy about a woman. I'm not crazy about her," he said, in reference to his ex.

"Ok, I believe you."

"You don't."

"I'm getting there." And I was. Sort of. I needed to hear him talk about that relationship in person. Body language, vocal tone, eye movement—it would tell me far more than whatever words he typed in that moment. Women often move on from past relationships more quickly than men, so his lingering confusion didn't surprise me. But that doesn't mean it didn't sting a bit.

"I think you wanted to preemptively sleep with someone in case I did the same this week," I concluded.

"Yeah, sure. All of it," he agreed dismissively. "And to conclude...you feel *blank* about it..." he prompted me.

"Confused."

I assured him I would remain confused until I met him in person.

He felt at liberty to remind me that I was currently on vacation with an ex-boyfriend, and his point was well-taken. It didn't feel right to throw stones.

"It was a defense mechanism," he said, still insisting on getting to the root of his actions. "I'm obviously freaked out a bit about what's going on here. I just don't get the impression that you'd deal with it in a sympathetic way."

His words were like a knife in me. I felt like I'd stepped into an emotional blender. He was manipulating me by preying on my insecurities in an effort to diminish his own bad behavior. I recognized what was happening, while still being susceptible to it. Perhaps I should have stepped away, shut down the conversation, and hit pause until we could meet in person. But I feared that leaving things unresolved might result in us never meeting. I was too invested. I couldn't risk that.

"You underestimate me. It's insulting. And hurtful. I'm sorry you slept with her, I'm sorry you told me, I'm sorry you didn't like my response." I couldn't take any more verbal or emotional tests. I surrendered.

"It's kind of sweet. We're arguing like a couple that has emerged from the honeymoon stage," he observed. "I still want to date you."

"I still want to meet you," I replied, emphasizing the distinction.

"Ladies and gentlemen, tonight's twisted conclusion," he announced to our imaginary audience.

The more I experienced him, the more guarded I became. He had a way of inserting playful levity into these horrible, cruel, dramatic moments. He knew how to kill, then disarm, all with words. All in a matter of minutes.

I had 12 percent battery remaining on my computer, so we agreed to chat until it died. We'd done it again. Talked all night. This time it felt like we packed three months of dating into those intense hours. Ethan was right: We'd sped through the honeymoon period and landed squarely in the power-struggle phase of the relationship. All. Before. Meeting.

It was the strangest forty-eight hours of my life. I was exhausted.

CHAPTER 6

Five-Day Countdown

January 2, 2011

The persistently crappy weather matched my mood. After what was the first time I'd had an extended virtual fight with a stranger I cared way too much about, I felt emotionally hungover. It was cold and damp outside, and I was stuck inside with Surfer Dude, while I replayed the love-hate exchange I'd had with Ethan from across the country. It all felt like a dream. Or a nightmare. Maybe both.

I fired up my computer to find an email from Ethan awaiting me. The subject was "1-5."

> I've been rewinding through last night. I'm a bit floored by it from a variety of angles.
>
> 1 — I think you're great.
>
> 2 — I think I like fighting with you, because you're all the sweeter afterwards.
>
> 3 — I don't think I regret the way we've met. I think as nervous as we'll be at the end of the week, what we're working on now means that we don't have to start at the very laborious beginning. We can just leap forward to the part where we like each other already.

4—I'm sorry for hurting you. I think we both need to work on keeping our defense mechanisms at bay.

5—I think you're great. And I'm more attracted to you than I ever was before.

In the week (which felt like a year) since meeting Ethan, I'd learned I could always count on these timely (albeit questionable) reflections after any sort of friction popped up. Even when I didn't agree with every word, his eagerness to reflect on our relationship and lay it all out for me in such a precise and elaborate fashion was a huge turn-on. And while I appreciated his reparations, Thursday—airport pickup day—couldn't come fast enough. I was hitting a wall. I checked in on the New York weather and asked about the snow-melting progress; I didn't want any obstacles impeding our date.

"Snow is melting, but streets are dangerously slippery. I might have to carry you," he informed me.

"I need to wear heels."

"If you wear heels, make sure you bring your medical insurance. We'll be making a pit-stop at the emergency room."

We joked about what it would be like if I met his very Jewish, very Russian extended family. "It will be Guess Who's Coming to Dinner," he said, insinuating that I would be Sidney Poitier in this scenario. We came from different worlds, but neither of us fit neatly into those worlds, so merging the two felt both natural and exciting.

*   *   *

We were occupying a lot of each other's time, and yet I wanted to pace things, given that the emotional intimacy was moving much faster than anything physical. So I made it clear we should continue to explore other options for a while, even after we met.

Ethan was not in agreement. Rather, he believed that "you meet someone, and if there's a particular connection, both of you know, and there's an implicit agreement that both of you have no interest in anyone else, so by the time you sleep together, you're exclusive."

"I'm old-fashioned in terms of dating," he informed me. "With most other women I'm interested in, I wouldn't even consider sleeping with them when there's a definite possibility that we're not exclusive."

"Well, I think we agreed to a mandatory non-exclusive phase, right? That doesn't mean it's mandatory that either of us hookup with other people, but that we have the right to do so," I clarified.

"Yeah, we agreed, and that's why I said you're going to force me far outside of myself," he replied, seemingly agitated. "And you think that is good for dating?"

"In the very beginning, yes. It makes both parties work hard to earn the other person and keeps things in perspective. But that's not a forever period."

"Being out in the wild gets old quickly. You can't share anything legitimate and worthwhile with someone from way out there," he countered.

Once again, I didn't disagree. Was I just guarded and cynical? I began to rethink my approach to dating.

As a compromise, I suggested we commit to a three-date grace period before we jumped to any conclusions. That seemed more than reasonable and hardly commitment-phobic.

Ethan disagreed. "I don't need a grace period. If we're happy enough with our dynamic to sleep together, we should be happy enough with our dynamic to be exclusive."

This felt like a trap.

"Is there someone else who's an option you're considering?" He would not let it go.

"I don't have any interest in pursuing anyone until I have a better understanding of our dynamic," I clarified.

"You should be more honest about it and just say you have loose ends," he pushed.

I felt strongly for Ethan, but he was pushing the boundaries of premeeting expectations beyond my comfort zone.

"I should get some sleep. Have a drive ahead of me in the morning. Sleep well, Anna," he said abruptly, clearly not getting the responses he was hoping for.

I just wanted to remain grounded and realistic about our expectations—at least until we met.

"In an ideal world, you would do what feels right, and I would do what feels right. The only difference is, in this world, what feels right to you, doesn't feel right to me." He was speaking in riddles again. But, he promised, "I'll sleep on it and it will be fine tomorrow."

January 3, 2011

Subject: PSA

OkC account deleted.

That is the email that greeted me the next morning, as well as a separate email, with the subject "Addendum":

"And on a separate, but related, note—I think I'm going insane as a result of all of this. Maybe we should both do a little reevaluation."

Huh? Confusing contradictions abounded. I tried to address one issue at a time.

"Wherever we land, I am grateful for this strange and absorbing time," I replied. "It's many things to me, but perhaps two are most salient: 1) it's reminded me of my desirability, beyond the physical, and 2) it's reminded me that there are people like you out there, which is exciting. However, it is my hope that this is just a prelude, not the main event."

That seemed to momentarily satiate him. But it was clear the expectation was for me to follow suit and also delete my profile, despite his refusal to request it directly.

"I don't care if you do the same or not, but I do care that you start acting like the men who were in your life don't need to continue to be until you figure out whether we can create a healthy relationship together. For me, it's just a matter of putting some thought into exactly which values I'm comfortable relinquishing for the sake of yours."

None of this was sitting well with me.

Perhaps realizing he was crossing a line, he pivoted slightly in exasperation: "Grace period exists till you deem it extraneous. I'm off OkC. You can be on OkC, as you want. You can date as you want. Fuck as you want. We've agreed."

Not exactly the sweetest proposal of exclusivity I'd ever received, but I tried to focus on the intent: his desire to be with me and only me. Had I ever considered such a thing *before* meeting someone? No, that sounded crazy. But this was not your average get-to-know-you week. Perhaps I was adhering to old habits that simply did not apply to this situation. I probed for more clarity:

"So, if two people are already committed to exploring only that one person for the time being, at what point does that person transition into boyfriend/girlfriend?"

"I think people can start throwing labels on it when it's not just an exclusivity of the moment, but an exclusivity that assumes a long term duration. It's the point where both of you feel comfortable making plans about houseswapping in August because the assumption is that you'll be together. Shit happens, but it needs to be unexpected shit."

As usual, Ethan made a lot of sense. Plus, isn't this the approach to dating most women hope for? Who was I to dismiss it when it came knocking? Did I have anything to lose by going along with it? The usual dating rules never felt quite right for me. Ethan was giving me a chance to write my own.

Even beyond dating, I prided myself on meeting people in unexpected ways. I'd crashed weddings (I'm an *excellent* uninvited guest), hosted "stranger parties" (where all of my friends brought a stranger as their plus-one, resulting in several enduring friendships), invited a guy I met online to my Thanksgiving dinner party for our first date (we dated for months afterward), engaged in regular house swaps with strangers, and bonded with a guy I met in an airport (he played his guitar and we sang songs together while our flight was delayed; we've since vacationed together and are still friends). I opened myself to meaningful connections that required a leap of faith in as many ways and places as I possibly could. My life was much richer for it, and in all of these examples, I had zero regrets. Why should this be any different?

Ethan was asking for a few weeks of exclusivity while we explored a connection—not marriage. I could live with that.

*   *   *

Seventy-two hours until I was back in NYC and in Ethan's presence. I tried not to lose sight of the electricity of the connection and just how close we were to finally meeting.

Ethan said he was leaning toward trying to kiss me before we reached his car at the airport, and I was more than OK with that. "Though, I might throw up from nervousness," I warned. We acknowledged that the airport is not exactly the sexiest environment—the crowds, the chaos, the brightness!

We played out our respective anticipated internal and physical states to each other. "I'll smell like plane," I acknowledged. "I have to shave tomorrow so I'll have the right amount of scruff," he said, planning ahead. "I just got a pedicure," I shared, as if to excite him with the thought of my freshly groomed feet. We discussed the perfect car ride music; he said he'd make us a playlist.

I was grateful for a reprieve from the heaviness. This is how it will be, I told myself. It's the distance that's messing with our heads. All will be fine—and possibly great—once we meet.

As we psyched ourselves up for Thursday, he suggested I come home early. I was miserable in San Diego, but I had people in my apartment, so it wasn't really an option. "Come home early and stay with me," he suggested casually. The idea of staying with a stranger might be creepy to some people, but this was the era of Couchsurfing, and I'd stayed over at the apartments of people I knew far less well than I did Ethan. So I briefly considered it. But by the time I changed my flight, I wouldn't depart until

Wednesday, only a day early. It didn't seem worth the expense. "Plus, you need time to grow your stubble," I reminded him.

"Are you ready for this?" he asked, sensing the mounting expectations and my growing anxiety.

"My toes are. But I'm not," I replied honestly.

"Well, inch by inch," he assured me.

As the days and hours wore on, our virtual chats became more intimate and sexually charged. My friend went to a launch party where they gave out sex-themed goody bags, complete with a vibrator that attached to your iPod and pulsed to the beat of the music. She'd given it to me.

"Have you used it?" he asked excitedly.

"I had some fun with it one weekend. Then I was over it. It was more laughter-inducing than sexy."

"These next few days will kill me."

January 4, 2011

> Hey you, just wanted to let you know there's an emergency at work I have to handle. Won't be responding as diligently as I usually do during the day...I'll miss you though. Feel free to serenade me while I'm dealing with the crisis.

Another day, another dramatic email upon waking. I was just grateful this one had nothing to do with me.

"What kind of emergency?" I asked. "There isn't a global financial meltdown, is there? Cause you know that already happened... It's still sort of a mystery to me what you do exactly, so I'll look forward to hearing more."

We dipped a bit deeper into the details of his work: He was employed by the U.S. government, but he also worked for Morgan Stanley in New York. An interesting combination, and one I couldn't wait to hear more about. Both of those worlds demanded extremely long hours. I knew what I was getting into.

In the absence of our real-time IM chats, I emailed him a list of some observations that popped into my head that morning:

- I'm genuinely concerned about your sleep deprivation.
- I'm beginning to think that we're characters in each other's novels. But then the movie comes out, and it ruins everything. I hope the movie doesn't ruin everything.
- It feels like Thursday is Christmas. [I know, you're a Jew. I got the memo. Just try to relate.] All highly anticipated and full of surprises and possibilities. I love Christmas.
- Have you told anyone about me? No one really knows about you except the girlfriend of Surfer's friend from New Year's and this guy I'm working on a project with, and he only knows bits and pieces. Anyway, just curious if you have someone you confide in and tell these things to.

He said he anticipated having to work through the night, but wanted to chat at some point. We compared schedules and decided they didn't align—the weather had finally turned, and I was happy to get in a little beach time—so we continued to email each other periodically throughout the day. In between crises, he told me the work stress was making him lose his hair, so to cheer himself up, he'd splurged on a fountain pen; he loved fountain pens.

I sent him a link to a beautiful house on the water in Connecticut that I planned to exchange with in February. "It excites me to go to these domestic spots some weekends. I feel like I'm playing house. Especially when there's a fireplace."

"Trying on all sorts of identities, huh?" he replied.

January 5, 2011

The final day. *Finally.* I had to clean the house and get everything in order before my flight the next day; plus I wanted to squeeze in a bit more beach and yoga. I was grateful these last few hours would pass quickly. I had only a forty-five-minute layover in Chicago, so I worried about making my connection. I didn't want anything to derail our much-anticipated airport-pickup first date.

"What happens in the slight chance I can't make it back to NY in time?" Ethan asked. He'd be driving in from DC.

"Oh, no problem. I'll just take a cab." Not the end of the world.

"I just hope I can get out of here by 5 p.m. tomorrow," he said hopefully.

"Things still crazy?" I asked.

"Yeah."

"Have you slept yet?" I already knew the answer.

"Barely…So if I get in late, still want me to get in touch? Or just wait to take you out Friday?" he asked, apparently anticipating a disruption.

"Depends how late you get in." I was saddened by the thought of waiting an extra day, but I tried to be practical. "If it's midnight before either of us gets home, maybe just wait til the next day, as we'll both be exhausted."

He had to be at work by 9 Friday morning, and I didn't anticipate our first meeting running short, so I thought better to wait until we had more time, if necessary.

"Yeah, but I'd want to see you. I miss you in a weird way," he added.

"I know. It's strange." Strange was an understatement. "Keep me posted on the airport pickup."

"Either way, you'll have your proposal to read tomorrow," he said, referring to the courtship letter he'd promised me earlier in the week. "So you can decide if we're allowed to date or not."

"Oh yes, the proposal! I will read it over and over and over on the plane. I can't wait."

"Keep in mind that I'm not at my creative best," he demurred.

"I know," I said, acknowledging the toll the work crisis had taken on him. "I'll understand if you want to defer the exercise."

"No, I already might have to postpone the meeting. I don't want to defer anything else."

January 6, 2011

In anticipation of my flight, Ethan sent me the Tefilat Haderech, the Jewish traveler's prayer, which he said had particular significance to him. "Read it to yourself when taking off," he instructed. I promised to do so, and my sincere interest in it seemed to delight him.

I was thrilled to be heading to the airport, away from Surfer Dude and toward Ethan. I couldn't help but gloat about winning our bet: Nothing sexual had occurred in San Diego. "I'm officially the winner. (God, I love to win.) Please start working out your pecs now, cause I want you to get lots of attention when you prance through the streets."

"What do you think is the likelihood that you'll pick me up? 50/50?" I asked eagerly around noon, just before takeoff, barely able to contain my excitement.

No response, but I knew he was focused on trying to get out of the office on time, so I didn't mind.

As I monitored my inbox in anticipation of Ethan's response—or, better yet, the "proposal" essay—I received another, less favorable 750-word letter. It was from Surfer Dude, labeled "final correspondence." Oy. I wasn't sure if that was a threat or a promise, but I braced for impact. He was fed up, frustrated, DONE...sort of. If I reconsidered my stance toward him, he might be interested once more. I didn't reply.

At takeoff, Ethan reemerged and my mood shifted. He wished me a safe flight and assured me the proposal letter would be in my inbox by the time I reached Chicago. I opened the prayer he'd sent me and read it several times.

I arrived in Chicago to another email: "GAH. Disastrous night...and doubtful that I'll be able to pick you up. I'm really hating it."

It was disappointing, but I knew this might happen. He had warned me. So I tried to focus on the other email I'd received upon landing: his "proposal." It was not an essay, he assured me, but a letter, "a missive which gives you a deeper insight into my intentions, goals, and romantic motivations."

In it, he made it clear that he understood I wanted to feel courted and appreciated—not just at the beginning of our relationship, but ongoing—and so he proposed not just this letter, but a series of letters: "monthly reminders and renewals of my motivations and desires to date you." Every month he would submit a new letter stating his request to date for an additional month. "You will have every freedom to accept or deny my request," he explained. "So Ms. Akbari, I introduce you to the first of, hopefully, many submissions."

It wasn't a "proposal" in the sense of asking for something or convincing me of anything. Rather, it articulated to me just how well he'd come to know me in a matter of twelve days, without ever seeing or touching me.

> I know that your fascination with social identities, manipulation, and transformation of these identities stems from your innate curiosity and fascination with the human experience. You're looking for someone who is as fascinated with the human experience as you are, but also loves you enough to be content with the very normal, predictable, lounge-on-the-living-room-couch human experience that you share together.

He knew I wanted a man ("not a boy in boxer shorts") who would push boundaries, challenge norms, and go beyond his comfort zone with me. He wanted to peel back the layers and melt my defenses to access my heart. "I want to be the source of your encouragement," he wrote.

"Please entertain my request for dating you in Month 1," he closed, adding the word count to punctuate the ridiculous formality of it all: 771.

It was the best thing anyone had ever written to me. I was smitten.

"I accept," I replied. "Looking forward to Month 1. xo"

CHAPTER 7

Reasonable Deadlines

January 7, 2011

The airport pickup date was a bust. Despite my disappointment, I tried to focus on how much more confident I'd feel meeting for the first time when not stepping off a plane. A night of rest and a hot shower would be a blessing. Maybe this wasn't such a bad thing.

By Friday night, Ethan was still stuck in DC working, making plan B—dinner and the opera—unlikely.

I asked Ethan how he felt about bull riding, suggesting that perhaps we could check out the rodeo that was coming to Madison Square Garden that weekend. It was one of my favorite annual events. I promised to wear my cowboy hat and boots. Maybe that could be plan C.

"Ha—that's great! Ugh, I'm still in D.C. I'll keep you updated."

Accepting defeat on plan B, I attempted to calm my anxiety with a yoga class, but when Ethan and I logged on to IM later that day, I didn't feel too together: "I'm losing it," I admitted. "It's like a sick joke. You're still a myth." I felt completely out of balance.

"I'm a myth, which is kind of cool," he replied, taking it as a compliment. "That makes me sound like a god."

"I mean a sick cosmic joke," I clarified, annoyed. There was so much buildup, so much anticipation; I didn't know if I could take more delays. I tried to find just a little more patience. It will be worth it, I told myself.

"Sick cosmic jokes have a way of working out," he assured me. "I want to leave tomorrow morning. I'm planning on it."

"I showed your photo to a few friends," he continued.

"Do they think you're crazy?"

"No, they think you're hot."

"Well, I guess that's the response one hopes for," I acknowledged. Then he asked, "If you had to, would you be able to come to D.C.?"

University classes didn't resume for two more weeks, so my schedule was pretty flexible. "And by 'had to,' you mean..."

"If I asked you to."

"Right. Then yes. When were you thinking?"

"If I worked through the weekend, you'd just about kill me. Rightfully so."

"I would. I'd actually cut ties for the time being. Can't take anymore," I said, being explicit about my shrinking patience and timeline. This was the deal I'd been negotiating with myself. The winter storm, my trip—these were unfortunate delays that I could justify and endure. But now that I was back and all of our dates, planned with precision and heightened emotion, were delayed indefinitely, I needed to recalibrate. I was in an unsustainable headspace.

"That's fair," he acknowledged.

"I can't focus on anything." It was an embarrassing and increasingly isolating reality. This relationship was preoccupying me and the only remedy was to meet—and soon. "Are you considering working through the weekend?"

"I'm not considering anything. It's just the program I designed isn't working, and I've been busting my ass to fix whatever's wrong. It's not coming together."

"Aw, I'm sorry," I said, trying to empathize, but not feeling very charitable. "Any end in sight?"

"End = how quickly I can find the code error. I have a team working under me."

"A big team of mathletes can't do it?" I was trying to make light of it, but

I was also wondering how many superbrains it might take to deliver him to me by the weekend.

"I'm the supreme mathlete. We will eventually," he said optimistically. "I understand if you need to break ties."

"Noooo, I'm just being extreme." I suddenly felt silly for my impatience. "If we'd already met, this would be a non-issue. It's that we HAVEN'T MET YET that's killing me." And it was. It didn't make sense, but every hour that passed without meeting him felt like a slow death.

"I know," he acknowledged.

"How is this not driving you crazy?"

"It is. But what can I do about it?" he replied practically. "I just don't want you to go loco on me about this unfortunate progression of events."

"I know. And the fact that I can't tell anyone kills me." I longed to tell people, but feared what they might say. *So, you met this guy online, and he seems too good to be true—*

"Ok, I know, Anna. What can I do? Tell me…"

—and he's canceled on your first few dates… I continued playing out the voices in my head. "I'm not mad at you, I promise," I assured him. "I know it sounds that way. I'm sorry."

"No, it's ok. Tell me what to do," he asked again.

"I'm just frustrated and feeling silly. There's nothing you can do. I don't expect you to do anything other than what you are doing. It's just such a rollercoaster." Patience was never my strong suit, and emotionally avoidant ex-boyfriends had scolded me for pushing too hard for movement, so I worried I was being unreasonable in my expectations and repeatedly apologized for them. This was his job, I reminded myself. It mattered more than some girl he'd never met. I was as frustrated with my impatience as I was with his delays. If I could just get a timeline, that would help me manage my expectations—and my sanity.

"What is the likelihood you will come back tomorrow morning?" I asked. "Realistically."

"It's just a matter of troubleshooting. The moment it works, I'm done. I don't care if I have to drive overnight."

"So you might finish tonight, or you might finish in 2012. Impossible to predict, right?" I said, my hopefulness turning to cynicism.

Ethan suggested that we set a "reasonable deadline," at which point, if he still wasn't finished, I would come to DC and he'd take a few hours off for dinner so I wouldn't think he was "a sick joke." It was a far cry from a night at the opera or a day at the rodeo, but at that point, I would have been happy with a trip to the corner deli and a chat on a park bench.

"Ok, that works." Rationality, flexibility; this was workable. We were just two busy people trying to make romance happen between life obligations. "What's a reasonable deadline?"

"You set it."

"I don't know...I have a meeting with a client on Monday that I could probably reschedule. And I have other stuff scheduled next week—but it's all pretty flexible."

"So then let's say by Sunday morning? Or Tuesday morning?"

"Oh man, Tuesday. That's a really long time." Suddenly the prospect of waiting four more days felt like an eternity.

"So Sunday," he confirmed.

"It doesn't make sense for me to sit in your apartment while you work." I started anticipating how odd that would feel.

"Completely up to you. I just want you to feel more secure. We don't have to do it this way. We can wait it out and see how it goes," he offered, trying to comfort me.

The whole thing was depressing me.

"Let's just take it as it goes. Day by day. It won't take too long. I'm doing my best," he assured me.

I was equal parts sympathetic and sulky. I was also starting to feel stupid. Did I seem pathetic? I was so emotionally invested, I didn't trust myself to see any of it clearly.

Sensing my frustration (and possibly fed up with hearing about it), Ethan asked if I wanted to "cool things off" until he was back in town.

Again, I felt torn and self-conscious. Breaking ties and waiting both felt equally excruciating. "I don't know. I've just been really trusting and open, and even though I know you're legit, I can't help but think I'm being a naive little girl."

"Ok, Anna. Let's cool things down. I just don't want you doubting things and my authenticity. I'm okay with this; you're not."

His words pained me. I was embarrassed. He was so enviably calm and rational, while I felt like a total mess. I was the one who went to California for a week, missing his mellow downtime over the holidays. Now work was taking priority, and that had nothing to do with me. It's not that I was skeptical of his excuses, but I did worry I was being a little bit gullible. Was I more invested than him? Did this matter more to me? Was I setting myself up for disappointment? Was I turning him off by projecting all of this angst onto him?

I suggested that perhaps I should fade a bit until he returned. He had a job to do that was occupying his every waking moment, but for me time was frozen.

"I'm not going to lose interest any time soon. I signed up for a month of wanting you, and the month hasn't even started," he reminded me.

I needed to pull it together. Despite his physical absence, Ethan was more present with me and more intentional about our potential relationship than any guy I'd dated in a long time. I needed to take stock of the situation to better manage my own expectations. Was this week exceptional or the norm? Was his schedule always unpredictable? Was he always hard to make (and keep) plans with? Either way, I needed to know what I was signing up for. Knowing always soothed my nerves, regardless of the reality. It was the uncertainty that killed me.

Ethan assured me that this was atypical. "Just stick through this, even if you need a bit of distance. What's the worst that can happen?" he asked, trying to cheer me up.

The worst? Oh, just looking like a pathetic fool while also experiencing emotional devastation. Other than that, I had nothing to lose! "Don't you have any apprehensions?" I was amazed and annoyed by his calm demeanor.

"No. I know that I want you and I know these are just temporary obstacles."

Why did he seem like the practical one? I was practical, too! I was trying to be completely practical *and* take a leap of faith in the name of love. The cognitive dissonance was making me crazy.

"You can suspend disbelief with me. It's ok…I'm a good guy. I don't want to hurt you or leave you disappointed. You're a hopeless romantic jaded by experience."

Was I? Maybe Ethan was right. How could I not be a little jaded after more than a decade of dating in New York City? I didn't want to be cynical any more than I wanted to be a needy baby. I vowed to suck it up a little longer.

Self-conscious about the image I was projecting, I defended myself: I'm not generally a jaded person. I'm the eternal optimist. But I was at war with myself. I was not playing it cool. Thankfully, Ethan didn't mock or belittle me for it; he appreciated that this was affecting me so profoundly; it meant I cared.

"I wouldn't hold it against you if you needed a time out," he offered.

"I know. But I'd miss you."

"I'd miss you, too," he agreed.

"And so…here we are," I said. Right back where we started.

I suggested we were in a modern version of *You've Got Mail*, the film where Tom Hanks and Meg Ryan have an extended correspondence before ever meeting. In an effort to self-soothe, I grasped for examples of where this unusual type of dating preamble didn't end disastrously.

"I will probably be over 40 by the time we finally meet," I theorized.

"You'll freeze some eggs," he said, playing along. Then he told me he'd donated sperm to a sperm bank when he was younger. Later, when the brother of his British ex, the other Anna, had cancer, and the chemo wiped out his sperm, Ethan considered offering his sperm.

A sweet gesture, but somehow that story did not comfort me.

Throughout the day, Ethan kept in touch with me regularly while multitasking with his team. He told me about the first Thanksgiving his ex-wife spent with his family. He was in the other room as the food was being passed around, and when he returned, she had filled his plate in abundance (which proved to his mother that she was a suitable wife and demonstrated to him how devoted she was). I told him that if I were in a comparable situation, I'd dish him up anything that I knew he liked or that was running out, and then maybe call into the kitchen to ask him if he wanted the rest—or just wait until he returned. My casualness about the plate filling angered him beyond belief and somehow further demonstrated my unJewishness. A generous person (and wife) fills the plate of another first. How could I be so selfish?

"There are a lot of variables and I can't say, 'I'm the girl who fills the plate'—it's not that simple for me. I'd think about all those other things in relation to you." This went on at length.

"You think too much," he informed me.

"You need a simpler woman. A 'plate filler,'" I retorted. "Any other tests you'd like me to fail this evening?"

"I'll get in touch when I'm in town." That had escalated quickly.

"If you leave it like that, I'm not sure what my response will be."

"You're a grown woman. You can control your response."

"Yes, I can. And I know how I respond when someone treats me like this. You've taken me from wanting you to feeling interrogated and rejected."

"I guess I'm just that good," he said, seemingly self-satisfied.

I was livid. I was self-critical about my growing impatience with his work obligations, but his insistence on turning the most banal detail into proof that I was too this or not enough of that enraged me. The unfair judgments killed my confidence. Those were the moments when I questioned if any of this was worth it.

"Ugh, I'm sorry. I'm a prick sometimes. You don't react to things in the same way a Jewish girl would. I think sometimes I'm hard on you because I'm trying to bring you closer to that."

He needed to make a choice and stop punishing me for who I couldn't be.

"I really do want you. Anna, I'm sorry. It's just my stuff. It's my fault. Are you sick of me yet?"

I was. And yet. It was too late to turn back now. Insatiable curiosity and a nagging what-if got the best of me. Not to mention very real feelings and a deepening emotional attachment. I *would* meet this man in person.

"You just wreck my head. And my heart," I told him.

"Totaaaaaalllllly head on chest time," he said, trying to soothe the moment. "Sleep well, beautiful. I'll keep you updated."

He knocked me down, only to create an opportunity for him to pick up the pieces. It felt icky. The emotional drama was taking a toll.

"Let me know in the morning if I'm jogging or if you're driving—cause either way, it's on."

January 8, 2011

The next morning, Ethan told me to prep my running shoes. He was still stuck in DC, but he promised cereal bars upon my arrival.

Meanwhile, in New York, there was dirty sewer water dripping from the overhead light in my bathroom, thanks to my upstairs neighbor's overflowing toilet. If I needed yet another excuse to flee to DC, this was it.

So I sent Ethan an email laying out my travel options:

I've done some research. Here's what I've learned:

FOOT: It will take me approximately 24 hours of continuous running to arrive in D.C. I'm mentally up for the challenge, but my body and already-tattered running shoes may object, and I will most likely collapse upon arrival. [Pro: Fitness. Con: Too exhausted for sex.]

BUS: There are buses, but I have a gentleman's agreement with myself that, after paying my dues on bus trips from hell, I will never ride a bus that goes further than the M86 crosstown. [Pro: Economical. Con: Suicide.]

TRAIN: Trains travel with regular frequency between NY and DC in around 1/3 of the time that we spend fighting on an average IM session. Unfortunately, the trains are stupid expensive and cost about the same as a flight to California. [Pro: Speed. Con: Poverty.]

So, that said, the train would be the most probable solution. Several factors would influence that decision:

Would you even have time to see me?

Do you think you might come back tomorrow? (If so, I would wait.)

What flavor are the cereal bars?

Ethan was amused and assured me he would cover the train expenses. As for his return to New York, he anticipated Tuesday, based on the progress they'd made. He also informed me he'd changed the dates of the opera tickets, so we'd get a redo on that. "The cereal bars will always be apple. Unless you prefer strawberry. I can live with both," he concluded.

"I don't eat cereal bars. So apple is always perfect."

I told him that Tuesday felt…too long, and given the current state of my apartment, I was eager to escape. But I was also willing to wait until Tuesday, if that was preferable. Nothing I said made sense. I was willing to do almost anything just to get this man in front of me. Finally looking each other in the eye would be a relief, whether I found myself wanting to rip his clothes off of him or just give him a big, platonic hug. I was fine either way, but I simply needed to know. And to know, we had to meet.

Ultimately, he decided my joining him in DC would require a lot of unnecessary travel, so we made a firm date for Tuesday. He'd head straight to me upon returning to the city, and he planned to take the rest of the week off. To ensure he'd make it out on time, he'd tell his team he had an urgent doctor's appointment.

"I think we'll survive until Tuesday. No more broken dates," he promised.

*   *   *

Later that night, Ethan sent me a series of emails.

"Are you around? I'm drunk…"

"Come on, be around. I want to talk to you."

I was irritated.

"Yoooooooooooo. Come talkto me." Ethan's messages never had typos. He was definitely drunk.

We switched to IM and he informed me that he was working, but then someone dragged him to a thirtieth birthday party. He drank too much Scotch. Some girls left lipstick on him.

I was in no mood to hear about this turn of events after I'd offered to visit and he'd declined.

"Ah uck world is spinning," he replied, unable to process anything I was saying.

"I drank too mcuch. Stop not liking me," he pleaded.

I reminded him of my crappy day, in which literal shit fell from my ceiling, requiring some unsavory cleanup, and my laundry place gave my clothes to someone else, forcing me to sift through someone else's laundry to find my underwear. "And I had plans with you," I continued. "And tried to visit, but that was rejected. Now you message me that you have lipstick on your face and want me to be excited about it."

It was a breaking point for me. Something in me snapped. Anger swelled. He was either fucking with me or taking me for granted. Neither sat well with me.

"I think I need to throw up," he informed me. "But my balls are too cold for me to move."

I'd had enough for the evening and signed off.

January 9, 2011

I woke up to an email with the subject "Damage control."

"What's the status? I'm assuming you're unimpressed, but beyond that . . . ?"

Indeed, I was—unimpressed. I didn't reply.

Five minutes later, he sent another email, assuring me that he hadn't planned to go to the party, didn't stay long, but the effects of the alcohol were intensified by sleep and food deprivation. The lipstick, he recalled, was from some game—not from any sort of amorous encounter. "I have a pounding headache right now," he informed me, as if to assure me he was being punished for his sins.

I did not reply.

Four hours later, another email.

> Hey, Thinking about you ... Feel a little anxious about your reaction when you wake up. Say hi as soon as you do, please.

> —Ethan

"I'm annoyed, but it's fine. Heading to yoga. Hope you feel better," I replied later that day.

That afternoon, he sent me a link to Adele's remake of "Make You Feel My Love."

"If this were 1991, I'd make you a mixtape. (Although probably at some point, I actually will.) 20 years later, I'll have to settle for this," he said, referring to the MP3 he'd attached. "I'm feeling a bit odd about things between us right now—a bit sad, a bit angry with myself, a bit disheartened. This song came on the radio and made me think of you. Pathetic, sappy, maybe...but after you roll your eyes, maybe you'll at least smile. Several of the lyrics seem to apply."

The previous night had mentally and emotionally given me an out. His bad behavior nudged me toward calling it quits. When guys behaved like that, they were usually sending a signal: I'm not that into you. And that was my cue to leave. But Ethan was a man of perpetually mixed signals, and he loved a romantic gesture. Sure, sending a song wasn't like coming home to a house full of roses or, better yet, him finally appearing on my doorstep. But the sentimental song, plus words of contrition and his repeated attempts to get back in my good graces, wore me down. Maybe he was overwhelmed by the depth of our connection and was acting out? He certainly wouldn't be the first man to do so. But I could count on him to atone and try to make it up to me. Maybe that was enough—for now? Maybe I was overreacting.

We connected on IM later that night.

"You were drunk. I've been drunk before. I get it," I said, trying to move past it.

"I'm sorry, I really want to do this right. I like that you call me on all my shitty patterns," he said.

"I don't want to feel like the mom. Always nagging and telling you to stop being a prick."

"This isn't nagging. This is you telling me to get my shit together or I lose out," he said, affirming my feelings. "Anna, I've been worried about this all night/today, I don't want to fuck up with you. I'm sorry for being a prick. I'm rusty at this."

We made plans to meet Tuesday after 5 p.m. I once again assured myself that these issues would resolve themselves once we met in person. I would not bail until we met.

"You know what I'm going to ask my one-day wife to do?" he asked out of nowhere. "You've heard of a mikvah?"

"That bath?" I asked, not entirely sure what it was. "It's to cleanse? Does it revirginate you or something?"

"Yeah," he confirmed.

"I wonder how many mikvahs I'd need…" I pondered sarcastically.

"Haha it's really a rebirth."

"But only the woman gets cleansed?" I was skeptical.

"Yeah. Obviously," he said. "Religion is patriarchal."

"I'd want there to be some sort of comparable cleansing for the man. I like the idea of a rebirth. I'd gladly rock the mikvah, just don't want to pretend I'm the only soiled party."

"I can't expect to marry a virgin, but I think I can expect a woman to want to become a virgin again for me," he continued. By his logic, if you knew you would meet the man of your dreams, who was sure to fulfill all of your sexual fantasies by age thirty-five, then you would happily just wait for him.

Interesting theory. I did not agree. I certainly didn't think any man would patiently wait to have sex until age thirty-five if he knew he would eventually get to marry me. Though it didn't surprise me that a man—especially one as confident as Ethan—might think that he was worth the wait.

"I appreciate the experiences and the pleasure and the pain that helped me to evolve into that person. I don't think we're fully formed and then stop. I wouldn't be that person for him—and he wouldn't be that person for me—if I hadn't had those experiences," I countered.

While we differed on whether we preferred to marry a virgin, we discovered we were on the same page when it came to wedding rings: simple gold bands for both would suffice.

"Hey, let's take a vacation," he suggested, as if we were a normal, established couple who did things like plan trips together.

"We haven't met and we're planning vacations?" I was incapable of being shocked by anything he said at this point.

"Sure. First week of February. Scotland," he proposed. He was going whiskey tasting with two Irish buddies that week.

"I have to teach Mondays and Wednesdays," I informed him, dampening the mood by acknowledging reality: I did have a life beyond Ethan, as much as I'd been neglecting it.

"Why don't you come to Scotland for the weekend? The 3rd through the 6th."

I told him I'd consider it, but was not really in a financial position for international weekend getaways on my academic budget. I also made it clear I didn't want him to foot the bill. But he insisted.

"We're crazy—you realize this, right?" I confirmed, stating the obvious. "Ok, if we can find a way to make that happen, I'd be game." I'd once flown to Hong Kong for a second date to spend the week with someone, and we ended up dating for a while, so by the time February rolled around, I felt confident I'd be far beyond my second date with Ethan. Maybe I'd be going to Scotland in a few weeks.

* * *

Later that day, I logged on to OkCupid. I was with a friend who was thinking of joining, and she wanted to see my profile. Ethan deleted his the previous week, which I had verified, but I never deleted mine, so I had accumulated several new messages. I took a look at them, but nothing captured my interest in the way that Ethan did. I wasn't missing anything. I'd done enough online dating to know that if this didn't work out, they'd probably all still be there when I returned.

Out of curiosity, I decided to see if Ethan was still absent and looked him up.

There he was.

I emailed him to ask him if he'd deleted his account.

Ha...Knew this would happen. I did, of course, and then had to look up an email today...Just of a chick who had emailed me with a question a while back. Signed on today and then needed to delete again, but I can't do it for another week. OkC won't let you delete for another week after signing on.

He wasn't wrong about that. OkCupid had this weird policy that locked you into staying on the site for a prescribed period. He assured me the email was not for a date, but rather an agent who wanted to consider him for a documentary about dating in New York.

I told him I believed him and deleted my profile.

January 10, 2011

"Oh man. I just had the worst dream," I wrote to Ethan upon waking. "I dreamt that I finally met you and it wasn't you at all. It was some pasty kid with a buzz cut who'd stolen your photos and pretended to be you. He was awful. I was crushed.

"I know you're you," I assured him, but mostly myself. Reality was increasingly elusive. Everything felt like a dream. "Phew. So good to wake up."

In anticipation of our date the next day, I sent him a link to the song "Tomorrow" from the musical *Annie* (my childhood obsession).

Tomorrow. At last.

*   *   *

That afternoon, while with a friend who had an OkCupid profile, I told her about Ethan. She wanted to see him, so we looked him up. He was online, a mere day after he'd promised he was done. My heart sank. Again.

*   *   *

"Gah. Gah. Gah. Massive Gah. I really don't know why I even bothered to waste time perusing OkC. My go-to mechanism with dealing with nerves or whatever when it comes to girls is distracting myself with other random girls. Misguided gut reaction. No one interested me in the slightest. I need to get over myself and my habitual responses. I'm truly sorry."

I'd met (and dated) many NYC "players" over the years, so I knew it when I saw it. Despite saying everything I wanted to hear—that he was looking for something serious, that he was interested in pursuing me—Ethan was increasingly seeming like just another player, only with more eloquent and convincing cover-up stories. There was always a plausible excuse. And always a charming message to smooth it over. Whether I wanted to or not, I still cared about him deeply. I told myself that meeting in person would be the catalyst to merge his words of intention with his actions. And if that didn't happen, at least I'd know I stayed open and tried.

Miraculously, he was able to disable his account in under a week this time—which I verified. I was not in the habit of asking men to delete their dating profiles before I met them, but given the lengthy, heated discussions we'd had on the topic, his behavior was more than a little hypocritical. But, whatever—all I cared about was meeting him the following day. Then we could worry about the rest.

January 10, 2011

I attended the premiere of Paul Giamatti's new film, *Barney's Version*, at the Paris Theater. As much as I longed to be with Ethan, the screening was a fancy affair in a theater that I loved, and I was excited to take my mind off of him for a few hours. Unfortunately, it was the exact wrong movie for that moment: It featured a Scotch-drinking, boxers-wearing Jewish divorcé who meets the New York sophisticate of his dreams. There are all these obstacles for them to be together; then when it finally seems like it might work, he keeps fucking up, but she loves him anyway—until he gets careless and, in a very "accidental" incident, cheats on her, which ruins everything. There was truly no escaping Ethan.

"That movie is eerie in its parallels, aye?" he observed when I described the plot to him.

"I thought I was being Punk'd," I told him, not entirely kidding.

January 11, 2011

It was Tuesday, the new guaranteed date night.

The East Coast weather report called for six to ten inches of snow by 6 p.m.

Seriously? FUCK. ME.

Ethan's promise to tell his team he had a doctor's appointment that day did not pan out, as he had some last-minute work to finish up. I encouraged him to leave as early in the day as possible, as the weather report looked grim.

In between weather updates and logistics reports, Ethan informed me that the other Anna, the British ex, reached out to ask if he wanted to see her while he was in Scotland. "I was pretty convinced by the end of the conversation that you two are complete polar opposites—and I'm entirely attracted in your direction," he assured me.

I didn't love that they were in touch, but I did appreciate his transparency. And he seemed emotionally detached from her by this point.

All of his work obligations were complete, but he anticipated arriving a bit later than expected due to the roads. He planned to leave around 3, hopefully arriving in New York by 7.

At 3:36 p.m., he emailed to say he was on the road and the conditions were horrible. "Hopefully my car can handle this weather."

* * *

Throughout the afternoon and well into the evening, Ethan sent me periodic text updates. It was extremely slippery, and he had some close calls as he inched his way from DC to New York along I-95. Traffic was not moving, and when it did, it moved in unpredictable ways. I knew he was sleep-deprived and mentally exhausted, so the weather, coupled with his physical and mental condition, set my nerves on fire as he pushed to make it back to the city.

Eventually, finding conditions too dangerous to continue, he stopped in New Jersey to stay with a friend and let the storm pass.

Another date, thwarted by weather.

January 12, 2011

I woke up conflicted. On the one hand, I had been incredibly distraught by the real-time text messages I received from Ethan the night before. It was a wild and dangerous scene that he painted, and I waited anxiously for each new update.

On the other hand, we'd now postponed meeting somewhere around five times. Yes, the weather was real. Yes, I left for ten days. Yes, his job was demanding and unpredictable. But this extended virtual courtship was disrupting both my schedule and my life. I had no reason to think everything wasn't exactly as it seemed, but I was perpetually on edge. The emotional roller coaster was too much to endure. At the very least, I deserved a phone call. Something, anything to make it feel like our relationship was progressing. I wrote him a lengthy email explaining my frustration.

Ethan, however, was more calm about the circumstantial delays—and a bit irritated by my increasing impatience.

"Anna, I worked at twice the pace that any sane person should have to work. I don't think you realize how few hours of sleep I've had in the past week. And it wasn't entirely because I had to. A large part of it was because I felt you staring at me from 400 miles away."

Had I been impatient and demanding? It was a genuine fear I had in relationships: being too much. When I like someone, I get really excited—like a human golden retriever—so I regularly checked myself and tried to be the opposite of impatient and demanding with guys (though I didn't always succeed). But in this weird scenario, I lacked the ability to gauge if I was expecting too much or not enough.

"The pressure was fine," he said, putting me slightly at ease. "I want to see you. And now I get to enjoy a D.C.-free next few weeks.

"I got in the car and drove when I knew I shouldn't have, partly because I know you wanted me to, partly because I wanted to see you, too. I don't know how you could interpret that as a lack of interest," he continued.

I reminded him that I'd offered to come to DC days earlier.

"I wouldn't be a good man if I let you do it. Because I was raised to believe that a man shouldn't let a woman labor herself if he can help it."

I guess that was chivalry, right? It was like something straight out of the notorious dating book *The Rules*: Don't meet him halfway. If he won't travel to see you, then you just don't see him. *Was I becoming a Rules Girl?*

"Basically, all forces of nature have been working against us from every angle," I summarized.

"Right, and instead of getting frustrated, I've tried my best to work around it," he assured me, knowing I had no way of verifying his efforts. "And the fact that I was driving for 7 hours yesterday and still didn't hit NY doesn't make me less eager to see you."

And yet, I still needed reassurance. *What was wrong with me?*

"Anna, I'm crazy about you, I'm sorry we've had so many obstacles, but I'm not deterred from it... Winter sucks, snow sucks, driving sucks, but to me that seems temporary. I'm ok with dealing with obstacles to get to you."

All of this was very, very hard to argue with.

But instead of making a firm new plan, Ethan shifted to a "when I show up, I show up" mindset. "I'll give you a call when I make it to my apartment and you can tell me when I can come by," he casually suggested.

I resisted, wanting something confirmed.

"What's the worst that can happen? I tell you I'm in my apartment, you say, oh I'm out with friends; I'll say, ok, I'll meet you in 2 hours when you're home."

Well. When he put it that way. I felt a bit unnecessarily dramatic. So we settled on Friday night at the latest.

He reminded me that he was a patient person, and that I should not mistake his patience for a lack of passion.

Fine.

*   *   *

The sun came out that afternoon, and by evening the snow in the city had melted into slush. Temperatures were above freezing, so I figured there was little chance of ice on the highway. Ethan informed me that he would have dinner and head out.

*   *   *

Late that night, I received an email saying he was still in New Jersey.

I was annoyed. And confused.

"Can you please explain something to me? Why would you spend the last three weeks trying to win me over, to get me to commit to you before I've even met you, to ultimately be crazy about you—and then be so 'meh' about finally getting the chance to materialize? It's baffling to me."

"I'M NOT MEH!!!" he replied, clearly irritated. "I'M DOING THE BEST I CAN!!! FUCKING HELL. JUST CHILL UNTIL FRIDAY. I DON'T KNOW WHAT ELSE TO TELL YOU."

I recoiled. My rational mind told me that I'd done nothing to deserve his ire and that it was not OK for him to speak to me like that, but emotionally I was hooked. Ethan felt more like a drug than a boyfriend. (*Was he my boyfriend?*) I was so invested, I cared so much—I *really* wanted this to work. Normally a confident, ballsy, takes-no-shit professional woman, I folded in on myself until I was nothing more than a wounded child, unable to advocate on her own behalf. Ethan owned me. Sadness overtook me.

He informed me he was going to sleep. He did not enjoy the conversation and didn't see a positive outcome.

The fact that he'd heroically tried to make it home by Tuesday only to casually delay until Friday made no sense.

"I'm clearly not understanding all the facts." I continued to give him the benefit of the doubt.

No response.

Yes, his words crippled me, but it was his silence that broke me. I can't handle avoidance. It's my Achilles' heel. I'd rather have someone scream in my face than refuse to engage.

Feeling pushed to my absolute limit, I texted him: "I can't do this anymore."

Moments later, I received an email: "The roads were rough and I decided to stop by my parents' to help them shovel since my dad pulled his back last time. Instead of texting me with 'I can't do this anymore' you could have just asked me what happened."

And risk him lashing out again?

He explained his silence by saying he'd fallen asleep earlier. He didn't want me to bail. "I don't walk away from conversations."

Things were tense. We decided to reconnect in the morning.

January 13, 2011

"Let me know when you're up..." he messaged me the next day.

"Morning," I replied.

Twelve hours passed. No response.

I reached out again.

"??? Is everything ok?"

Nothing.

* * *

I'd struggled with insomnia for years, and when I wasn't up all night talking to Ethan, I was up all night worrying about Ethan. I needed sleep. I also couldn't take the isolation anymore. My bustling life came to a screeching halt when I met him. Most friends were away for the holidays and were just now returning. Ethan felt like my sexy, covert communication partner during the holiday slowdown, but the giddiness had worn off and I needed support. It was time to share what was happening with someone else.

I emailed Virginia, the same friend who'd met her fiancé on Craigslist. If anyone could appreciate this situation, it was her. She loved hearing about my latest relationship drama and always brought an open mind to the conversation, eager to analyze and support. That was exactly what I needed right then. She also happened to be an astrologer, so her first question, whenever I mentioned a new guy, was always, *When's his birthday?* Without offering any context about Ethan or our relationship, I said I'd met someone and sent her his birth details: July 10, 1975, 6 p.m. EST, New York, New York. She replied enthusiastically with various questions and initial insights: Did we love talking to each other? Was he a bit more conservative than me? What was he seeking? What was his name?

I wasn't ready to fill in all the blanks for her just yet, but merely sharing that I'd met someone gave me comfort. I hoped to tell her everything after meeting him the following day.

January 14, 2011

The day had finally arrived. The obstacles were cleared. Nothing could keep us from finally being together physically. Or so I thought.

In the previous two days, Ethan had been distant and hard to reach. I figured he was exhausted from his marathon workweek in DC and was just settling back into his apartment. I tried to be patient.

"Yes—how are you? How was your day?" he casually replied to my email from the day before.

I was stressed and anxious, but I didn't want to rock the boat. I refused to say or do anything that might give him an excuse to back out or postpone. I *had* to meet Ethan. And it had to be today.

I tried to play it cool. "Very productive. Yours?" I would not acknowledge the radio silence. "When do I see you today?"

I had an old friend in town, and she didn't want to be out late, so I suggested that I would have dinner with her and then meet him after. In three weeks, we'd progressed from a dramatic airport pickup followed by the opera to a casual drink. Whatever. I didn't care at this point. As long as I saw him in the flesh.

"Where?" I asked.

Silence.

*   *   *

Ethan hadn't responded to the email I'd sent at noon that day, trying to pin down a meeting place and time. I sent a text, but no response.

I met my friend for dinner near Union Square in a truly horrible mindset. I tried to explain the situation to her (which felt increasingly difficult to do), but she dismissed him as just another New York player.

By the time we finished dinner, I still hadn't heard from him. I was losing my mind.

I texted again, asking where we should meet. He replied immediately, saying he needed a second. Fifteen minutes passed, then thirty. He stopped replying.

I began to freak out. Not meeting was *not* an option. I had invested too much, and I couldn't endure another delay. I no longer cared what he thought of me. I needed to see who this man was. I could not rest until that happened.

I continued to text and call, leaving multiple voicemails, updating him on my whereabouts and demanding that he meet me. Needless to say, I was no longer playing it cool.

Nothing.

I eventually went home and emailed him: "Wow hmmm ok." After hundreds of hours of correspondence, that was as articulate as I could be. I had no words left.

I passed out and awoke to his reply: "What the hell happened?"

Huh? You're asking *me*?

"So you definitely went off your rocker a bit. But I probably pushed you there," he observed. "You hardly give someone the benefit of the doubt."

Benefit of the doubt? *Benefit of the doubt?!* I was on fire. How many passes could I give this guy? I wanted to scream in his face and inflict bodily harm on him. If I knew where he was, I would sprint to him and rip his clothes off of him—not out of passion, but uncontrollable rage. I thought I might crawl out of my own skin with anger. I needed to understand what was going on. It no longer felt like an amorous meetup. This was a battle of wills, and I was determined to get him to materialize.

"How was texting you going off my rocker? What happened to you?" I was delirious and hungover. "You should be flattered I still care at this point. And you're paying this month's phone bill." Fuck his expensive Irish phone and fuck him. He reminded me that he planned to pay for it.

"I backed out—no real reason, just that I'm a douche," he responded, dismissing his actions.

I thought my head might explode. But despite my anger, I once again became small. How could he not want to meet me? After all that? It was heartbreaking.

"I do want to meet you. They're my issues... Not your problem."

Huh? He had made it my problem. It was time for an ultimatum: We would meet that day or I'd disappear. The end.

There was nothing he could say that could convince me to keep torturing myself with this insanity. No work emergency or family obligation, no crisis of confidence—nothing. I had earned some face time and I wouldn't accept anything short of that. Plus, he was seriously interfering with my ability to live my life. He messaged me day and night, and I didn't have the capacity to ignore his messages (and I knew he'd message again if I didn't reply). He was my captor, and I feared I had developed Stockholm syndrome. The only escape from this mental hell was meeting. No more digital limbo.

He continued to be coy: It wasn't for lack of interest, he insisted, but perhaps it wasn't the best time for us to get involved. We'd been communicating for weeks, and suddenly *now* it wasn't the best time?

"Because it's a new advancement."

"What the hell does that mean?" The switch had flipped. I gave myself permission to be as demanding and bitchy as I wanted. Restraint clearly hadn't worked. Time for a different tack.

"The timing is off," he said, still being vague. "Can you please at least tell me what you look like right now—are you giving me the impatient hand-crossed stare down, rolling your eyes, ready to kill me?"

I was not amused.

He inched closer to the truth, dropping little breadcrumbs. Personal stuff... have to deal with some things... just found out... health stuff.

I flashed back to the biopsy he'd had done as I left for California. Oh no. How had I not asked him what was happening with that?

It was his throat. He needed surgery immediately.

I didn't want to make the situation about me, but I also didn't understand how that development would make him hesitant to meet me. Did he think I would run if he told me? Had his own insecurities flared up, so he was pushing me away before we met? I begged him to have a little faith in me. Of course I still wanted to meet him. This didn't change things for me. If anything, it made me more empathetic. No wonder he'd been lashing out and hard to pin down. He was scared about circumstances that had nothing to do with me. I needed to stop personalizing his actions and just be there for him. I reverted to beating myself up for my behavior.

"It doesn't make me a sexy alternative. And you don't owe me anything," he said, trying to dissuade me.

"I'm looking for real—not 24/7 sexy," I reminded him. I was fine with a friendship, if that made him more comfortable. But it needed to be an in-person friendship. On that I would not compromise.

He agreed. Good. Coffee? Brunch? I'd take anything. We needed to meet.

"Can I think about the best way to do this? And I'll let you know today."

"This does not deter me," I reiterated. "But I do wish you'd told me earlier."

His vague withholding transformed into anger. Not at me, but the situation. It fucked everything up and pissed him off. My commitment to stick with him through it offered little consolation. This was not the love story he had envisioned.

The surgery, which was scheduled for the coming Tuesday, was only the start. Afterward, he would need chemo. It was esophageal cancer.

This was really, *really* serious.

"I'd like to see you before then so I can hug you." I had no idea how else to respond. I just wanted him to know I cared.

"That's EXACTLY what I've spent weeks thinking about receiving from you." His worst fear was that we'd be a physical mismatch and become "buddies." Now, his medical diagnosis was pushing us in that direction. I was open to more, but it was clear he didn't know what he wanted.

"I'm really angry," he repeated. He said he was going for a run to clear his head and would be in touch.

I felt more attached to him than ever. I didn't know what role he wanted me to play, but I was certain I couldn't abandon him now. He knew I'd recently lost my grandfather to cancer and was still raw from that loss. If we couldn't be romantic partners for the time being, we could still be important players in one another's lives. I would support him no matter what. What kind of person would I be if I bailed at this moment?

Adversity has a way of bringing people closer. I already felt a strong bond with him, and I believed this would strengthen us, not tear us apart. My life had been a long series of obstacles, and I'd built up some resilience. Big, messy, intense life stuff didn't scare me. I didn't seek or demand perfection; I just wanted real. I wanted *him*.

January 15, 2011

"I've been doing a lot of thinking, Anna. I just can't bring myself to meet you before this surgery. For a variety of reasons. I'm really so sorry."

I was crushed.

CHAPTER 8

Tainted Love Talk

January 16, 2011

E than went silent. After telling me he didn't want to meet me before his surgery and promising to explain the reasoning in detail, he completely disappeared. Every hour of silence stripped away another layer of my self-confidence. In my head, I wrote and rewrote what I thought I might say to him, until we eventually connected on IM the following day.

"Why don't you want to meet me? I need to understand." It came out less poetic than I'd imagined.

"Let me write an email about it later today so I can organize my thoughts," he offered.

We were three weeks in, and despite my profound concern for his health, I was over Ethan's flowery email treatises. He could organize his thoughts—and I would organize mine.

* * *

Desperate for an outlet for analyzing the emotional turmoil, I emailed a friend to spill everything: how we'd connected, the obstacles to meeting, culminating with the cancer diagnosis. I needed someone to reassure me and help me make sense of it all. But it was also time to dig into some details I'd hoped to clear up in person.

Ethan was thirty-five, so by my calculations, he'd likely graduated from Stuyvesant in 1994, a year after my friend Matt. The fact that Matt didn't know him didn't seem like a big deal. There are more than three thousand students in that school; it would be impossible to know everyone. So I mentally set that information aside.

Now that Ethan had delayed our meeting indefinitely, I started obsessively scrutinizing every piece of the Ethan Schuman puzzle. His refusal to meet unleashed the sleuth in me.

Had he actually graduated from Stuy in 1994? And what about the Irish phone number? There was nothing glaringly suspicious about either of these things, but for my own sanity, I needed to start verifying pieces of his story if I was going to continue to stay invested throughout his illness. I realized that confronting someone with a recent cancer diagnosis about their biography could backfire. Was I being selfish and insensitive? Quite possibly. Had he shown himself to be anything other than someone who worked a lot and who now faced a very scary medical crisis? No. He was so communicative, so eager to share every facet of his life with me, that I felt a bit ashamed that I was thinking about anything other than his well-being in that moment. Yes, he had been a tremendous asshole on more than one occasion, but I felt guilty for insisting on putting my own mind at ease before determining if I could stick with him.

First, I had to try one last time to get him to meet.

I told Ethan that I planned to pull back significantly in our communication and likely disappear unless he agreed to meet me—a suggestion he deemed "a bit harsh." Then, without a smooth segue, I asked if he could answer a few questions for me.

"When did you graduate from Stuy?" (OK, so sneak interrogations were not my forte.)

"Uh?"

I repeated the question, trying to seem more casual about it and failing. Ethan was immediately suspicious.

"What's your train of thought here?"

I explained that I had some friends who were around his age and also went to the same schools as him. It would be cool if they all knew each other. I hoped I was conveying curiosity rather than skepticism, but Ethan was on to me.

"So you don't think I'm being honest with you."

I couldn't fake it. "I don't know at this point." Seeing I was getting nowhere with the school inquiry, I shifted to the other thing that nagged at me: his Irish phone. He'd been back in the United States for a while since he'd worked in Ireland, and using a foreign phone was expensive. Why hadn't he switched back?

"Because I need to finish off with Ireland. I have another trip I have to make, and after that I was going to cancel it and get a NY number. Makes no sense for me to have two numbers right now," he explained logically. He elaborated: Most of his business calls for his work with the government were with Ireland, so that was the number he used.

"Ok, I believe you," I concluded, as satisfied as I could be with that answer. I knew other high-level business professionals who did international work and used their phones in ways that would make my bank account collapse. So while it was expensive, it didn't seem implausible.

"I don't like the intent of this conversation," he warned.

"I just needed to clarify those two points so I didn't question anything," I explained.

"I agree that this has gotten pretty fucked up," he admitted. "If you're worried about your phone bill, I'll honestly pay for it."

"I am worried about it." I was. Very worried.

New York is priced for the rich, and I made very little money teaching. Ethan and I texted quite regularly, and while $0.50 to send me a message might not have fazed him, those messages carried a double layer of suffering for me: Each notification was a painful reminder of this man I wanted but couldn't have, accompanied by a financial burden. His foreign phone was more than a point of suspicion; it was an increasing source of stress.

"And you won't tell me if you graduated in 1994?" I didn't want to discuss money with him. So, like a dog with a bone, I returned to the original line of inquiry, insistent upon getting the information I needed. "Or maybe you're a prodigy and graduated early."

"I didn't graduate in 1994. I graduated a year early."

"Ok, I figured you were on the accelerated track," I said, stroking his ego, while mentally noting that didn't just put him in overlapping years with my friend Matt—*it meant they graduated from both schools the same year.*

"I don't know what to do about Anna #1," he said, apropos of nothing, as if that had been on his mind the entire time. "She wants to fly in and be here for the chemo."

The other Anna. Again. Far more so than his ex-wife, British Anna felt like the third wheel in our "relationship." Every mention of her stung. They had a history together. She was the one who got away. I knew they were in touch periodically, but flying in for his treatment? That felt very "girlfriend" to me, and he had insisted they were over. Clearly there were lingering feelings on both sides if he was considering it. Was I just the temporary replacement?

"I will try to answer that not as someone who has romantic interests in you, but as someone who has come to care about you as a person," I said, attempting to separate my advice from the emotional slap in the face he'd just given me. "I think that's a bad idea. It's very kind of her to want to do that, and the sentiment alone proves that she's a good person. But I don't think it would be helpful to your mental state. As your friend, I would advise you not to allow her to come."

"Yeah, I agree, but I also don't really know who to turn to, because I don't want my family to deal with it. And Anna's brother had it, so she knows what it's like."

Well at least he wasn't advocating for her to be there. That felt mildly promising. I knew he needed support, but he needn't look any further: There I was, begging him to let me be that person! Put me in, Coach! It was a role I was born to play—not just with anyone, but with someone I cared about. I'm the person people can count on. The protector. The caretaker.

I show up when it matters most. Sure, I had a ridiculous amount of stuff going on in my life, but I was good at juggling everything. And he was worth it.

But Ethan insisted that would hinder our chances at a long-term romantic relationship.

"Right, you'll really picture a guy naked who's throwing up all over your shoes." He didn't want caretaking from me; he wanted me to think of him as a sexual object.

"If she comes to care for you, I guarantee you two will get back together—so that squashes any chance we might have, also," I said, returning to the topic of Anna #1.

As if in the midst of a corporate negotiation, we took an hour break and then resumed the conversation. I had another angle to try.

"Since you don't want to meet me, but want to keep in touch, would you be willing to compromise on something? Could we talk on the phone? I'd like to hear your voice."

"Yeah, that's fair enough."

"Ok, can you talk now?" *No time like the present!*

"I'll give you a call before Tuesday, promise," he said, ignoring my impulsive suggestion.

"Ok, I'm going to hold you to that." Every time Ethan promised me something, my anxiety spiked. After so many canceled plans, it felt like more of a setup for disappointment than something to look forward to. I hated thinking like that; it wasn't my usual nature. But he'd given me no reason to believe this time would be different.

"I really miss you. Like I think about the stupid arguments we had, and it just seems so pointless, it's like we were testing each other the entire time. I was probably just trying to convince myself out of being crazy about you. But I failed with that. I'm totally hung up on you." Ethan could veer into cliché territory, but always with a knowing eye. This was different. He was clearly deep in his feelings. These comments were not accompanied by any of his usual wisecracks. Just raw emotion.

"I'll keep chasing you," he promised.

The issue of Anna #1 continued to weigh on my mind.

"I won't let her come," he concluded.

I was happy to hear this. "How is your family dealing with all of this?" I asked.

"Miserably."

"I can imagine. And you probably feel you have to be strong for them."

"Yeah."

His family was so close. This must be crushing them. It was all heartbreaking. I desperately wanted to hug him.

*   *   *

By midnight, he still hadn't sent me the promised explanation. I was growing impatient as conflicting emotions of empathy and suspicion waged a war in my head. Why did everything have to be so dramatic? We were both complicated people, but did every emotion and thought require a lengthy essay? And for once could he just do what he promised so I could set aside my doubts and fully support him during this difficult time?

With every delay, my mind started to wander, to replay and interrogate every drop of information. I'd googled him dozens of times over the previous weeks. The only Ethan Schuman I could find was a dentist in Missouri and an Ethan Schuman username for some sort of online video game. Graduating from high school in '93 and from college a few years later made him just old enough not to have an online footprint from school. And he'd made it clear that he didn't engage in any social media (Facebook was really the main platform at the time), and he kept a low profile online due to the sensitive nature of his job. So the underwhelming Google results didn't shock me.

The Irish phone number made enough sense given his work...but there was one other thing: I'd noticed that in some but not all of our email correspondence, the quoted text in his replies indicated an Irish time zone.

He was in Eastern Standard Time. Wouldn't the email platform correct accordingly? Or, I knew some platforms would allow you to keep it set to one time zone, regardless of where you were physically. Reluctantly, I decided to ask.

"Haven't changed the Irish time back yet. Geez..." he replied, less than thrilled by my question. "The 5th degree. I said I'd email you."

"You said you'd email me by 8pm last night," I reminded him, knowing that nagging might work against me. "You can't blame me for being skeptical when you refuse to meet me, refuse to talk to me, and don't keep your word on these things—especially without explanation. You wouldn't be giving me the benefit of the doubt this much. I want nothing more than to trust you 100%. Just don't keep giving me reasons to question everything."

January 17, 2011

"How are you?" he asked nonchalantly in an email subject line the following afternoon, with no text in the body of the email—completely ignoring my previous message.

I hadn't heard any more from him the night before, and I certainly didn't get the email explanation I was promised. Or the phone call. I deemed "How are you?" unworthy of a response—but it did prompt me to dig further into some inconsistencies.

"Something threw me off this afternoon," I said, initiating an IM chat. "I was hanging out at my friend Matt's house. He's an old friend of mine, graduated from Stuyvesant High School in 1993, and then went to Columbia. So I told him about you and thought it'd be fun to look at yearbook pics. You're not in either. Why is that?"

I lied. I was not at Matt's house, but I did call him and ask him to check his yearbooks. I was done being subservient. Cancer or not, I wanted answers.

"I don't know, Anna, I guess I don't exist."

"Well, it's a bit odd, no?"

"Yup. Completely odd," he agreed.

"Do you want to tell me what's going on?" I pressed.

"Nope. Not even a little."

"Why? I'd like to understand."

"Good luck with things, I have other shit to deal with right now."

Moments later, he followed up with an email: "You do fucking realize that tomorrow I'm having major surgery, right? I have other things on my mind beyond your trust issues."

"Well, whatever's going on, and even if that's not your name, I feel connected to you. So I wish you'd just tell me. What do you have to lose by just being honest with me?" I genuinely wanted to know, and I was doubling down on my assumption that he was lying about something. "Look, I wasn't *trying* to catch you in a lie."

"You didn't fucking 'catch me in a lie.'"

"I just thought it was sort of odd, so I thought I'd ask. That's all. It seems normal to inquire about something like that."

"Time and place," he retorted.

Was he asking to meet? *Yes!* "Today? I'm ready to meet whenever you are—would love nothing more. 30 minutes from now at Galaxy Cafe on 46th and 9th?"

"No, I meant that you should pick the time and place to ask about things that you think are 'sort of odd.'"

"If it's just a weird fluke, then I figured it wouldn't be a traumatic question. I just want to understand, to be there for you." I was being genuine—I did want to support him, *if* he was telling the truth. But I also shifted my energy and strategy. I would match him in whatever mind games he was playing. It seemed he'd underestimated me when, in reality, he'd chosen a worthy opponent.

"Your version of being there for me isn't what I need," he informed me.

"Can you please see the situation from my point of view? You won't see me, you won't talk to me, there are all these anomalies popping up—and still, I'm not going anywhere. All I'm asking is to better understand the situation. I want to support you. I can only imagine how traumatic this is for you. I just want to understand what's going on so I can stay in the picture for you however will be best for you." Demanding answers wouldn't work with him. I had to appeal to him emotionally.

"This isn't anywhere close to what I need right now," he reiterated.

But it was the day before his surgery and I was being kind of hard on him...Maybe I needed to extend him a little grace, while also staying mindful of protecting myself. That did not, however, erase the inconsistencies in his story.

"Even if you are lying to me about certain things," I continued, "I do believe that you are having this surgery tomorrow. I will be thinking about you intently. You're an amazing person, you're strong, and you will overcome this. I can only hope that I'll have the pleasure of meeting you one day." I believed everything I said to him, but by this point, I also believed he was manipulative and deceptive. About what and to what end, I didn't know. But there was something he wasn't telling me.

I started a separate email chain.

I'm sorry this didn't unfold how you'd like. It certainly isn't how I'd like it to be. I will be thinking about you all morning tomorrow and as you recover.

Someday I do hope to understand the mystery that is your identity—because, let's be honest, it's still a mystery to me—but in the meantime, all of my intentions and focus will be on your healing process.

"Honestly, let's keep our distance," he replied coldly.

I told him I'd respect his wishes if he didn't want me to contact him.

Ethan replied instantly. "I never told you not to contact me today, but you took that path. You really have no understanding of what I need from you." His words pained me—I *had* contacted him, just not in the exact way he desired. I wasn't a pro at navigating how to support a guy you've never met through cancer, but clearly I was failing. Even as I questioned his honesty, he still managed to make me ashamed that I wasn't handling this perfectly—whatever that meant.

In a futile attempt to set the record straight, I reminded him that I did reach out multiple times, but he said he would catch up with me later, so I wanted to be respectful and give him his distance.

Later that night, I tried a different approach. I sent him an Irish blessing and the hope that "from this storm, there will emerge an eventual rainbow. You are in my thoughts. If I can be there for you in any way, I am here."

It was cheesy, but Ethan loved cheesy.

I started thinking about a recent excerpt in the *New Yorker* from David Brooks's new book *The Social Animal*, which would be published that March. In it, he used a fictional couple to illustrate all the ways in which we demonstrate and observe signs of trustworthiness, competence, likability, and so much more in the first few seconds of meeting someone. The key was: *in person*. Romantic courtship, he wrote, was focused less on sexual compatibility and more on "sympathy displays." Well, that certainly seemed relevant. Couples are constantly testing each other on how compassionate they can be. Was I passing the test? I wasn't sure. I decided to share the article with Ethan.

"This article made me think of you, our relationship, and the missing physical link. Eventually, I'd love to hear your thoughts."

While it wouldn't be appropriate to send such a link to an average friend on the day of their surgery, Ethan was not an average friend. Brooks emphasized the importance of words in courtship, noting that the average couple exchanges ten million words in the first two years of courtship alone. It felt like Ethan and I were already creeping up on the ten-million-word mark—and yet, there were so many words I still needed to hear. Preferably in person.

I read this scientific analysis of human relationships in search of answers and advice. I was out of my depth. I simply didn't know how to proceed. I wanted someone to tell me what to do. What to say. How to feel. I naturally slipped into sociologist mode. Perhaps if I could better understand the human dynamics at work, I could be more effective in whatever role I was trying to play. The problem was I had no idea what that role was.

In the absence of our physical bodies, what were the forces bonding us together in such a profound way? Ethan was a man of science, so I wanted him to understand just how crucial it was for us to see each other, hear each other's voices, and bond via scent. There was so much that words alone could not do.

And yet, in that moment, words were all we had. I was frustrated, confused, and angry with Ethan. But I also felt other equally strong emotions. Something more tender, more vulnerable. It was more than mere desire. I was pretty sure I was in love with him.

Is it possible to be in love with someone you've never met? If so, it was a first for me. Did it erase the weird discrepancies that I couldn't fully make sense of? Not at all. But I did know that the depth of affection I had for him could only be described as love. I wasn't sure it was the healthiest form of love, but love nonetheless. I'd always operated on the belief that when you feel that deeply for someone, you should tell them. So I did.

"I love you," I texted him, then quickly coupled it with other commentary to avoid calling too much attention to it. We'd already exchanged hundreds of thousands of words, yet these three terrified me the most.

I think some part of me hoped that being brave enough to say what I suspected we both felt would motivate him to do the same—and encourage him to want me physically with him. My expression of love was both genuine and calculated.

He didn't respond.

January 18, 2011

I never got the phone call he promised me (huge surprise). But around 1 a.m., hours before his surgery, Ethan finally sent me an explanation of why it was crucial to our relationship that we put off being together physically until after this ordeal was over.

Subject: The email I was too messed up to write.

Ethan had a very specific idea of what our relationship would and could be: romantic, sexual, and all-encompassing. He wanted that and nothing short of it. Me playing nurse to an ailing man disrupted that vision.

"I think I have an understanding of what will interest you, intrigue you, give you stomach flips. And it ain't this; it ain't me at this juncture in time."

He didn't want to ruin our chances at that ideal with the "stupid distraction of surgery." He assured me he still envisioned us together at the end of this, and hoped I shared that same vision and excitement.

But, despite the sweet reinforcements and future imaginings, he didn't miss an opportunity to scold me for not responding exactly the way he wanted: "You obviously distrust me right now, and when I'm going through such an ordeal, that's really the last thing I need on my plate."

Ouch. Maybe he was right. *Of course he was right!* This was no time to play Nancy Drew. That could wait. Every insecurity I'd developed during childhood surfaced. Instead of focusing on his bad behavior or unverifiable claims, I obsessed over my own lovability.

Unable to trust myself anymore, I searched for perspective. Between all the volatile miscommunication and canceled dates, one thing remained the same: Ethan's unwavering insistence that he wanted to be with me. Maybe I just needed to take him at his word.

*   *   *

"I'll be online when I feel a bit better," he said—clearly already online. "What are your thoughts right now?"

Barely out of surgery, and he was thinking about me and our relationship. It was both confusing and flattering.

"My thoughts are that I am first and foremost concerned about your recovery and grateful that you're out of surgery and doing ok—one hurdle down. I still have lots of questions, of course—that is my nature, but that is all secondary to my concern for you."

Even when faced with the possibility that this person was not exactly who he said he was, I still cared about what he thought of me. I needed him to know I was a good person acting from a good place.

I asked about the details of the surgery: Did they enter through the throat or his stomach? (Throat.) Was he in pain? (On painkillers.) What was the path to recovery from here? (Just taking it day by day.)

"If there's anything I can do, please let me know. I can send something to the hospital or go walk your dog. Whatever you need."

*   *   *

"What was that love talk yesterday?" he asked. Immediately embarrassed after I'd written it, I was mostly grateful we'd glossed over it the day before.

"Well, it's the only way I know how to describe this feeling, as f-ed up as it may sound, given the circumstances. I never thought it was possible to care so much about someone before meeting them in person. I now know that is not the case."

"Just wish you'd said it at a time when we weren't arguing. How about you take it back and say it some time in the future when you feel it again from the right place?" he said. Ethan loved do-overs.

Sure, I could do that. And maybe he'd be inclined to reciprocate by then.

"How about I wait to say it until I see you in person? That seems more appropriate."

*   *   *

Ethan's surgery was in New York at NYU hospital—at least I knew he was in Manhattan and I was pretty sure he was at NYU, as that was where his tests were done. A part of me really wanted to send flowers to him. The other part of me wanted to verify that he was in the hospital in the first place. I'd fully reconciled these competing motivations: I was equal parts lover and skeptic. The supportive sleuth. I vowed to pursue both equally in an attempt to hedge my bets. We'd either make it out of this thing as an unstoppable couple, or I'd dig deep enough and long enough to expose whatever he wasn't telling me.

So I called the hospital. No Ethan Schuman admitted. I called all the NYU locations. No Ethan Schuman. I tried all the other hospitals in New York, just to be sure. There was no Ethan Schuman.

January 19, 2011

Ethan had a rough night. He was in pain, coughing up blood, and had to be put on oxygen. In our email exchange that morning, I encouraged him to rest, but he insisted that he hated sleeping. "I've had enough health issues in the past to make me really appreciative of being awake."

I was curious about the particularities of his diagnosis. He told me he'd had issues with his stomach and esophagus over the years, and his mom had some stomach issues. "Just shitty luck in the genetic lottery," he concluded. As for how effective the surgery had been, he told me it depended on the outcome of the chemo. "Guess cancer is a whole different kettle of fish." He even had to store his sperm.

Despite his insistence on staying awake, I wanted to give him time to rest, and I had meetings and events to run to. My non-Ethan life rolled on. I checked in later to see how he was doing.

No reply.

I needed to set aside the ailments he'd just described to me. The hospital mystery nagged at me. I added it to an ever-growing list of oddities. Could he be at a non-NYU hospital? Possibly. But something about my inability to find him registered confirmed my hunch. Asking him for answers no longer sufficed. It was time to start investigating this person more seriously.

A friend of mine knew a former detective for the city and said she'd pass

THERE IS NO ETHAN

along Ethan's info to him: Ethan Schuman, 35, lives on the Upper West Side, his mom's name is Anna Schuman, and his parents live in Essex County, New Jersey. He says he graduated from Stuyvesant High School, then attended Columbia, then MIT (though I noted I couldn't find any record of him attending Stuy or Columbia). Works for the Department of the Treasury as an economic analyst and does consulting work for Morgan Stanley.

I just wanted to verify something, *anything*, about this guy.

"I will get Tony on this tomorrow," she promised. "I'm SURE he will be able to find something out."

I also emailed my friend David, a New York lawyer with an Israeli "cousin" who did various "jobs" for him, including some unofficial "detective" work. I remembered David speaking about him, but I never asked too many questions. I just knew he was good at producing results. I gave Ethan's info to David and said I needed to verify his identity, promising to explain the details when I saw him.

David told me, "I'll get this over to my cousin to see what he can find. I'll give him your cell number in case there are any questions. And no, I don't need any explanation. I'd prefer to let my imagination run wild."

The cousin was shady and mysterious and I knew he was the perfect man for the job. At the time, David was representing two girls who were conned by the same guy who claimed he went to Cornell. The guy wiped out their bank accounts. "Be careful," he warned me. "Or at least make sure the sex is good!"

If only, I thought.

January 20, 2011

I checked in with Ethan again. "How are you doing?"

"Surviving," he assured me. "Pain was insane."

Ethan was currently high on painkillers, and I was impressed by his level of coherence given the heavy medication. He said he'd been working a little, trying to keep busy.

He sent me a link to Brené Brown's TED talk on vulnerability. "Vulnerability is a challenge for me, and yet I crave it so deeply," I shared. "No doubt, part of my challenge with vulnerability stems from past experiences in which that vulnerability was betrayed."

Every word was calculated at this point.

My contacts were still searching for answers about Ethan Schuman, and my questions about his identity piled up. And yet... I still felt close to him. How could I not? He was—ironically—the most consistent, attentive person in my life. He wanted to know every detail of what I thought and did. I compartmentalized the unknowns and continued to connect with him while I sorted out the mystery. It was contradictory and practical, all at once. There was just so much day-to-day stuff happening for me that I wanted to share with Ethan—or whoever this guy was. I felt mildly schizophrenic.

"So share..." he encouraged.

I was juggling a lot of entrepreneurial ventures and passion projects, which was both exciting and daunting. Ethan marveled at my ability to handle so much uncertainty.

"Looking for more stability?" he prompted, clearly speaking beyond my professional life.

Yes, I was. And I understood the subtext.

"Ugh, Anna, I'm so crazy about you," he said out of nowhere. "It has become a chronic condition that I can't shake. (Can you see that I'm overwhelmed by the medical analogies?)"

I groaned, but appreciated he was in such good spirits.

"If I wanted to say it, I could say it," he teased mysteriously.

"???" I wasn't following.

"You know. It. IT."

"Oh... IT," I said, catching up. "The big relationship milestone IT. The forbidden IT." The IT that I'd already said to him, only to have it rejected—with a request for a redo at a more "opportune" time. *That IT.*

"I don't know why, but you're going to be a difficult woman to say it to.

I don't want to be a lovesick puppy around you," he said. "I'm very much lovesick."

"Ever since you've brought it up, that's all I've been replaying in my head, and then it clicked into place and I thought, fuck, *I do*," he explained.

He had not embraced my words of affection when I expressed them before his surgery, however, and it hurt, so I was grateful he'd warmed to them.

"It was a rough day. I didn't understand what you were saying exactly and where it was coming from. That made the day even rougher."

His words were daggers. The last thing I wanted to do was create more difficulty in his life during this traumatic time. Plus, I hated being misunderstood.

"If I told you right now that I plan to get back with Anna and marry her, would it kill you?"

What? Was he considering this? What a strange and cruel thing to say—and right after he alluded to being in love with me? Ethan's ability to pivot from hot to cold in an instant was chipping away at my sanity and my ability to emotionally self-regulate. People often told me I had a tough exterior, that I seemed like I could handle anything, but this felt cruel. Was Ethan casually suggesting this hypothetical as an intellectual exercise, believing it wouldn't affect me? Or was it meant to hurt me? Whatever his intentions, it immediately pushed me back into a wounded, fragile place.

"I would question the authenticity of your communication with me," I replied, not understanding where he was going with this and not letting on how upsetting his words were.

"Doesn't answer the question," he said, pushing further.

"I'd be very sad. How would you feel if I told you I'd met someone new?" I asked, turning the tables.

"It would kill me," he responded without hesitation.

It was difficult for me to entertain opening myself to other people at that moment.

"Is Anna going to come and help you out?" I asked, afraid to hear the answer.

"No, I told her that the woman I'm seeing wouldn't be happy about it."

My heart reopened a little. "Does she know we've never met?"

"No ;)"

I knew the timing wasn't ideal, but I also knew there would be no ideal moment anytime soon. So I decided to revisit my presurgery sleuthing.

"Can I ask you a question and have you promise not to get angry and just trust me?"

"Ok," he agreed.

"Promise?" I was not convinced.

"Uh...no."

"Ok then I won't ask."

"No, ask," he encouraged.

"Not unless you promise to trust me and not get angry."

"Fine," he said.

This was delicate; I needed to word it just right. "You're obviously brilliant. I have no doubt about you. I just want to understand as much about you as possible. So I'm curious why you're not in the yearbooks? Not curious cause I doubt you, just curious cause it's another piece of the puzzle that is you."

I braced for impact.

"So we're talking about all this other stuff—and THAT'S what you want to bring up?"

"Yes. Cause my curiosity (NOT my distrust) is still there."

"Hmmm." He didn't seem convinced. "Well, it's all true. I'll show you all the yearbooks you want that have me in them."

"But why isn't it under your name?" None of it made sense.

"It is."

"For 1993 at Stuy?"

"No."

"But that's what you said."

"Well I'll show you the yearbook that has me in it."

"Which year would that be?" I would not back down. "And why would you tell me a different year? I'm confused."

Silence.

"Don't shut down. I just want to understand."

"You're probing for stuff that isn't there. I haven't lied to you, I've been honest, don't know what else to say. I don't like being investigated. When you're over at my place and you want to see a yearbook, I'll hand it to you, but this is really unfair."

Was it? I was obsessed with figuring this out. If I could just understand why he wasn't in the yearbooks, I could stop torturing myself. Why wouldn't he tell me?

I went into explanatory overdrive in an effort to drag it out of him:

"I'm not trying to insinuate that you lied. I just figured it was some sort of fluke, so not really a big deal. But I still like to understand. My brain is such that it needs to understand things. I'm not a naturally suspicious person at all—in fact, I'm incredibly trusting. So if you said '93 and that's not correct, fine. Though I'm not sure why you'd say a different number . . . I don't see why this would be a sore topic—unless you explain it to me. You should feel free to ask me absolutely anything. If I doubted anything, I wouldn't still be communicating with you, nor would I still feel this way about you. So I hope you can accept that it's my curiosity and desire to know you."

I thought maybe if I just kept talking, he would answer honestly out of sheer exhaustion. I was exhausting myself at this point.

"Well obviously this specific curiosity bothers me," he replied with markedly more brevity than me. "I've been open with you, too, and this looks a lot like a witch hunt to me."

Time for damage control.

"Not at all. Total coincidence that a group of my close friends went to Stuy and Columbia those same years. That excites me, actually. Makes me feel like you're already part of my network."

It was true. I liked the prospect of him being part of this group of friends I'd known since I first arrived in New York. They were some of the best people I knew. But I also needed to know why he wasn't in the yearbook. I couldn't trust anything he said to me until I got a straight answer.

"I didn't graduate in '93. I graduated early, we went through this," he explained, irritated to be revisiting the topic.

"I asked if you graduated in '94. You said you graduated a year early."

"Earlier than '94," he corrected me.

See, the thing with textual communication is there's a record. *OF EVERYTHING.* He'd said "a year early."

Sensing that was a dead end, he took a different approach. "Your math is off," he informed me.

"I know, math isn't my forte. Help me out?" I begged, making him feel like a big, strong mathlete.

"I'm 35." (Yes. I knew this.) "I should have graduated in 93. Different birthdays," he said, indicating that where his birthday fell changed the year he would have started school.

"So you graduated in 92."

"Right."

It still didn't account for the earlier correction of "a year earlier" than '94. Was he drunk or high when he'd answered that question? Or was he purposefully hiding something? I had no idea, but I knew this was the only answer I was going to get from him.

"Did you finish college in 3 years, too?"

"Yeah."

"I'm starting to feel like an underachiever," I admitted, not doubting his brilliance.

"I'm just good at math."

"How old were you when you finished your PhD?"

"26."

"That is super young." I hadn't finished mine until age twenty-nine. Twenty-six was impressive.

"Doesn't make life any more exciting."

"Ok, well, thanks for answering these questions."

I was late for a meeting and had to run. I wasn't fully satisfied with the responses, but they did offer more pieces of the puzzle for me to work with.

January 21, 2011

As usual, I woke up and checked my email, expecting to see Ethan's name in my inbox.

There he was.

Subject: Can't sleep very well.

I love you.

CHAPTER 9

Expiration Dates

January 23, 2011

"Awake yet?" he messaged me on IM. We hadn't spoken the previous day because the nausea was getting to him, but he was feeling a bit better.

"I over-jerkied." I'd just returned from a jerky-tasting brunch (why I thought that was a good idea, I do not know). "What's with your status message?" Ethan often changed his G-chat status with links to articles or quotes he stumbled upon.

"It was a quote from a religious community," he replied. "The rabbi thought that a woman being educated was evil." He sent me the link to the article on Ynet, an Israeli news outlet. It was a report about a rabbi who wanted to lower the legal marriage age from seventeen to fifteen to ease the financial burden on large families and offer an alternative to women who didn't want to study. Ethan seemingly thought it was a bad idea, thankfully.

"Interesting that the article reports that Ahmadinejad is also in favor of lowering the marriage age," I noted, referring to the then president of Iran. So nice to see the Jews and Persians finding common ground.

The fact that he updated his IM status so regularly led me to believe he was communicating with a wide enough audience to make that effort worthwhile. And it further supported the notion that he was, in fact, Ethan Schuman—despite my lingering questions.

He was still in the hospital, but said he expected to be released Wednesday or Thursday. Spending over a week in the hospital was … serious. *Which hospital was it again?*

"You've been distant," he said, clearly seeking a fight. I reminded him I'd been reaching out multiple times a day to chat but hadn't gotten a reply.

"I don't know what you'd expect from someone in the hospital," he snipped.

So … reach out more, but don't expect a reply. Got it.

I sensed he was mad about something. By this point I'd learned that whenever he started to point out my shortcomings, something else was bubbling beneath the surface.

"Have you been on any dates?" he asked. So *that* was what this was about. Perhaps he had too much time on his hands in the hospital, and his imagination was getting the better of him.

While I hadn't been on any official dates, I decided to test the waters by telling him about the speed-dating event I'd attended the night before with my friend Nicole, who was recently out of a bad relationship. The men were mostly guys who lived in Jersey and worked in IT. We'd gone half as a funny social experiment and half in the hope we might be pleasantly surprised.

"Any love connections?" He was baiting me.

"No. There was one guy who liked me and was definitely the best of the bunch. Maybe I'll go out with him. I don't know."

"Cool," he said casually—though I knew he would find me dating other people anything but "cool."

This was getting weird(er). The man who'd just told me he loved me was cheering on my new love life, which did not include him. He insisted the idea of me dating other people did not bother him and asked that I let him know when I went out with Speeddater. There was a lot I still didn't know about Ethan, but I did know that dishing on my love life like I was gossiping with girlfriends was not something he could handle. Plus, why did he want to know? What was to be gained with that knowledge? I was not buying his act of indifference. "You're still the person I'd prefer to be dating," I reminded him.

"Sorry—I need to go—family is here." He was clearly blowing me off.

"I'm trying very hard to stay in close contact."

"While you fuck around in the interim," he finished.

"Huh? Why are you making accusations? That's not fair."

"Not accusations, so much as foretelling the future."

He had explicitly told me to keep dating while he continued to pursue me. Those were his terms, not mine. Did he not realize I had a digital record of these statements?

"I need to go. I'll talk to you tomorrow."

*　　*　　*

Later that night, he sent me an email wishing me luck on my first day of classes. "I just want to tell you this no man's land is difficult for me," he added.

Always the same formula: something sweet, paired with something salty. Somehow, he could bring any topic back to him.

January 24, 2011

Ethan messaged me first thing the next morning, seemingly far more excited about the first day of classes than I was. "Pumped? It's the eye of the tiger," he said, referencing the rock anthem from *Rocky*.

"Still sort of groggy. Excitement building slowly," I typed out, still half awake. "Can you bring me breakfast? I have no food in my apartment."

"Sorry for being a jerk. As usual," he said while I ordered food from the corner deli.

We took a quick detour into analyzing my eating habits, but I brought us back to the topic at hand. "So why were you being so mean to me?"

"I wasn't MEAN, just not as nice as usual. You're pretty self-sufficient, you don't need me to be nice all the time."

What kind of psychotic comment was that?

"I'm going through a really difficult time. Just try to be supportive. I'm trying to find my grounding here. Give me a break."

Ethan's cuts at me were taking a toll, and I told him as much. I couldn't take much more nastiness, cancer or not. I hadn't heard from the private investigator or David's cousin, but I prayed they would uncover something soon.

January 25, 2011

I received a call from a number I didn't recognize, so I didn't answer it. Moments later, Speeddater emailed me:

> Miss blogosphere, I tried calling you and realized phone conversations are probably too old school for you, being the technologically savvy academic and all (oxymoron, no?). After some modern stalking (ie google) you appear to be quite a bit more than a fashion intellectual. My interest has been piqued. Let's continue our past Saturday conversation over coffee sometime.

A phone call? And a plan to meet in person? I was ready to marry this guy.

*   *   *

Ethan and I caught up on IM, and I was grateful the tone was much lighter than the previous day. I told him about making it into the interview round for a startup competition and also shared an anonymous blog I'd started, where I told funny and unbelievable stories of things that had happened to me as a professor. Ethan loved it and wanted to pass it around to his "people." "Just don't use my name!" I warned.

I told him about my first day of class, which delighted him to no end. He loved hearing about the girl in one of my classes who rolled her eyes in an exaggerated fashion every time I said something she found ridiculous—like "You can't text in class" or "Please stay awake." "You know, crazy requests like that," I told him. "I believe she already dropped out. But then—and this is the best part—after rolling her eyes all during class, she came up to me at the end and explained that she's waitlisted for my other class, and could I please let her in?"

"And you said?" Ethan asked expectantly.

"'This class didn't seem to please you too much, no?' She then sort of mumbled something. Another girl pulled me aside after class and told me she'll be interning for Vogue 33 hours per week this semester, plus taking 4 classes. So would she have to work hard in this class? If so, she thought maybe she shouldn't take it."

"You must make these kids pee in their pants," Ethan said gleefully.

He was in a good mood; he was being released from the hospital that day. He would stay with his parents for a few nights, so he'd have assistance, but then he would move back into his apartment. "Pretty excited to get the hell out of here," he said, particularly anticipating a nice shower.

"Are you experiencing discomfort?" I asked, not sure what the recovery process was like for something like this.

"Trying not to think about it. I'm not 100%. I just want to get out of here and feel like myself and see you." Tease. I wasn't holding my breath, but he promised we would see each other before he started the chemo.

"Babe, I need to get some bloods taken—will be back in a bit, hope to catch you."

*   *   *

Later that day, I brought the conversation back to an anticipation of (finally!) meeting in person. Unsurprisingly, Ethan felt conflicted.

"You make me feel 100 things and none of them are ever straightforward," he told me. (I was mostly immune to these declarations at this point.) "I don't feel cared about," he continued. "I feel like a marginal thought to you." Sigh. I had become detached since his surgery, he informed me. Detached and divested.

And maybe I was. It was a form of necessary self-preservation. I still felt deep affection for him and was emotionally entangled, but before his surgery, Ethan consumed me. I wasn't sleeping or eating. It was not healthy.

I had since rebalanced. I could check in with him, exchange some funny words, take my daily beating about not living up to his expectations in one way or another, let him apologize, and then go on with my life. Instead of letting him hijack my thoughts and emotions, I stepped into and out of Ethanland. It was like I had split myself in two. It was weird and more than a little dysfunctional, but it was far more sustainable. Meanwhile, I continued to investigate who this mystery man was (without his knowledge). Whoever he was, he had a front-row seat to my life. The lows were really low with him, but our conversations were captivating. I enjoyed the rhythm of our banter so much that I decided I could tune out the rest. I was still hopeful that someday soon we'd meet in person and I'd get some answers, and in the meantime, I'd continue living my life.

Ethan did not approve of this newfound balance, however.

"Ok, Anna. I get that you're busy. I get that this is strange. I get that you need to detach for self-preservation. I get all of that."

"Well, if you can find someone who cares this much about you and puts themselves out there as I have and can also be more perfect in this situation, then I'd snatch them up. I'm sorry I fall short." What was he going to do—walk away? Unlikely.

I felt empowered for the first time since I'd met him. Maybe it was because classes were back in session. It reminded me that I was a respected academic teaching at a top university. Maybe some of the confidence I brought to the classroom was finally seeping into my relationship with Ethan. Meeting Speeddater also reminded me there were other men out there who were willing and interested in connecting in person—something I never previously thought I'd lose sight of. I hadn't eliminated Ethan from my life, and he did continue to feel like an abusive weight I couldn't shake, but at least I (mostly) felt like myself again.

Ethan could smell my confidence. So he reverted to his secret weapon: the other Anna. That Anna would've been giving him all the warmth, he reminded me. He'd chosen the wrong Anna.

"I just need to feel like I actually affect you," he concluded. What a weird turn of phrase.

"Even if I'm not supposed to say it, I do love you. Just marry me," he said in jest.

"Sure, when? I'll check when I'm free." I was so accustomed to these erratic emotional flip-flops that I'd learned to play along and avoid more conflict.

"We have a few weddings to go to. Might as well steal their officiants."

He asked for my anonymous blog link again and told me he'd just sent it to a bunch of people, including an ex-girlfriend who was also a professor. "She will be VERY grateful to know she's not alone!"

January 26, 2011

I mentioned a book I'd just finished reading: *The Happiness Advantage*.

"I can't read that book," Ethan informed me.

It had the word "happiness" in it, which, evidently, made it "a chick book."

"Imagine I am riding the subway, engrossed in a book about happiness. I'll never get a date again." Ethan's concept of masculinity was questionable.

"Ah, get over it." I was not in the mood to argue this point.

"You have very little grasp on who I am." (Oh, was that a true statement!) "For a sociologist, you're not all that accurate in reading people." Ever the flatterer.

"I gave you a whole letter about who you are," he went on. "Tell me who I am."

I was being set up to fail.

"I'm not asking you to write me poetry," he assured me snarkily.

Who was Ethan Schuman? That really *was* the question. I honestly didn't know. But I did understand who he'd presented himself to be, and why that person appealed to me so much.

"You are traditional and responsible, yet have an incredible sense of adventure and want to test boundaries. That is part of why you're attracted to me. Your agility with language is gorgeous and, especially given the nature of our first month 'together,' a huge foundation for my continued draw to you."

"Why thank you," he said, flattered. "I'm yet another New Yorker working on yet another book."

What? This was a new one. I made a mental note to revisit this.

I continued on with a list of frequently contradictory yet compelling traits I recognized in Ethan: what he wanted in a partner, his commitment to being a better person, his hypersensitivity, and the current challenges he faced. I also listed some of the many things I was yet to discover—the way he socialized, our potential chemistry, his physical ticks and quirks, his laugh, his smell.

"Shit. My apples just exploded," I said, interrupting my digital monologue. I'd neglected the apples I was baking.

Then I continued: "I don't know what sort of wine you like. I don't know if you floss. I don't know if you will ultimately, one day, just decide that you want a Jewish girl and call it a day. I don't know if I can trust you not to cheat on me."

How accurate was I?

"It was dead-on," he assured me.

He told me about the dream he'd had about me the night before. "I hardly ever dream about women," he said, as if to tell me his subconscious was hyperfocused on me. "It was so great. You had just finished lecturing." Ethan described the scene in detail. "I remember how hard my heart was racing when I saw you that first time, stuffing your papers into your briefcase."

"When do you think we can try to recreate that feeling in person?" Despite his stalling, I continued to believe we would eventually meet. How could we not? New York was a small big city. He couldn't hide forever. Plus, why would he want to? Despite all my insecurities—and there were many—I believed I would ultimately prove too irresistible for him to avoid. If not out of passion, then curiosity. Curiosity was also a huge piece of what continued to drive me. I couldn't say if my need to meet the "real" Ethan was motivated more by some lingering hope that he was the man he'd presented himself to be or simply an obsession with knowing the truth. It was probably equally both.

"Definitely Valentine's Day weekend," he promised. Not before? "I have to see how I'm healing. I want to look/feel like a human before, you know."

I told him I had a home exchange in Connecticut that weekend. And while he was game for a weekend together, he was not thrilled by his doctor's insistence that he wait six weeks to have sex.

"We'll see if people can really fall in love without sex," he said.

"Well, we've given it a hell of a try so far," I replied.

There was something old-fashioned about this bizarro courtship: First, we learned to love each other; then, we'd (hopefully, eventually) find physical passion. It was like I was playing a role when I was with Ethan virtually—the loving girlfriend, the confidant, the future life partner— and when I logged off, I shifted into analytical mode, determined to get to the bottom of the Ethan mystery. It wasn't rational, this lingering hope I had. But it did fuel both my continued communication with him and my ongoing investigations.

He assured me we would be fine in the sex department, before turning more serious. "I'm not a sexual idiot. I don't have a small penis. And I'm crazy about you. I feel like I have so much at stake here. There's nothing as unveiling as cancer."

January 27, 2011

I asked Ethan about the book he mentioned, the one he said he was writing.

"My book is fiction—Talented Mr. Ripley meets Brighton Beach Memoirs. About a guy who's working at a coffee shop, feels very ostracized for many reasons, and lives a double-life where he takes on the roles of the narrators of the conversations he overhears."

I wasn't entirely sure what that meant, but I went with it. "Book sounds really intriguing. How far along are you? I'm surprised you haven't mentioned it before. Can I read some excerpts? Double life, eh? I hope you're not trying out any of the characters with me...I'm working on blind faith here!" I was not joking.

"Nope. This is that single life thing that makes it all the scarier. In a double-life there's always a way to restart, to go back to the beginning, to get yourself a blank slate. When you're living your one and only life, there's everything at stake—lasting memories, lasting pain." He was nothing if not a Russian writer.

He said he worked on the manuscript for around five years, mostly during grad school, and it had been awaiting an opening and a concluding chapter since then. So far, no one had read it. He wasn't even sure he wanted to publish it. "I mean...how many well-respected government employees have written novels about loneliness?" he asked. He promised to share an excerpt with me eventually, but he preferred to wait until we were together and I was "madly in love" with him. It wasn't the literary critique he feared, but he didn't want to risk any misunderstanding. "It's like handing someone my journal," he said dramatically. "It's handing someone a photo of your soul and their reaction just being, 'Oh, that's a bit blurry.'"

Ethan dangled a new carrot: The following week he would feel better and we could have dinner.

January 28, 2011

After a bit of phone tag, Speeddater called again. We talked for forty-five minutes and made plans to meet at the Ace Hotel that Sunday. I learned he (rather predictably) lived in Murray Hill, that finance bro wasteland, and commuted to Greenwich daily. *But*, to his credit, he was super apologetic about the unfortunate location of his apartment and assured me he was not a fan. His body, which seemed plucked from the gods, was well-earned: He was doing some sort of twelve-mile run/obstacle course in Austin that weekend. In short, I wasn't sure I wanted to have his children, but I definitely wanted to make out with him.

I forwarded his email to Nicole, my friend who'd attended the speed-dating event with me. She hadn't been a fan of his that night. Too preppy. Too finance-y. But now she was reconsidering her stance.

"Hmm. Perhaps I misjudged. I am really into how he has called you twice. He appears to have balls, which is a major bonus. Judging from his semi-affected email that he wrote you, he also seems to be intelligent."

Yes. And most important: I knew he was real.

January 29, 2011

Ethan was on antibiotics. He had some sort of infection. He also had too much time on his hands, which led him to obsess over my upcoming date with Speeddater—a date he had accurately predicted would happen. He wanted details.

"Just think I should know," he said. "I am entitled to know."

Why?

"A guy telling you that he loves you deserves to know when you're dating some other guy."

Should I cancel my date? (I was not canceling my date. Ethan would not rain on my Speeddater parade.)

"No."

"If I were unable or unwilling to meet you in person until further notice, I would expect you to date other people until we could finally be together," I explained, trying to help him understand.

"Except you're fucking forgetting that I'm not out finding myself or traveling around the world for the hell of it. I'm fucking dealing with cancer." Yes, he was. Which was what made all of this that much more confusing.

"Can you answer a very straightforward question in a straightforward sentence?" he asked.

"Sure," I said, not at all sure.

"Why are you going on the date if you know that you want me?"

"Because I don't know when I'll actually get to be with you and I promised myself I would be open to dating people until that day arrived." That was true. Plus, he had specifically encouraged me to keep dating while he recovered.

"Why do you have to remain open? Why is that important to you?"

"There's a part of me that is scared that you're never going to want to meet me. That that day will never come, and I'll have been a huge fool for just waiting indefinitely." That was also true.

"You'll need to go out with me," I told him. "You understand that? There is an expiration date. For me out there by myself."

January 30, 2011

"You're going to KILL me tonight," he said, referring to my much-anticipated date with Speeddater. He begged me to send him a photo of what I was wearing. My phone couldn't yet take selfies, but I snapped a photo in the mirror and emailed it to him—the first and only time I did that. "Oh geez. With the open shoulder." He told me I looked like Jennifer Beals in *Flashdance*. I got that a lot. "Ah, fuck. Come on, change." He suggested I shave my head.

*   *   *

Going into the date, I wasn't entirely sure what to expect. Yes, I found Speeddater very attractive. Distractingly so. He was like a Roman statue come to life. Chiseled perfection. But aside from his beauty, what really sold me during the silly speed-date session was his playfulness and humor. Desperate to avoid boring conversations in the few minutes I had with each guy, I asked them all the same question: *What's your fake career?* Mine was as a taxidermist, complete with a taxidermy blog, a business card, and some actual taxidermy (that I didn't stuff) hidden in my closet. They looked at me like I was crazy (understandable), then told me they didn't need a fake career because they operated in the glitz and glamour of IT. But not Speeddater. He didn't try to sell me on the wild world of private equity; he explained his life in the circus. It was perfect, and the only conversation I didn't want to end.

So he seemed fairly promising—and didn't disappoint. He won me over with talk of his aspiring entrepreneurialism, his dedication to volunteering as a Big Brother, and his reflections on how a serious accident changed his outlook on life. We talked at length about how important it is to put aside technology and be present with people (I might have had an orgasm at that moment). His only strike was suggesting dinner at a place beyond my budget…and then letting me split the bill. But I would overlook that, since he'd given me a priceless gift: an entire night when I didn't think of Ethan once. I think those were the only four waking hours I'd had without communicating with or thinking about Ethan in over a month. And it was glorious.

My first post-Ethan date exceeded all expectations, but most important, he had something to offer me that Ethan wouldn't: his presence. I floated out of the Ace Hotel in a confused state, feeling guilty for my attraction to someone who was not Ethan. Here I was, laughing and flirting and forming a new connection, while Ethan was home in bed recovering from major surgery, in pain, coughing up blood, preparing to start chemo.

I was a terrible person.

And Ethan was sure to let me know I was terrible. Never mind the fact that he'd repeatedly encouraged me to keep dating—it was the very fact that I'd even *wanted* to date someone else that enraged him.

When he asked me how it went, I had the insensitive nerve to say it was nice (an intentional understatement). I'd disrespected him. I'd disrespected us. It changed everything for him. He was done.

"Anna, fuck you. Have a good night. Thanks for being so supportive. You broke my heart with the way you dealt with this situation. I can't forgive you for that."

I knew he was in a precarious state, and we had been on the precipice of what might have been a truly incredible connection. So to have that all ripped away in an instant due to circumstances outside of your control, and then watch as the woman you wanted to be with went out with another man—I knew that wasn't easy. This was far more complex than mere jealousy. So I tried to be as patient and understanding as possible, which felt easier than ever. I'd found the secret formula for managing Ethan: dating other people.

January 31, 2011

Ethan was still fuming. He sent repeated emails to remind me what a despicable person I was. He was shocked by how inappropriately I'd dealt with this situation. I could see him clutching his pearls through the computer.

He wasn't out "dilly-dallying," he reminded me, yet again. He was trying to recover from *cancer*. If I were an adult, rather than a self-absorbed child, I would be patient. Friendship was our only path forward, he concluded.

Meanwhile, he would be spending time with a girl he met before me: Sarah. They would meet the next day.

"You made plans with her immediately, but you wouldn't make a date with me when I begged for it? Now that's fucked up."

"Different situation. She's a doctor. This is what does it for her. The whole patient-doctor thing. And that's not the kind of dynamic I wanted with you." It didn't hurt that she was also a Jewish girl and was smitten with him. I knew what he was doing and why he was doing it. Protesting and rationalizing were pointless. I was pissed.

Ethan pressed for more details about Speeddater, fixating on his age: twenty-six. He lost it.

"The fact that you could even remotely stomach hurting me for the sake of a 26-year-old? It's the most insulting thing you could have done."

He was six years younger than me. This wasn't an epic age difference.

He would not stop. "Do you realize that I'm 35, that I've been married, that I've been working for 20 years now, that I have a lot to my name at this point, I've accomplished enough and I think in the scale of human worth, I've done a great deal?"

Yes. I realized all of this. At least I realized that was what he'd told me.

According to Ethan, he was destroyed, disrespected, and incredibly bitter. He said he would meet me for coffee—with his new girlfriend. Sometime in the near future.

His tirade showed no signs of slowing down. He kept firing off messages. For someone who was "done" with me, he sure didn't seem very done. Despite recognizing that he was unhinged, I didn't feel physically threatened. It never even crossed my mind. He'd have to appear in person to inflict any sort of bodily harm, and I mentally dared him to do so.

I was exhausted, hadn't eaten all day, hadn't showered, hadn't prepped the readings I was teaching later—and I had five hours of classes ahead of me.

"I've forgiven you enough times," he said, signing off dramatically.

Ditto. "Let me know when we can meet for coffee," I replied. Indifference was the only emotion I could give him. My focus was elsewhere—finally.

* * *

"I need to stop emailing you. I won't email you anymore. It just tortures both of us," he emailed me later that day.

"Goodbye. I wish I could say it was great getting to know you, but I can't say that anymore. The truth is that this failing has destroyed me."

Oy, the drama. Going out with Speeddater changed things for me. It broke the spell. Ethan's shenanigans no longer emotionally ravaged me. I knew he could feel the transformation. That was why *he* was the one spiraling for once. I no longer harbored romantic notions, but I was still wildly curious to meet him. I told him to just meet me for coffee once, then he never had to see me again.

"I'll meet you for coffee when I can bear to look at you."

February 1, 2011

I emailed Nicole. I was no longer expressing angst and loving concern. Not anymore. I'd stripped him of the name he loved so much and reduced him to a nickname: Internet Cancer Guy (ICG). "He actually wrote 'Fuck you. Fuck you. I hate you. You destroyed me,'" I told her. "I'm pretty sure a door slammed after that was typed. But then, miraculously, he decided to send me a text to see how my lectures went later tonight. *TOTALLY stable, clearly."*

*   *   *

Ethan was over it. Only a day had passed, but he wanted things to go back to "normal." He just needed me to understand that he and Speeddater were in two different leagues. Speeddater was a kid. Ethan was a man. Miss a few hours of this never-ending telenovela, and you've missed a lot.

"You know what Joanne Woodward said about being married to Paul Newman?"

No, I didn't. But I was pretty sure he was about to tell me. His quirky anecdotes no longer charmed me.

"She said that the reason they made it work is because each of them fell out of love with the other at exactly different times. So there was always a chaser."

That bit of trivia did not comfort me. Ethan's behavior felt...psycho. And yet, I continued to engage. I didn't have the emotional distance or mental clarity to draw a clear line. He had worn me down to the point of disorientation and inaction. Besides, even if I stopped responding or blocked him on IM, he would continue to find a way to contact me. Ethan refused to be ignored.

"I was extreme because there's no reason I should be with someone who could even consider choosing a 26-year-old over me." He was irrationally obsessed with Speeddater's age.

Desperate to change the topic, I mentioned the miserable state of my finances.

"Hey, if you ever need something to help you make ends meet, I'm ready and willing."

I declined.

"I can do March rent," he offered again. "Seriously, wouldn't be the end of the world if I helped out."

"I'm not looking for a sugar daddy," I reminded him. I needed the money desperately. But there was no scenario in which I'd accept it from Ethan.

*   *   *

"Is Connecticut still happening?" he asked later that evening, referencing the upcoming home exchange.

"You told me no." Among other choice words after my date.

"Now we're ok," he said nonchalantly.

Were we? Our views of the situation were not aligned.

February 4, 2011

It was Friday, and Ethan was back at his apartment. He still wasn't feeling well enough to get together.

But the following Wednesday we would be on.

For now, he was back on OkCupid. While I didn't have an active profile I was using, I had created a dummy account to check up on him. He was seemingly always on. I told him my friends regularly saw him on there, but in reality, it was me who saw him.

"Your friends check up on me? They've saved me as a favorite?" he asked, clearly not buying it.

"Yes. Because they care about me."

"Jesus. Sounds a bit psycho to me."

He told me he'd turned it back on during our fight. "I still promised that other woman Sarah," he added, reminding me of his doctor backup date.

"I'm going to lay down for a bit," he informed me.

February 6, 2011

It was Super Bowl Sunday and Ethan had friends over to watch the game.

"I had a bad dream last night that I had to sublet my apartment because I couldn't stay here. It really depressed me," I wrote to Ethan. I was freaking out for reasons that didn't involve Ethan. My vulnerability was at an all-time high.

"How much do you think you need?" he asked, throwing out numbers.

I refused to entertain the idea of a loan from a man who wouldn't meet me in person.

He reiterated that we'd get together on Wednesday and all would be fine.

He went into his room and shut the door. His friends were out in the living room, distracted by the game. He insisted that I tell him about this fantasy I'd mentioned. The timing felt weird, but in a moment of weakness, he convinced me.

We'd been communicating for six weeks at this point. There had been lots of sexual banter, but nothing explicit. This was the first and only time we'd taken it to the point of some sort of IM cybersex. Rage and lust can intertwine in dysfunctional relationships. Perhaps I thought that climaxing—even if reached digitally, without ever touching—might be yet another way to solidify the relationship and make it just a little more real (and a little more justifiable).

"Alright, love, let me clean up and get back to them. Don't stress about things. We'll figure it out."

In that moment of what felt like mutual satisfaction, our complicated, frustrating relationship reached a new point of connection, and I held on just a bit longer.

February 8, 2011

Ethan seemed distant. Again.

I started to panic. Again.

"Why are you panicking?" he asked.

"Turns out waiting 6.5 weeks to meet someone is anxiety-inducing."

February 9, 2011

Wednesday. Meeting day.

"Hey babe, doing my best," he emailed me. "Just feeling crappy. Trying to drug myself up till I feel better."

I offered to come over. No need to go out. We'd made a pact to meet up and I was not backing down. If he was well enough to have friends over, he was well enough to see me.

By 6 p.m., he had completely disappeared.

"It's a huge deal for me that I'm not seeing you tonight," I wrote him. No reply.

February 10, 2011

Not only had he stood me up and ghosted me the night before, but now we were only one day out from my Connecticut home exchange. There was no way I was going to take him there without first meeting. I needed to know what was happening and notify the exchange partners if the weekend was off. It wasn't so much that I'd believed he would actually materialize at this point. It was more a mental metric for myself: It was one thing for him to repeatedly disappoint me. It was another for him to mess with other people's lives. I would have to lie to them on his behalf, and that didn't sit well with me. I wouldn't let him compromise my integrity. It felt impossible to cut him off while he was sick, but my patience and compassion had reached their limits. If he tried to cancel on this, it would make it easier for me to finally walk away.

I clearly laid out my list of demands:

> I've reached my limit and I'm going to lay out for you what I need in the next 2 days if you want me to continue to invest in you:
>
> 1) I have an interview at 10am tomorrow. I need you to meet me on-line to talk at 9am. No work excuses, no silent treatment. Just be there.
>
> 2) We are meeting up tomorrow night. I don't care if that means that I come sit on your couch while you sleep. I will be in your presence tomorrow evening if you'd ever like me to be in your presence in the future. When we talk in the morning, please be ready to set a specific time and place. I'm free at 7:30pm.

3) We need to discuss this weekend. If you bail on me at the last minute, it will be extremely upsetting.

These are more than reasonable requests at this point. I've been patient for 7 weeks and endured innumerable broken promises. You see me or I go away. It's simple and it's your choice. I truly hope you will think that I'm worth it, trust in our connection, and not choose to lose me—because, unlike other women, I won't come back.

"I don't respond well to ultimatums," he replied. "I'm not 100%. I'm sorry."
"It's canceled," I informed him.
Finally. I was done.

February 15, 2011

"How are you, Anna?" he emailed me for the first time in five days.
    I did not reply.
    "Hi," he tried to IM me hours later.
    I did not reply.

February 19, 2011

"You really don't feel like responding at all?"
    "Unless your correspondence includes an apology and a definitive invitation to meet up, I will never feel like responding," I replied.

March 1, 2011

It was the day Ethan was scheduled to start chemo. I felt a lump in my stomach. I wanted to reach out to him, but this person clearly didn't want to meet me for reasons beyond his illness. And yet, he was still quite possibly someone with a life-threatening condition, and I was abandoning him. I remained silent and tried not to think about him.

PART 2:

THE OTHER WOMEN

CHAPTER 10

British Anna

In September 2008, Anna half-heartedly continued her search for a guy on JDate. She'd broken up with her first-ever Jewish boyfriend, a South African, and thought maybe she'd search for another one—but not just any Jewish guy. Her mother always wanted her to date a Jewish guy, and avoiding them was her way of rebelling. But as time went on, she warmed to the idea of sharing her culture with her partner. She avoided the London Jewish scene, however, because she found it to be a bit too superficial for her tastes, and Judaism alone wasn't enough to bridge that gap. She was a worldly woman with diverse tastes. So, after her favorable experience with the South African, she decided non-British Jewish guys were the way forward!

While browsing for new suitors one Sunday night, she stumbled upon Ethan Schuman from New York. He was thirty-six—just one year older than her—extremely witty and articulate, and he definitely piqued her interest. He worked as a research mathematician at Morgan Stanley, living and working between New York, DC, and Pittsburgh. Long distance wasn't ideal, but she reminded herself to stay open.

Anna and Ethan messaged on the JDate instant messenger platform for a while, then quickly switched to G-chat, where their first conversation stretched on for hours. By the time she logged off, she was already quite taken with her rapport with Ethan and his willingness to get to know a woman from across the Atlantic.

They connected over their Russian roots and their boredom with the usual Jewish scenes in their respective countries. He admitted that he'd married a "nice Jewish girl" to please his parents, only to grow frustrated and eventually cheat on her, leading to a divorce. Anna loved his music taste, which aligned closely with her own. They also bonded over their similar educational paths: She was studying for her doctorate in psychology, and he had a PhD from MIT. They were aligned in what they wanted in a relationship, in a partner, and how they wanted to live their lives. Family was very important to him, as it was to her, and he made that clear from the start. He especially loved that her name was the same as his mother's, and he knew she'd be readily accepted by his parents with their similar backgrounds.

Over the next few days, their chats continued and the two grew closer as their exchanges built in intensity. Ethan wanted her to know every facet of his life, his strengths, his vulnerabilities—he was just so disarmingly open and communicative.

By the time they'd corresponded for a week, she began to take this American seriously.

*   *   *

Anna was a confident, dynamic person. In addition to pursuing her PhD in psychology, she trained as a horse whisperer in Johannesburg and had a side career as a soulful house singer-songwriter. She performed at big summer music festivals, spoke French and Italian, and led a full and thriving life.

So she wasn't shy about stating what she wanted: a real relationship with the goal of marriage and a family. Ethan agreed. He made it clear he wanted a Jewish girl, but the *right* one this time. He wasn't about to repeat past mistakes. And while he was a bit more traditional than Anna, none of it was a dealbreaker for her.

Ethan emailed persistently and consistently, which Anna found to be a refreshing change from the emotionally self-absorbed flakiness she'd encountered so many times in the online dating world. Ethan convincingly declared himself the exact opposite, and his tenacity seemed to confirm it. He did the chasing, and Anna never wondered whether he would be in touch. Despite the intensity of his career, he made time to craft thoughtful, funny emails, regardless of his workload. Their correspondence accelerated, and he was soon writing her the most eloquent and beautifully written love letters she had ever received.

*   *   *

While Anna loved their written correspondence, she was eager to connect with Ethan more fully, even if they couldn't physically be together yet. Not all computers had internal webcams at the time, and Ethan initially didn't have an external webcam for video calls on Skype, as his had broken. But he promised he'd go shopping for one just as soon as he could get away from the office. He worked incredibly long hours, which Anna understood, no stranger to extended work hours herself. And while the webcam didn't materialize, Ethan's presence in Anna's life remained constant.

He was transparent about his past relationships. He'd dated Ava, a Jewish U.S. Navy girl, for a year after he separated from his wife. She was great, but not for him, because of their differing backgrounds, commitments, and lifestyles. His certainty that she wasn't a fit was comforting for Anna, as was the fact that he'd had a relationship after his wife: It reassured her that she wasn't a postmarriage rebound.

Ethan portrayed his career as a multifaceted, fast-paced, international position that moved him between high-level academic environments and sophisticated government projects. He dazzled her with huge amounts of seemingly flawless detail about doctoral-level mathematical modeling and the inner workings of his corporate environment. His knowledge of postgraduate-level math was astounding, and his prowess came out in their endless G-chats, where he would share his various math and science theories. Anna loved his intellectual side and the fact that he teased her when she said that statistics made her want to hide behind the sofa. But it was clear he also admired her intellect. They were equals, with strengths in different areas, and that idea really appealed to her.

Their intimate, personal chats continued for weeks, and they connected with increasing frequency. They talked all day and all night on G-chat, both of them lingering at their offices long after they'd completed work, not wanting to log off. Then, one day, flowers arrived at her house with a note: *Thank you for your patience and for having faith in me.—E.S.* It melted her heart.

While she found his refusal to fix the webcam issue an irritant, it was truly another era for technology—long-distance communication was riddled with hiccups and complications. Plus, her usual dating rules and logic were hushed by the intensity and spark of their connection. In her mind, a relationship couldn't exist unless two people met in person, so any lying on his end seemed pointless. He would eventually have to materialize. As an early adopter of online dating, she had plenty of positive experiences to give her faith in the process. No, "catfishing" wasn't yet part of the cultural vernacular, but she wasn't naive. Ethan's fluency and the level of detail he consistently provided in response to every question, combined with his constant availability to chat, all added up to the picture he presented: someone who had thrown himself into work after his marriage broke down and who led a geographically complex life, traveling frequently for work.

Ethan asked nothing of her except her time, openness, and emotional vulnerability; he wanted to be part of her life, to know her as intimately as possible. He was also investing huge amounts of time in her and sharing every part of himself. For the moment, that was enough, she told herself.

*   *   *

A month into their virtual courtship, Ethan assured Anna that the webcam issue would shortly be irrelevant, as he would be in New York during the week she would be in Boston to attend a family bat mitzvah, so he would drive to see her. He planned everything down to the last detail, and they spent hours imagining how wonderful it would be to finally meet after corresponding for so long. She worried about whether they would have the same chemistry in person that they did online, but she decided she would deal with that when the time came. She was just thrilled to finally meet him.

Unrelated to her, he had been hoping for a transfer to the Morgan Stanley London office, and that position seemed increasingly more likely, so long distance didn't seem like a permanent state. He assured her he'd been thinking about this for a while, as he wanted to test out living in London, regardless of what happened with them. This was encouraging to Anna, but also made the possibility of their relationship feel that much more real.

They excitedly planned what they would do if he got the position in London, all while retaining an appropriate level of reality check: They wouldn't put pressure on themselves, promising to just let things take their natural course. But first, Boston.

*   *   *

Four days before she left for Boston, Ethan sent her an email with the subject, "Dueling with a double-edged sword."

"Oh, Anna. I don't even know where to begin."

He broke up his lengthy email into three sections: "The Good," "The Bad," and "The Ugly."

The Good: Morgan Stanley was offering him an incredible position. "They're starting a task force to deal with the effects of international bail out plans on the Morgan Stanley credit crunch," he explained, referring to the current financial crisis. Morgan Stanley offices across the globe would assess the rescue plans of various markets in relation to the future of the company. Ethan had been tapped to be their "math-heavy" research scientist. He'd work internationally, across Europe, Asia, and South Africa. "It's at the crux of everything going on in the world—and I can't complain about the salary at all," he said excitedly. There was also growth potential into emerging markets, which fascinated Ethan.

The Bad: They wanted him to fly to Tokyo the week he was supposed to meet Anna in Boston. "I don't know if you've heard, but the Japanese have granted Morgan Stanley about $10 billion in liquid assets," he explained. That was the task force's priority, and since they wanted him to start the position immediately, he needed to fly to Tokyo as soon as possible.

The Ugly: The offer was only on the table for the next day, as they needed to fill the position immediately. He wanted her to tell him how she felt about all of it. The trip would, however, bode well for a future posting in London, he assured her.

During her time in Boston, Ethan emailed her photos from his Japanese trip and organized times to chat with her on the hotel computers. She didn't expect him to call, because it was logistically problematic and things were chaotic for him at work, so online chatting still seemed acceptable. Her family knew all about him by this point, and everyone thought he sounded great. She had finally met A Suitable Jewish Boy—and she wasn't going to let this unexpected business trip stand in the way of being with him. Besides, this trip meant he would be spending a lot of time in London. She was OK with a little delayed gratification if it meant he'd soon be living locally.

She arrived back home in London to a ten-page, handwritten letter, which Ethan said he wrote on the plane between Japan and New York. It was scrawled on lined paper in masculine, spidery handwriting, complete with chocolate smudges, which he identified with little arrows (he was a self-proclaimed chocoholic). It stated, in no uncertain terms, why Ethan was so hopeful about their relationship and how their connection had illuminated his life in a way that he had long ago given up on.

When she read it, her heart stopped. She couldn't believe she had connected with someone so perfect for her. She read it out loud to her brother and sister-in-law, whom she was living with at the time. They'd heard all about Ethan Schuman by this point, and after hearing that letter, they understood why she was smitten. Anna was prepared to wait a little longer to meet this guy, to find out if he really was the person she imagined him to be. His intent, his depth of feeling, and their connection were unquestionable.

*   *   *

On October 15, he forwarded an email he'd sent to his sister, Riva. The subject was "The Confessional," and in it, he shared his excitement about this incredible new woman he'd met.

"The last time I wrote you a confessional email like this I told you that it was I who overdosed Gabe on grape jellybeans, leading to the marathon vomiting spree. This confession is less guilt-stricken, but maybe equally as nausea-inducing," he prefaced his email, referring to his nephew, Gabe.

"You're no stranger to my long battle with/against/in the spirit of love," he continued.

He admitted to falling for women simply because they "smelled the right way" in the past, lighting up, and then losing interest just as quickly. But this time, things were different.

"In the most unforeseeable of ways, I found a woman who is everything you've wanted me to find for myself," he gushed. He sang Anna's praises: She was educated, accomplished, beautiful, sweet, and generous. He thought she was wonderful, "and for some inexplicable reason," she felt the same about him.

He acknowledged the geographic distance but noted that a job opportunity was presenting itself in London, and things were really aligning. "There is no pressure. There are no expectations," he assured his sister. "I just know, quite simply, that I need to be with her. I need to give it my best shot or I'll regret it for a long time to come." He asked for her support as he followed his heart.

Ethan closed with a mention of Tokyo, indicating he'd already notified her of his upcoming trip. He alluded to her being pregnant, said he'd try to bring their mom a bonsai plant (if customs didn't confiscate it), and joked that he would see if he could afford a geisha for their dad. "And I'm not bringing back leg warmers for Dave," he closed.

It was so flattering, so kind and genuine—her anticipation mounted.

They continued to talk every day, with their Skype messenger and G-chat sessions lasting upward of seven hours a night (neither of them slept much at this point). Ethan planned to correct the Boston mishap by flying to London in a few weeks. But his life grew increasingly complicated, which put stress on their growing relationship.

Ethan frequently mentioned the other women in his life—both past and present. Anna knew this was normal, given they hadn't even met in person and couldn't physically be together yet—plus, he was a man who had led a full life before connecting with her. But they'd been communicating constantly for more than a month at this point, so it was difficult for her to hear about these women, despite the fact that he never wavered in his declared commitment to her.

At the end of October, Ava, the Navy ex, turned up on his doorstep in Pittsburgh unannounced, hoping to get back together with him. He allowed her to stay overnight because he couldn't bring himself to slam the door in her face—it just wasn't in line with his gentlemanly code of conduct to turn her away.

During that night, he chatted constantly with Anna. So while she felt sick with jealousy and worry, he wasn't absent long enough for her to think that anything had happened between them before he drove the ex to the airport in the morning. The level of detail he gave Anna about their interaction, about how he felt moment to moment, where the ex was and what she was saying to him, and how he rebuffed her from behind his closed bedroom door, was unparalleled. Ethan somehow managed to navigate the situation with just the right amount of honesty and vulnerability to keep Anna on tenterhooks, but still on his team.

He knew her well enough to know that loyalty was important, and despite the unusual nature of their relationship, she wouldn't tolerate cheating or blurred boundaries with other women. They were both emotionally invested at this point. However, he knew Anna wouldn't want him to turn a brokenhearted girl out into the night. She agreed that it would be unkind, but trusted him by this point. Even in the most unsettling of situations, Ethan's transparency and communication were reassuring.

The drama continued to mount. A few days later, Ethan was back in DC and was mugged, suffering a stab wound. It was horrifying; she couldn't imagine how terrified he must've been. As he recovered, he looked to Anna for guidance on how to dress his wounds and speed the healing process.

Despite these complications, Anna remained focused on his impending visit in mid-November. They would spend a couple of days in London, then go to New York for a few days to pack up his apartment, meet his family, and move him to London to start his new position. It was all such a whirlwind.

Two days before his arrival, she sent her friend a long email, telling her all about her new guy. "I know it sounds crazy, and I know it sounds like I've lost my mind, but it could be the best love story ever, right?!" she wrote. Anna assured her friend that she didn't feel stressed at all about his move. ("I figure he's the one doing the moving, not me. What do I have to lose?") She estimated they'd already exchanged a year's worth of conversations, so she knew him better than most guys she'd dated.

"There are just no red flags," she proclaimed confidently. "I've seen too many photos of him, his family, etc., and if he were sending me someone else's photos, he'd be a dumbass to move countries," she wrote flippantly.

*　　*　　*

Anna booked time off from work in anticipation of Ethan's visit and scheduled a visit to her doctor to restock her birth control pills. Knowing the unpredictability of his work schedule, she waited anxiously for him to confirm that he bought his ticket. As the weeks passed, her anxiety mounted. Ethan complained about his heavy workload, which made her feel selfish for pressing him while he was in the office eighteen hours a day. He would get around to it eventually, she told herself. They chose a hotel together and everything seemed fine. Not to worry, he said—he would definitely buy his ticket in time. As promised, Ethan forwarded her a link confirming his booking, and she breathed a sigh of relief. *This was happening.*

Finally, the day arrived. Her entire office knew about his impending arrival, and she practically skipped into work, ready to wrap things up for her week off. As the day went on, Ethan became increasingly distant, and she started to worry. His email replies, which were usually instantaneous, were now delayed, although they reassured her that he was just tying up loose ends and would soon be on the way to the airport. He seemed hassled and a little short with her, but she told herself he was just stressed—and possibly a little nervous. There was a lot riding on this trip by then.

By the time he should have been heading to the airport, his replies ceased altogether, despite her increasingly emotional pleas for confirmation that he was on his way. By the end of the day, she felt sick and paralyzed, not knowing what to do. She was glued to her computer, unable to move in case he replied, but feeling that something was terribly wrong. By 8 p.m., she was an emotional wreck. The plane had departed, but she had no idea if he was on it.

Anna stared at her inbox in a panic, stunned. And then, after hours without any correspondence, it appeared: an email from Ethan Schuman that made her stomach drop through the floor. He didn't get on the plane.

In classic Ethan style, told through emotionally moving and dramatic prose, he explained how tortured he was. It was a crisis of confidence, he said. He wasn't good enough for her, and he feared rejection once they met in person. And so, he backed out.

That normally would have been her cue to walk away and never look back, but Ethan was skilled at pressing just the right buttons and displaying the perfect amount of vulnerability to somehow stop otherwise rational people from behaving normally. His masterful cunning, combined with the intensity of their emotional connection, heightened by months of anticipation, allowed her to show him unprecedented levels of understanding and empathy, and to continue talking to him, instead of writing him off.

She spent that week—the one she'd booked off from work to spend with Ethan—in bed, feeling utterly depressed and humiliated. How would she explain to everyone that Ethan just never arrived? And yet, she had to. It was crushing.

This was unlike anything she had ever experienced. There was no playbook or life experience to prepare her for how to navigate Ethan Schuman.

By then, he had become her constant support and companion, messaging her practically every minute of every day, perpetually interested in her life, eager to share it all. The thought of not hearing from him was unthinkable. They would sneak away from friends to text each other, to share a thought or a joke, or from family gatherings, to talk about how they would spend future Jewish holidays together with their families.

Ethan's failure to fly to London that day was the first one in a long line of incidents that left Anna unsettled and riddled with confusion, overcome with stomach-wrenching emotional turmoil. Life with Ethan was a constant page-turner. She wouldn't have tolerated it with a lesser man, but Ethan was just that incredible.

* * *

Ethan rebooked his trip for just after Christmas, forwarding her a hotel booking for the Park Lane Hotel in London. But Anna was cautious, and rightfully so. She called the hotel to verify, but there was no booking.

Once again, he canceled.

Just as she was about to give up on him, he came clean about why he kept failing to appear: He hadn't used his real photos. He had stolen some photos from an older friend named Brian. He was not actually thirty-six, he was twenty-seven, and his real photos would give him away. Once it became clear they were so well suited and developed a strong connection, he was afraid she might pull the plug if he revealed the truth.

Anna was stunned.

Twenty-seven was well outside her usual age range, but he was clearly bright and accomplished, and the fact that he'd already been married established him as someone who had experienced the world more fully than the average twenty-seven-year-old. So their eight-year age gap was not a dealbreaker.

The photos he'd initially sent were clean-cut and classically handsome, very much Anna's type. But far more than the age difference, she worried the physical spark might not be there. Then Ethan shared his real photos—lots of them. There were photos with his sister, with his ex-wife, a portrait series his ex made him do, photos with friends, vacation pictures. He went to great lengths to paint a visual picture of his life.

Anna was relieved. He didn't fit her typical type quite as much as the first photos but was still a very attractive guy. And when you combined his appearance with the emotional bond they'd already created, she had no concerns about their in-person compatibility.

She was grateful to finally know the truth and move forward with him with no more secrets or lies.

Ethan's sister, Riva, came forward to corroborate his story, as well as to get to know this incredible woman her brother kept gushing about. When Ava, the Navy ex, emailed Riva to disparage Anna—"This is your brother's new flavor of the month"—Riva forwarded the email to Ethan, making light of it and complimenting Anna. (She also mentioned mundane sibling stuff. "Are you coming home soon? Gabe needs some math help. He told me he doesn't remember his numbers until you come by and show him.")

When Anna made one of her many unsuccessful attempts to call Ethan, Riva picked up the phone. They had a long conversation where she explained how her brother was a complicated-but-good guy and spoke to her in a way that made sense of all the things he had told her—everything aligned perfectly. Hearing Riva's voice made Anna think she finally had access to a real piece of Ethan's life.

*   *   *

By February 2009, it seemed that Anna's patience had finally paid off: Ethan's trip to Japan was a success, and he was being transferred to Morgan Stanley's London office. He forwarded her an elaborate email chain between him and a local London real estate broker who was facilitating his search for an apartment. They were nearly six months in, and she was losing faith, so the news bolstered her belief in what they were building.

"I have no doubts about you," he assured her. "Let me reiterate that. I have absolutely no doubts about you or us. It's all about us, Anna."

His confidence in them relieved her. "You have no idea how wonderful that is to know."

"Do you want further proof I have the position in London?" he offered, unprompted. "They set up my network ID—you can email me at ejschuman@morganstanleylondon.com."

"Can I? Really??"

"Yeah, I mean it's not the one I use the most, but you can."

Up to that point, they'd only communicated via his personal email and Skype, so receiving his new work email address was affirming. This man was real. This job was real. It was finally all coming together.

And yet. She was cautious. After the initial incorrect photos and lies about his age, Ethan had proven himself to be less than trustworthy. So, desperate for further validation, she did a little research and looked up the morganstanleylondon.com domain:

Domain Name.........morganstanleylondon.com
Creation Date........2009-02-15
Registration Date....2009-02-15
Expiry Date..........2010-02-15

The domain had been created that day and was not registered to Morgan Stanley, but to a woman named Emily Slutsky.

Anna emailed Ethan immediately. "Is anything you've told me true? Has it been fun for you to deceive me like this? Have you lost sleep and stayed awake nights for months just to make a fool out of an honest woman? To make her fall in love with you, give her heart to you and trust you like she's never trusted anyone, just to make a fool out of her? Really? Really??? After swearing to me, time and time again that you're for real? My god, do you care about me at all?"

"There is nothing about this that is a joke for me," he responded, seemingly unaffected by her rage.

"That is not a Morgan Stanley email," she reminded him. "It's registered to a private person TODAY."

"Well, I got it two days ago . . . so . . . I'm not sure how it's registered today. I AM COMING," he reconfirmed, irritated. "I'm not lying to you."

"It is not only not registered to Morgan Stanley, but it's registered to Emily Slutsky."

"I am not lying to you," Ethan repeated.

"WELL WHO IS SHE? Is that your wife? Your sister? Your friend? Tell me the truth!!"

"Anna stop it. I think we're following very unhealthy patterns, so we need to stop it right now," he warned, as if Anna's behavior were completely irrational and unprovoked. "Let's just keep away from each other until I buy the damn plane ticket."

They argued at length, with Anna pushing for answers and Ethan saying they should discuss in person. She begged him to get on Skype to speak with her, but he refused. He didn't want to hear her sound "all hurt."

"You really have me in this place where I'm constantly feeling like I have to prove everything to you," he said, pointing the blame at her.

After extensive pleading by Anna, Ethan finally admitted to creating the email address, despite having the Morgan Stanley job "100 billion %," because Anna was overly anxious that he wasn't coming. So, while he would eventually have his new email address, he wanted to give her peace of mind now. He was being thoughtful, really.

Fake email aside, she continued to press him for more information as to who this woman was and why she would assist him with this lie.

"It's not a long story, and it's not a dirty explanation, I just don't want to give it," he replied.

"I don't get why you would do something that would make me distrust you now," she asked, more confused than ever.

"You already distrust me! I HATE THAT YOU DISTRUST ME NOWWWWWWWWWWWWWWWWWW," he scream-typed.

Well, he wasn't wrong there. She did distrust him. But that wasn't an explanation. She quickly googled Emily, but aside from revealing that she went to MIT, nothing about the results provided much clarity.

Instead of focusing on the lies, Ethan did what he was so masterful at doing: He shifted the entire focus back on Anna. Her emotions, her anger, and how he couldn't deal with them. It was too much. She needed to cool down, stop overreacting, and then, only then, would he reengage with her. But not yet.

*   *   *

Anna could not easily dismiss the Morgan Stanley incident. But fortunately for Ethan, a new distraction popped up in the following week, which diverted their attention away from the lingering answers she was seeking.

Eighteen months earlier, Anna had connected with a guy named Ben on JDate. She quickly knew he wasn't for her, but he had an extra ticket to an all-expenses-paid trip to an event in Newfoundland with a group of friends. It sounded fun, but she needed to make sure she and Ben were on the same page: She made it abundantly clear it would be a purely platonic trip, and he agreed. Anna hit it off with the other women, and they spent the weekend together, largely separate from Ben and the other guys. Ben became disgruntled, as the weekend didn't unfold the way he'd hoped, and the two lost touch. Over the course of Anna's lengthy correspondence with Ethan, she mentioned this incident.

Then, by chance, Ava, Ethan's Navy ex, met Ben in a JDate chat room in early 2009. As their conversations continued, Ava mentioned Anna, the British woman who had stolen Ethan from her. It didn't take long for them to piece together that it was the same Anna who'd rejected him. Like a game of online-dating telephone, word traveled back to Ethan, who then communicated it all to Anna. Anna was upset about how Ben portrayed her in his conversations with Ava, and Ethan was irate. So he took it upon himself to write lengthy, scolding emails to both Ava and Ben in an effort to defend her honor.

"Don't call her a British cunt. I won't let you vilify Anna anymore," he emailed to Ava and forwarded to Anna. "The reason I chose her is because she's healthy. She's positive. She's not embittered toward life. I chose her because she makes me feel like a man in a way you never could."

"You know the caliber of woman that Anna is," he then wrote Ben indignantly, also forwarding the message to Anna. "What could you possibly offer a woman like Anna? If she backed away from your friendship, it's because you screwed up."

Ethan went on at length, admonishing Ben and Ava for their behavior, belittling them, and singing Anna's praises. No one was going to talk about his woman like that.

*   *   *

For the first nine months after meeting Ethan, Anna was so wrapped up in him, so deeply invested, that she couldn't fathom dating anyone else. Despite the frustrations, she held on to the belief that this was something special, and that belief lingered longer than she ever wanted to admit. But by the summer of 2009, she knew it was time to open herself to other men. Her dynamic with Ethan was toxic, but she couldn't resist responding whenever he reached out. The least she could do for herself was to keep dating and try to compartmentalize Ethan until he finally arrived.

She met a new English guy online and they started dating. He was recently divorced and not entirely ready for something serious, but she was only half-available anyway, so it worked. They dated for six months; she managed to hide it fully from Ethan, and he had no idea Ethan existed. She kept each relationship entirely separate.

Maybe it was the slight bit of distance she was able to carve out during this time, but by August 2009, Anna decided to dig deeper into the woman who colluded with Ethan to deceive her with the Morgan Stanley email stunt six months earlier. She'd accepted that he was just crazy enough to create an email address to satiate her until his work transfer, but she never got a clear answer about the woman who registered the domain on his behalf. She often suspected he was secretly in a relationship and that was why he wouldn't materialize. But surely a wife or girlfriend wouldn't assist with something like that. Would he dare to use his wife's name to register it? But why? She had to know, so she confronted Ethan again.

"Emily Slutsky. Please just tell me who she is to you," she demanded.

"You tell me what you think she is—you're confusing me. I have no idea what she has to do with anything. You have an assertion. Stand behind it and tell me. If you give me the assertion, I'll tell you the truth." God, he was infuriating.

Anna continued to press, ultimately getting him to admit that Emily was a friend from MIT whom he'd briefly lived with—as a platonic roommate, not a girlfriend. Desperate to prove himself to Anna, he'd asked Emily how to register a domain, and she'd done it for him.

"This conversation is really not worth our time," Ethan concluded.

But Anna wasn't done. She'd done quite a bit of online digging on Emily Slutsky, and there were more than a few overlaps in her life and Ethan's. They both went to Columbia and MIT, both did Tae Kwon Do, she was Facebook friends with some of the friends Ethan had mentioned, and her mentor had the same name as Ethan's uncle, Joseph Malinsky. Also, her mother was named Anna. "You even have the same initials," she noted.

"Oh, please," he said, dismissing her. "I have not lied to you and I'm not Emily."

"You're just denying. You're not telling me the real story."

"My denial is a statement of truth!" (Was it?) "I am telling you the truth. You always do this, explode when you don't know what you're exploding about. Calm down. I haven't lied to you."

"Why won't you let me hear you? If you're a woman and you've lied to me all this time, I feel sick."

"OH COME ON." Ethan was not having it. And if Anna was honest with herself, as much as these details confused her, even she didn't believe what she was accusing him of. She didn't fully understand why this woman would help him lie to her (if he even told her the truth about why he'd created the domain), but if there was one thing she was confident in, it was that this person—whoever they were—was a man. Was he stealing the details of this person's life? And if so, why?

"I'll amend it all," he promised, clarifying that he'd amend her displeasure, but not the lies—there were no lies. "You're going to be disappointed that I've told you the truth about my life. I don't know what you're searching for, but I have. Please just calm down."

She pressed on, repeating all the details and overlaps and points of confusion, then stopped herself. "Why am I doing all the talking? Fucking tell me."

"Because you're overreacting," he chimed in. "And that usually means you'll be doing all the talking."

"You talk," she demanded.

"She worked with my uncle, I knew about her, we met later on when she was in Boston, she's younger than me, some of her friends are my friends, because I introduced her to a bunch of people, we went to MIT and Columbia, but I did it in reverse. That's it. You do need to shut up though. I'll talk to you later."

She exploded and demanded an apology, prompting him to throw it back at her, calling her "nasty." She was getting nowhere and she had a migraine.

"I'm sorry about the migraine. I'm not sorry about everything else, because I haven't lied," he informed her, unsympathetically signing off.

The next day, he sent her a full confessional:

> Anna,
>
> This is the truth.
>
> I am 28. My name is Ethan Schuman, and I do want to be with you.

But Ethan didn't dive directly into the full truth. First, he wanted her to understand why he did what he did: He was struggling with how to allow her to enter his world. He was afraid of getting into another serious relationship. He wanted everything to be perfect for them, but feared he might fall short in that quest.

"This isn't a farce. This is my life. I didn't steal Emily's life. We have a similar life only because we're related. I should have been honest with you when you asked me, but I get nervous when it comes to really introducing you to my life."

He explained that Emily was a distant cousin ("Mom has a cousin. From my grandmother's side. Grandmother's sibling. Cousin's kid is Emily."), but they grew up together and had mutual friends, then lived together in Boston. He assured her that Emily had nothing to do with the life they were building together. He wanted to overcome these mental hurdles that were sabotaging their relationship, but he was terrified he would mess it up. He'd already messed it up with one woman—if he lost Anna, too, he'd have nothing left. He wanted stability and permanence. But he worried he wouldn't be the right man for her.

"I know you feel suspicious right now. I know you're hurt, but I will try to do the best that I can to really let you enter my life. I will not make any promises I can't keep, or feed you anything questionable or deceptive."

While he worked on these issues—and awaited his much-anticipated transfer to London—he suggested that they continue to stay connected, but encouraged her to continue living her life. She asked him what he was going to do to work through all of this.

"I'm being a pussy. I'm going to stop being a pussy."

*   *   *

As the months went on, she continued living her life, as Ethan encouraged, but he never let her out of his grasp. A number of serious medical issues arose, and he turned to her for support. Back in late 2008, he had reported having cardiac spasms—which required ongoing medication, constant monitoring, and a 14 mm stent—and he later had pneumonia, both of which landed him in the hospital. He mentioned some ongoing esophageal issues. He narrated several of those episodes to her, then backed them up with photos of his esophageal scans, combined with details of his appointments with a gastroenterologist (whose identity Anna verified).

Later, he was in a car accident on a journey from Boston to New York and briefly disappeared, but he offered a full medical breakdown of the incident and his physical condition postaccident. He told her about the pain while on G-chat, and complained about how it hurt to get dressed.

His sister, Riva, had a host of medical issues, and Ethan described them in detail. He told Anna about the drugs she was on, as well as the likely progression if the drugs stopped working. Ethan asked her to do some research on the condition to help Riva, as he was too distressed to do it himself. Extremely concerned, Anna dedicated a great deal of time to doing as much research as she possibly could. She wanted to do anything she could to help.

Ethan's health concerned Anna greatly. But over time, despite her empathy for him, she started to question herself as much as him. In the moments when she dared to express more doubt due to constant obstacles to meeting or his refusal to talk on the phone or the previous lies she caught him in, Ethan's nasty side came out. He responded with fits of rage, followed by extraordinary measures to convince her he was telling the truth. It seems he wasn't entirely the gentleman he painted himself to be. His unhinged anger and defensiveness led to threats to leave the relationship, followed by apologies and plausible, detailed explanations that left her with no idea what to believe.

But Ethan always had ample evidence to support whatever hurdle he was currently overcoming or story he was telling. He sent dozens of photos that featured him with his family and friends, accompanied by detailed explanations of each of them. He forwarded email exchanges with his sister, as well as exchanges with his Navy ex. He photographed his New York driver's license and sent it to Anna. He forwarded multiple professional documents, like a copy of his thesis, complete with a supervisor's signature (a verifiable MIT professor who supervised this particular academic area) next to Ethan's name. He sent an incredibly intricate infographic explaining "advanced fuel assembly potential design," which he'd created with Pavel Hejzlar, a scientist who also studied nuclear engineering at MIT the same years as Ethan. He took her through the day that he orally defended his dissertation at MIT with a level of sophistication, knowledge, and eloquence that simply couldn't have been faked. While cleansing his ex-wife's computer of a virus, he found and sent a thirty-four-slide PowerPoint presentation on financial modeling that he did for Morgan Stanley (complete with a Morgan Stanley logo on each slide): "Ethan Schuman, PhD; VP, Research and Development, Morgan Stanley."

He forwarded an email exchange with a real estate broker in London for renting an apartment there. For one of his planned visits to London, he booked a short-term apartment and had Anna stop by to inspect the place with the manager, only to later cancel it. It was simply too much proof to dismiss.

Ethan's personal life was never simple. He always seemed to have a "near miss" situation when he sensed she was getting to the point where she was about to leave—just enough to make her feel insecure or jealous enough to stay interested in him. Often, it involved other women.

When Ethan and Anna met, he'd been separated from his wife, Katie, for more than a year. She'd gotten pregnant while they were dating, and that prompted them to marry quickly. Nonetheless, he encouraged her to get an abortion—he knew he didn't want to have a child with her, and, ultimately, he knew she just wasn't for him. A few years later, they officially separated and he filed for divorce. Until the divorce was finalized, Katie remained in the apartment that he owned in New York, where he stayed whenever he was in town for work (which was not too often at that point). He assured Anna that they lived separate lives and that Katie knew about her. As usual, Ethan was in constant contact with Anna whenever Katie was around, which eased her mind.

Then, one evening, he admitted that the two had slept together again. He said it was weird and meant nothing, but divorce is messy, and these things happen. Anna was torn up about it but tried to remain calm. She knew the end of relationships can bring up wildly contradictory emotions. She just wanted their divorce to be over.

Katie's father was making it more difficult to finalize their divorce. Ethan described in detail the meetings they had with the lawyers, how much it was costing him, and the terms they were negotiating—all under the watchful eye of Katie's father, who was present at every meeting, putting further pressure on him.

One night, a Skype chat window popped up on Anna's computer. The words "This is Katie" appeared in the little box. Her stomach dropped. It caught Anna completely off guard. Not knowing what else to do, she replied and chatted with her for a few minutes. It was both weird and comforting.

Katie said Ethan had gone out, and she looked at his computer because he'd told her he met someone else. She was curious about Anna and wanted to know something about who she was. It was difficult for her, despite the fact that she was also in a new relationship. Katie came across as a woman who knew her relationship was over but who was also understandably sad. They'd known each other for so long that she couldn't help but mourn the end. She was timid and sweet, exactly as Ethan had described, and she begged Anna not to tell Ethan about their conversation. So Anna didn't.

Then, just prior to the divorce, Ethan and Katie took a weekend vacation together. She'd decided she still wanted to make it work, so he appeased her with the vacation—it was his way of going through the motions and showing Katie and his family that he'd tried. He assured Anna she had nothing to worry about. Nonetheless, that weekend was torture for her.

Ethan asked Anna to fly to DC to be with him for the much-anticipated divorce, but she declined, saying she couldn't bear to mentally prepare for such a significant event, only to have him cancel at the last minute again. The day of the divorce finally arrived: October 16, 2009. By then, Anna and Ethan's relationship was so intimate, so connected, that he offered real-time narration of their divorce proceedings. ("We are just outside. We just spoke to the judge and are waiting to go back in.") He later narrated her through the coffee he had with Katie after it was all over, as they both attempted to get closure. Anna was with him every step of the way.

But that week was difficult for Ethan, and he constantly picked fights with Anna. His messages grew increasingly nasty: "I just got divorced. Lay off me. I've done my best to communicate with you, but lay off me. If you don't trust what I look like or who I am, then stop fantasizing. Simple as that. Don't pretend to have accepted me and trusted me. I have a really shit week ahead of me, and I'm in no emotional state to deal with your tantrums."

Anna had a habit of lingering a bit too long in relationships, even once she knew they should end. She'd had one abusive boyfriend in the past. A super-controlling man she lived with and feared. About a year into that relationship, she found herself sitting in her car crying. She no longer knew who she was, but she knew she needed to get out, so she did. Several years later, he called her after his mother died. She'd blocked his old number, but he'd called from a new one. He wanted to clear the air with anyone he had bad blood with. After she hung up the phone, she realized how easily she'd slipped into their old dynamic—minimizing herself, acting polite, catering to him. It was a type of PTSD.

And now, she found herself in that same loop with Ethan. The way he masterfully gaslighted her accusations whenever she caught him in a lie, making her question her sanity. Or the way he abruptly disappeared every time they were supposed to meet, activating her anxiety attachment wounds, only to eventually reemerge with a compelling story that demanded her sympathy. That cycle paralyzed her. She could never leave. So, despite any lingering doubts or frustrations, she stayed.

*   *   *

Ethan's arrival in London for work was significantly delayed. By this point, their connection was strained, but she was desperate to see who this person was. His parents were coming to visit, and they'd all planned to meet for dinner once they arrived, but Anna had a horrible feeling that, once again, the plans would fall through. So, knowing their arrival details, she headed to Heathrow to see if she could catch a glimpse of them. No luck. He invited her over to where he was staying—only to then refuse to come down and meet her, leaving her to sit in her car and wait for him. He regularly went on early morning "bike club" outings, then relayed his routes in great detail (all of which checked out with the actual bike club). One morning, determined to catch him, she got up at 6 a.m. to go to the station he departed from and returned to, just to see if she could catch a glimpse of him. But there was no Ethan.

On her birthday, he planned to meet her. The night would be so special that he gave her strict instructions not to plan anything with her friends and family. But she'd been down this road with him before, and she didn't trust his promises, so she arranged a celebration with her friends and family (unbeknownst to him). Ethan, of course, did not show up as planned.

Over the course of two years, she bought gifts, planned trips, and booked time off from work, all in anticipation of their time together. He'd sent verifiable proof—hotel reservations, flight details, emails from colleagues—that all of this was happening, but plans always changed, leaving her gutted.

Her time, attention, energy, and money were all wasted. Of course, Ethan knew in great detail the amount of effort she made on all of these occasions. He also knew exactly what she went through each time he let her down. It felt cruel. Why was he doing this?

Ethan felt bad for keeping Anna from dating while he sorted his life out so they could be together, so he put her on Match.com, creating her profile, filtering emails, sending her updates about users who "winked" at her or emailed her. If he couldn't be with her, he'd look for a suitable man for her.

Once he was back in the United States, he encouraged her to transfer her doctorate to the U.S. and attend Columbia to be closer to him. His power of persuasion was strong, and eventually Anna started investigating potential programs, sending initial exploratory emails, looking into necessary entrance exams—all of which pleased Ethan.

It became hard for her to watch any show that featured New York—a reminder that he was there and she wasn't. She cried in her car when one of their songs came on the radio. She missed him—a man she'd never met, but whom she felt she knew better than just about anyone on the planet.

What made it all so much harder was that for every fight or cancellation or harsh comment, Ethan did or said something kind to counteract it. He sent her several hundred pounds via Western Union (using the name Ethan Schuman) to offset an unexpected veterinary bill for one of her horses and provided emotional support when the horse was ill and she was terrified it might die. But then, when she received an emergency call in the middle of the night from the stable to report that her beloved childhood pet likely wouldn't make it through the night, Anna drove an hour to the stable beside herself with fear. Ethan was her confidant at the time, and she begged him to call her. It was during that drive that he confessed that he couldn't call because he was with Katie. Anna was devastated.

Then, inevitably, he'd do something to make it up to her soon after. Ethan kept her company while she wrote essays, assisting with tedious reference formatting as needed. He spent hours compiling music playlists for her, finding movies for them to watch together online, doing research into jobs she was interested in postgraduation, and helping her imagine where her career could go. He picked songs for them that were mainstays on the radio, so that she would be reminded of him when she heard them. Those moments of kindness eased her doubts and convinced her Ethan had to exist; this couldn't be a scam.

He seemed to want nothing from her but her time and emotional investment, which was why she couldn't rationalize why he wouldn't just *appear*. He swore repeatedly that he wasn't in a relationship, and time after time, his constant presence reassured her that it wasn't physically possible to be with someone else *and* talk to her all the time. It just didn't add up.

Anna was confident, vibrant, and highly social—the opposite of the person you might picture sitting in their bedroom, having a virtual relationship when there were so many real ones out there to be had. She had one toxic boyfriend in her past, but otherwise, she had a long history of normal, healthy relationships. And yet, somehow, the weeks turned into months, and months turned into years, as she waited for the time she would finally meet Ethan.

Technology bred more patience back then. The absence of selfies and the nascent nature of video chats worked heavily in Ethan's favor. Sure, she longed not only to see him in person but also to speak with him on the phone. But there was always an excuse. Always a delay. After a while, she found herself so mentally abused that she simply accepted it. That was what Ethan's brand of psychological abuse did to her: It slowly, gradually deteriorated her to a point where she found herself accepting things that would've seemed unthinkable a year prior. Before meeting Ethan, she was practical and calm. But Ethan plucked away her sanity, one thread at a time, weaving in enough humiliating incidents that she couldn't fathom sharing any of it with another person. He was her secret, her abuser, and her confidant, all at once. His medical issues and dramatic life events further chained her to him. He didn't hold back in letting her know how hideous she was whenever she wavered during his times of need. As time ticked on, she found herself perpetually anxious and deeply depressed.

By early 2010, Anna's brother's cancer returned and she was in a very bad place. She'd asked Ethan to finally show up and be there for her, but once again, he failed her.

That was the final straw. She was done.

Ethan forwarded Anna many emails from Ava over the years, and in January 2010, Anna reached out to Ava to tell her much of what Ethan was saying was a lie, but that she hadn't yet uncovered the truth. She shared how hard her brother's illness had been on her, leaving her to presume he had "no humanity or conscience at all, to keep lying, even in that situation."

She did her best to appeal to Ava, alert her to Ethan's lies, and sympathize with his skilled ability to always, eventually, find a way back in.

> He is not 37. He is 28, but that may be a lie, too. I can't find ANY evidence of his existence under that name on any public records, at any of the places he's said he worked at (and yes, I've been in such a bad place that I've actually looked/called these places, because I couldn't believe someone was being such a liar. I mean, why would they?).
>
> All the photos he initially sent are fake. I have a million other photos of another guy, but I'm really not sure if that's him either.

Maybe it's his best friend and that's why he has pictures. Everything about his life seems to be fake. Pictures of his family, everything. I'm not even sure his name is what he says it is.

I told him to fuck off soooo many times and always he wormed his way back in by being "friendly" and going on and on about how much he couldn't get over me. I wanted to believe he was a good person, just immature and mixed up.

She lamented that Ethan had so effectively pitted them against each other. She wanted to be allies with Ava, not enemies. But Ava wasn't receptive.

A few weeks later, he forwarded Anna an email he'd sent Ava:

I owe both of you your own, personal set of apologies. I need to be clear that Anna is no nutjob. I'm sure both of you will agree that I'm the only nutjob in this situation. And for once, I'd agree. I hope you end up being someone else's genuine, healthy addiction.

And yet, his correspondence with both of them continued. He persisted until they relented.

In April 2010, Ethan continued to steadily bombard Anna with messages, despite knowing her health and well-being were suffering. As a backlash for her attempt to break it off with him, he regularly tortured her with tales of various women. Angry about his latest tryst with some Irish girl and still unsure how to distinguish fact from fiction with Ethan, she called Morgan Stanley and asked to speak with him. The receptionist said she didn't have anyone there by that name. When she told Ethan, he scolded her. Repeatedly. "You were completely inappropriate," he informed her over and over. He admitted to acting stupid when he was lazy and horny and drunk, but she was being inappropriate.

"Stop expecting shit from me," he concluded, before signing off after hours of back-and-forth.

Three days later, Ethan sent another confessional email that admitted to a series of unidentified lies over the previous year and a half. He assured her that, however disappointed she was, he was equally or more so.

"Years from now, when you've long past forgiven, forgotten, and maybe even laughed over it, I will still hold onto it," he told her. "It represents a dark, ugly time for me and correspondingly, a dark, ugly era in my treatment of you."

He was embarrassed and repulsed by himself. And while he never offered specifics—Why was it dark? Why did he treat her so horribly if it embarrassed him so much?—he likened himself to a psychopathic serial killer: "I feel like Dexter sometimes because of it. Like I'm always riding through life with this dark passenger, this relic from past mistakes and horribly wrong decisions." It was a reference to the show *Dexter*, in which the lead character of the same name has an overpowering need to kill, which he refers to as his "dark passenger."

"I really see myself in Dexter in a way that you'd probably laugh at—like I'm always having to work doubly as hard to keep my ugly desires and stupid decisions at bay," he confessed.

He regretted how he'd behaved, but he had no regrets in meeting her. He pleaded for her to have faith in who he was and how much he cared:

"I'm not lying to you about who I am, where I am, what I look like, or what I want with you." The lies were to cover his own insecurities, but were never made out of malice. Yes, he could be a coward, but his biggest fear was disappointing her.

"You might say that I'm critical of you at times, but there is no one in this world that I am more critical of than myself. And I think you know that."

Ethan never stopped making an appeal for just one more shot. Yes, he was flawed, but how could she ever doubt how deeply he felt for her?

A few weeks later, he sent another email, detailing the long conversation he had with his parents, finally telling them all about Anna, how much she meant to him, and how his own "failure to jump" was holding them back.

"My mother seemed to come to your defense consistently. I think she was mostly relating to the situation like a female ally, rather than an overprotective mother. My father just listened—not one for giving any helpful advice in situations like these. Though I did appreciate the fact that he stayed out of it. At least now you can be comforted by the fact that you have a few allies, and you can bet she'll be asking me consistently about the Anna situation."

Ethan's fits of rage after being caught in a lie were always followed by the same sentiment: He was not cavalier, he was ashamed. His shortcomings drove him to hide things, including himself. In his eyes, he was just as much a victim as she was. He knew this worked on her, provoking empathy and keeping her engaged.

After these dramatic moments, when Ethan could tell he was losing her, he'd slowly rope her back in with the promise of some momentous occasion, just on the horizon. In October 2010, Ethan informed her that Riva spoke to their parents about Anna, suggesting she meet them in Spain the following month. The Schumans still hadn't given up hope that Anna would someday be part of their family—so did she really want to walk away now?

*　　*　　*

Time stretched on, and Ethan kept Anna in a permanent state of emotional turmoil. He became increasingly more demanding of her time and attention, and she slowly began to feel less and less like the vibrant woman she once was and more like an emotional wreck. She couldn't sleep. Her health and well-being suffered. She failed assignments at school. She stopped eating properly. She spent hours crying from a mix of disappointment and confusion. Ethan often messaged her right around midnight, just as she was about to go to bed, then turned nasty, calling her selfish for prioritizing her sleep over him. Her family worried about the changes they witnessed in her and were concerned she was withdrawing more and more as she invested larger chunks of her day to talking with Ethan—a man who still hadn't materialized. Her family, who knew about him initially, had thought that relationship fizzled long ago. She was too embarrassed to tell them the truth. The cycle of lies, cover-ups, personal drama, and abusive behavior persisted. And so did Ethan's pull on her.

In those moments when she pulled back, Ethan would bombard her with correspondence on every available virtual medium, leaning into the details of his various medical dramas. Ethan knew how distressed she was. Why would anyone intentionally do that to another person? What could he *possibly* get out of it? She knew she could try blocking him across all the technology over which they communicated, but she was confident he would just find another way of contacting her. Plus, she was hooked. She was in such a psychologically compromised place that she needed to know who this was. Shutting him out and pretending he didn't exist didn't feel like an option. Though she did try. Only to be greeted with hostile retaliations:

"Don't fucking question my maturity. Don't fucking tell me I'm playing power games. I've told you never to do both of these things and you persist. No, I've said my goodbye," he wrote her in December 2010 after she failed to show up to chat with him.

In one of his fits of rage, he said that if she didn't believe that he loved her, he would just go out with someone local. He'd met a sociologist at a club in New York—another Anna. They'd chatted online awhile ago and she was reaching out again, eager to rekindle. She wasn't Jewish, however, so of course he could never be serious about her. And yet, he brought her up to illustrate how offended he was that Anna would ever doubt him or give up on him.

But there was another element that kept her going, beyond any desire to be with Ethan: It was a compulsion to know the truth. If he was lying, she needed to ensure that he didn't get away with it and disappear. She'd invested so much; he had to be held accountable.

Anna knew there was more to the story, but she had no idea what he wasn't telling her. She knew he was ungoogleable, though he had a Facebook page for a while, and it seemed legitimate: His friends also had friends, so she concluded they *had* to be real people. She tried reverse IP address look-ups and reverse phone number look-ups, but nothing worked.

Everything he'd told her either included some sort of verification or, at the very least, a detailed explanation.

And yet, something was not right. She begged him not to continue to pursue her relentlessly if he wasn't going to appear, giving him every opportunity to get out. She made it clear just how seriously his endless pursuit was affecting her—her physical and mental well-being and every other aspect of her life were suffering. He also knew she was in her midthirties and wanted a partner and a family. He was wasting important years for her.

But this was precisely *why* he was still pursuing her, he insisted: He would never maintain this communication if he wasn't serious about her. He understood that these were real consequences in her life, and he wouldn't do that to her. He cared about her too much.

Ethan put her at war with herself over why she couldn't just cut him loose. It felt impossible and she felt helpless. She had this conversation with herself over and over—she needed this to end, it *had* to. And yet, he wouldn't let her go and she couldn't get away. He knew just what to say, and given her sleep deprivation and emotional exhaustion, his words always hooked her back in, despite her best intentions. She had constant emotional whiplash. Despite her intelligence, she was no match for someone like Ethan Schuman.

*   *   *

Gradually, she set about emotionally disentangling herself from him. She'd stopped responding to his virtual onslaught as much as possible, as difficult as it was, and she picked herself up and pushed herself out into the dating world.

The more people she met, the easier it became to start living again. Though still very connected to Ethan, she had a bit more emotional distance by late 2010, and she made a bargain with herself that she would resign herself to living an emotional double life: dating and connecting in ways that felt healthy and normal, while never fully giving up on knowing the truth about Ethan.

By February 2011, she was returning to her old self again, and she'd just met a guy she really liked. Life was good.

Then, one Saturday morning, a few weeks later, she got a Facebook friend request from the other Anna, the New York sociologist. She almost didn't respond, but curiosity got the better of her. That response changed everything.

CHAPTER 11

Gina

Gina Dallago met Ethan Schuman on OkCupid on February 3, 2011. The previous year, she took a break from the online-dating shuffle to date a guy she'd met on the site, but once that relationship ended, she was ready to put herself out there again. "BeyondSleeping" popped up on her favorites and she visited his profile. She'd seen him there during her previous stint on the site and had her eye on him.

Moments later, a message appeared in her inbox:

You stopped by, but didn't write? What gives?

—Ethan.

*   *   *

Gina is a night owl who hates mornings, a self-described workaholic, and an all-around perfectionist. She loves indie rock and fashion, and by 2011, at age thirty, she was finally living a life she loved in an apartment she *really* loved. Though she was working as an architect at the time, her apartment—located on one of the best blocks in Philadelphia—was her testing ground for her future career pivot into interior design. She was learning to express herself in her space, and as an architect, she swooned over the 1,200-square-foot brownstone with skylights, original oak floors, and high ceilings. It was so big she could ride her bike inside. It was also the epicenter of her bustling social life, her space for hosting regular parties and dinner parties. Life was good. She finally felt ready to meet a serious partner.

But it had been a long road there.

After finishing undergrad at Princeton in 2002, Gina took a year off before moving to Boston for an MA in architecture at Harvard. She met her fiancé, Ray, her senior year of college. It wasn't a bad relationship, but it wasn't…great. For a long time, she couldn't put her finger on what felt off about it. It was stable and healthy, but something was missing. Ray was overly critical and not the most passionate, but more than anything, Gina never felt she could fully be herself with him. The relationship wasn't expansive enough, not growth oriented. She wanted more.

Despite these nagging thoughts, Gina tried to power on with Ray. In 2007, her mom's sister died and Gina finished grad school. Her mother was in need of an escape and Gina wanted to celebrate her accomplishment, so they planned a vacation together with her brother to the Dominican Republic. Ray, however, did not approve. He thought it was financially irresponsible—not of Gina, but of her mother. Gina couldn't figure out why Ray felt it was his place to decide how her mother should spend her money, and the unsolicited critique created even more doubts about the relationship for Gina. Ultimately, Ray opted not to join them; he was also an architect and felt he had too much work to take a vacation. His disapproving attitude cast a cloud over the trip, and Gina felt relieved to be free from him for a week. She also realized that wasn't how she wanted to feel about her fiancé.

In the Dominican Republic, Gina met a French guy named Mathéo (though he insisted that she call him Matthew). He was the first person who had romantically sparked her interest in six years. Unlike Ray, Matthew was over-the-top romantic. He came on *strong*; some might call him a love-bomber, but she excused it as just being French. They spent innocent time together on the Caribbean beaches, and despite Matthew's romantic gestures, nothing inappropriate happened. It all just felt playful and surreal, an escape from her actual reality. She told herself it was nothing more than a fleeting vacation flirtation.

Gina returned to Boston and grappled with her rapidly dissolving feelings for Ray. She started seeing a therapist, and eventually called off the engagement. She was ready to be alone for a while.

Matthew reached out periodically to say hello, and the two exchanged emails every few weeks. Gina enjoyed their correspondence, but she was focused on transitioning her life out of Boston and to Philadelphia, where she'd recently gotten a job. The plan was not to be with Matthew; it was just *not* to be with Ray.

Almost a year into their correspondence, a few weeks passed before Gina replied to Matthew's most recent email. She wasn't sure if she'd respond. It seemed their interactions would eventually fade. But just as she was pushing him from her mind, she received an email in broken English from a French girl claiming to be Matthew's girlfriend. They were in love, she informed Gina, and he was hers.

Without that email, Matthew likely would have remained a vacation flirtation. But the drama of the email increased their interactions. Who *was* this girl? According to Matthew, she was his ex-girlfriend who had cheated on him and broken his heart—but according to her, she was the current girlfriend, and Gina was an unwanted interloper.

Gina was twenty-six at the time, and when she'd met Matthew, he told her he was twenty-three. She later learned, via a long confessional letter, that he was only twenty; the (ex?) girlfriend was only nineteen. *Who are these French children?* she wondered, more than a little intrigued. The girl's message made Matthew indignant. He wanted to be with Gina, and he made that clear via very flowery, over-the-top correspondence.

His extended overtures eventually worked. He seemed so utterly and ridiculously in love with her that she couldn't believe he could also be doing all these deceptive things behind her back. His power of persuasion was impressive.

Over the following year, Gina found herself in France four times, and Matthew visited her in the United States even more frequently. She met his family and visited their homes in Paris and St. Tropez. Matthew worked for his father's company in the United States in the summer and stayed with Gina. Two years after they met and one year after they began dating, Matthew proposed.

Gina felt weird getting engaged a second time, especially to a foreign guy she had so many doubts about. She hadn't been on the hunt for a new fiancé, but it just felt like the natural progression of their relationship. And yet, she was conflicted. She felt tremendous embarrassment about calling off her first engagement, so part of her thought perhaps this second chance would erase the feelings of failure she still had from the first one. She wanted a family, but not immediately, so there was no rush there. But Matthew wanted her to be his wife. And she said yes. He'd been living in France, but after the proposal, they applied for a fiancé visa so he could move to the United States and apply for his green card.

Things were going well. Sort of.

Despite the fact that Matthew portrayed himself as a sick puppy in love around her friends and family, Gina had her doubts. There were lots of texts and online messages with other women. Eventually, another email arrived from a different French girl, claiming that Matthew dated her friend for years and was a pathological liar. More drama, more mystery. Something wasn't adding up. But Matthew always had an excuse and was smooth enough to know how to win her back. Just as he was about to fly back to Paris for a month, he bought her a big bouquet of roses the day after this latest email accusation landed in her inbox. She didn't even particularly care about flowers, but those gestures, on top of his extensively long emails and letters in which he professed his love and reassured her he wanted to spend his life with her, wore her down. She wanted the fight to be over and wanted his words to be true so badly that she allowed herself to believe him, despite having a sick feeling in the pit of her stomach. She couldn't fathom someone going to such great lengths, exerting so much energy and being so cruel, as a form of manipulation. He was also good at playing the pity card, always finding a weakness to endear him to her.

The final straw came after their engagement "honeymoon." They'd just spent a romantic week celebrating their upcoming wedding in the Dominican Republic—the place where they'd first met. They parted ways in the United States, with Gina heading back to Philly and Matthew flying to Paris for a few weeks. While he was still at the Philly airport, she opened Facebook on her laptop to find that Matthew was still logged in. He had given her plenty of reasons to be suspicious before, so she checked his inbox and sent messages: She found dozens of emails between him and a French girl she knew to be his "friend." But the emails told a very different story.

She called him immediately to scream at him and demand to know what was going on. He said he knew nothing about these emails—he did not write them! Gina did not believe anything he was saying, and he immediately canceled his flight and returned to her apartment (incurring a $1,000 rebooking fee). He begged her to believe him. He swore on his grandmother's grave, his sisters' lives. He swore he did *not* write these emails. He swore and swore and swore. His story was so implausible, so unintelligible, no one would believe it. And yet, she could not reconcile how this man, after they spent a romantic week together, could lie to her face so boldly. "I guess I have to believe you. Because you are either telling the truth or you are 100% FUCKING EVIL," she informed him.

By chance, Gina's brother's girlfriend was also French. Despite her embarrassment about these repeated incidents, she was desperate to get to the bottom of her mounting questions and suspicions. So she printed out some of the Facebook messages and emails with other women that he'd left open on her computer. (He regularly left his accounts open on her computer; he was not good at hiding his tracks.) Since it was all in French, she asked her brother's girlfriend, Emmanuelle, to read it. "Am I missing something?" Gina asked. "Is it all just innocent flirtations?"

Emmanuelle read the messages in horror. "Oh my god, he's cheating on you," she gasped. "Now what?"

Gina was shattered. She broke it off with Matthew and started seeing a therapist. After their breakup, she experienced extreme emotional upheaval. First, a sort of manic euphoria, unleashed from the relief of breaking free from him, followed by a crash and months of depression.

She questioned everything in her life that made her susceptible to someone like him. She learned what a sociopath was for the first time and became increasingly aware of how many "bad" people were out there. She didn't really understand it before, but Matthew opened her eyes to just how much people can and will lie to get what they want.

By 2011, when Ethan landed in her inbox, Gina was savvier and more world-weary. She wasn't the naive girl she'd been with Matthew. She was ready for whatever life threw at her. But mostly, she was ready for something real.

*   *   *

Post-Matthew, Gina tried out online dating. She tried Match.com for a month but didn't love it; all the guys were a bit too square for her. There was Plenty of Fish, but it had a weird MySpace integration and was crawling with internet trolls. There weren't many options to choose from back then, so when she saw an ad for a paid site called "Fitness Singles," she decided to check it out. She quickly realized, however, that it offered mostly long-distance matches (because there weren't enough users to find local connections), and everyone wanted to sext—which was new to Gina at the time. She received lots of requests for photographs, and since selfies weren't a thing yet, it meant taking a photo and uploading it to the site via her computer. That was not for her. She wanted to go on actual dates. When she found OkCupid in the summer of 2009, she instantly realized it had more guys who seemed like her type and wanted to meet up, with the added benefit of being free.

When OkCupid eventually launched a mobile website, it was a game-changer for her. The user experience still wasn't great, but she could check profiles and exchange messages while at the supermarket or out with friends, taking online dating from solitary to social.

So while OkCupid was her dating site of choice, it was not without its weirdos: At one point, a guy with photos of himself covered in cheese reached out to her. He was a local Philly guy known as the "Swiss Cheese Pervert," and he wanted her to jerk him off with cheese in exchange for $50. (*He needs to up that rate!* she thought.) Years later, he was arrested for driving around pantsless with cheese on his genitalia, flashing unsuspecting women.

But cheese perverts aside, OkCupid offered a good crop of men for Gina to date. By the fall, she had a new boyfriend from the site, so she deleted her account. He was a nice guy, but it didn't work out, and they broke up the following year. She continued to use OkCupid casually, going on dates here and there for many months. She was looking for someone in their late twenties or thirties, somewhere between Philadelphia and New York, and since she was five foot eleven, she wanted a guy she wouldn't tower over. OkCupid allowed you to select your preferred body type, but Gina remained open. She'd learned that all these precise premeeting dating criteria didn't always pan out. She just wanted someone whose photos appealed to her and who seemed relationship oriented.

Then she met Ethan.

*   *   *

Ethan was intense from the beginning. It was still pre-apps, so they were using the OkCupid mobile site, which was a nightmare for messaging. They quickly switched to email and G-chat for constant access to each other. "Do you know our G-chat was just 6 lines short of being 1,000 lines long?!?" she typed in awe. "That's the longest G-chat I've ever had, and I've had some bigguns!"

Ethan wanted to get all the facts of their respective lives out of the way so they could be sure there were no dealbreakers. He presented her with a questionnaire:

A—Heritage. Religion. Background.

B—Parents. Married. Separated.

C—Coffee. Tea. How.

D—Tennis. Sports. Tennis > Sports.

E—Last relationship. How long it lasted. Why it became a "last."

She giddily typed her answers from the tiny keyboard on her Motorola Droid X phone while walking home from work down Walnut Street in Philadelphia. She wasn't Jewish, which was important to him, but as long as she'd consider converting, they seemed extremely compatible. Matthew had also been Jewish, and religion wasn't important to her, so converting wasn't off the table. Plus, she had experience with guys from different cultures, as Matthew was French and Ray was Chinese American, so none of this seemed insurmountable.

He playfully assured her there would be an intense psychological grilling upon their first face-to-face meeting. "Bring it on!" she encouraged. "When will this be?" "I WANT TO BUY YOU A DRINK. This is CRAZY!" he rejoiced. Valentine's Day was rapidly approaching, but despite their excitement, Ethan thought it was too much pressure for a first date. Soon, though, he would come to Philly from New York and take her out.

Ethan commuted between DC and NYC, his hometown. He grew up on the Lower East Side, the oldest son of Russian immigrants, and his parents were proud he was born on American soil. He promised to take Gina to Henry Street, where he spent his youth. During Ethan's childhood, his father became a successful attorney, which Gina thought was a strange profession for a nonnative speaker. Ethan brushed it off and she didn't ruminate on it, but made a mental note. They bonded over the overlaps in their individual paths to success. Gina also came from humble beginnings, growing up in the projects in Pottsville, Pennsylvania, a small coal-mining town two hours outside of Philadelphia. They both felt like misfits as they worked their way into the upper echelons of American academia. This was not a superficial connection.

In their chats, Ethan always balanced abundant teasing with meaningful praise. He laughed at her Italian name and called her a "Jooisey princess," never missed an opportunity to correct even the smallest grammatical error, disparaged her hometown of Philly, and told her she dressed like a "trust fund hipster"—all in good humor, and she took it as such. He also shared her respect for architects and relished her good taste in books and music. He showered her with compliments when she sent him additional photos (per his request): "You have THE perfect body," he said approvingly. While he mocked her need to overachieve, he clearly admired it. They were similar in that way. He understood it. Neither of them settled for average.

Gina's non-Jewishness came up repeatedly. He'd told his mother about her, and she had strong reservations about Gina's Catholic heritage, despite being nonpracticing. His mother worried Gina's family would be rosary-carrying anti-Semites. But Gina understood how mothers could blow cultural differences out of proportion, so she assured him they'd work it all out in due time.

Ethan loved a good argument and didn't shy away from tense conversations. At one point in their exchanges, she asked if he was the type of guy her therapist warned her about: the type who knocks you down, only to pick you back up. "Switch therapists," he replied dryly. "I don't like the ones who warn you against me." Ethan also went to therapy for a while, but there was too much sexual tension with his therapist, so he stopped their sessions and asked her out instead. Nothing was an overshare with Ethan.

Ethan was not simply a distraction; he was different. It was the substance of their chats that grabbed her. Before meeting Ethan, Gina found that many guys she met online thought she was smart, but not sexy enough, and the ones who found her attractive wanted a snapshot of her butt—not what was happening inside her mind. Ethan, on the other hand, embraced her intelligence as desirable and endlessly wanted more of it (though he never missed an opportunity to recognize her beauty, as well). He was also equal parts sexy and smart, and just the right amount of flirtatious. They openly discussed sexuality, but never in the "send nudes" sort of way. It was a perfect balance of romance and intelligent sex appeal without crossing the line. Ethan seemed to understand what she wanted perfectly.

Ethan quickly felt more like a soulmate than a stranger. Their separation of some eighty miles wasn't ideal, but it wasn't a dealbreaker. And she already knew from past experience that digital correspondence could encourage a real bond. Two summers earlier, she carried on a three-week-long OkCupid email chain with a guy in Brooklyn who was planning a move back to Philadelphia. After hundreds of emails, they met and dated for nearly a year. So the email-based prelude to her relationship with Ethan didn't seem all that strange, and she suspected their eventual physical relationship might grow stronger because of the intellectual and emotional intimacy they first established virtually.

The snappy responses, the quick and verbose explanations—it just flowed. One of her biggest pet peeves in dating—which was then accentuated with online dating—was what bad conversationalists many guys are. They'd answer a question about themselves and then stop responding. Ethan, on the other hand, asked endless questions, often in a playful way. He made it clear he was interested, but it wasn't too much. His interest felt just right. She'd laughed at him, and he'd laughed right back. Ethan offered so much of what she'd always wanted in a man, but never seemed to find. Until now.

When she'd communicated with Matthew long-distance in 2008, that was the first time she got a taste of the thrill of receiving regular correspondence from a love interest. Back then, it was still quite rare to text and communicate with someone all the time. It's easy to crave that connection once you get a taste of the dopamine spike that comes with the ping of a new message. And Ethan seemed to have an endless appetite for amusing, thought-provoking, 24/7 messaging from the start. G-chat, which was spiking in popularity at the time, offered an even more satisfying stream of conversation than email. Ethan's love of messaging met its match in Gina: She loved it so much people would riff on her name and call her "G-chat."

Unlike most people back then, she didn't love talking on the phone. She preferred texting and adopted it as her go-to mode of communication as soon as it was introduced. But she made exceptions for guys she was dating seriously, and wanted to talk on the phone with Ethan. She suggested it early on, but Ethan deflected. She decided she was fine sticking with texting, as long as they met up soon.

Even by Gina's standards, her interactions with Ethan soon hit an unprecedented frequency and volume. A couple of weeks in, he sent her a link to a messaging app she hadn't heard of: WhatsApp. "Download this onto your phone tomorrow—that's an order!" he wrote, including the WhatsApp URL. Ethan used an Irish phone number, and WhatsApp allowed them to text endlessly for free. (A courtesy he did not extend to me.)

Gina and Ethan both worked late, so they talked at all hours leading up to their first date. "BeyondSleeping" had indeed been an apt moniker. Her work and concentration suffered as a result. It was rare that he didn't respond to a message within minutes. They chatted while he shaved in the morning, while she waited for a cab outside her office late at night, while they socialized with friends at a bar, and while they were in bed—alone, but always together.

That was the preamble, she told herself. Not the main event. She was looking for a partner, not a pen pal.

*　　*　　*

Ethan lived a full life when it came to women, and he was transparent about all of it: his failed marriage, the cheating, the divorce, and, most significantly, Anna, his ex in London. He was just starting to get over her when he met Gina. Anna was his lost opportunity, the one that got away. Everything had been right with their relationship, except they couldn't be together: Her life was in London, his on the East Coast. He'd been the "perfect boyfriend" to her, and it still didn't work. He'd bought her a ring and everything, but never got the chance to propose. This left him disillusioned in many ways, but Gina reminded him of her: They were both "feisty," "artsy fartsy," and well-endowed. (Ethan had a thing for boobs and wasn't shy about sharing that affinity.) Ethan was not without his hesitations, however. "Every rule in my dating history says that you shouldn't get too serious about a hot girl," he informed her. "And you're hipster Miss America."

There was another Anna in his life, as well: a sex sociologist from New York who came up regularly in conversation, as she was still popping into his life. Gina wasn't immediately turned off by this, however. It was common to talk about online dating while online-dating, and it wasn't taboo or unusual to recap some of your more colorful experiences. She'd shared some recent dates of her own. It wasn't jealousy-inducing in the same way that it might be to start talking about an ex to someone you've just met in a bar. The assumption was that everyone online was dating multiple people, and you were all just trying to find the right person. The trial and error component was both assumed and appreciated. It made the person seem more real.

Shortly after they began corresponding, Ethan told Gina he had to fulfill a promise he'd made to accompany New York Anna to Connecticut for a house swap over Valentine's Day weekend—despite the fact that he was no longer interested in her. He told Gina tales about his sexual adventures with Anna and labeled her a nymphomaniac. He only dated her for the adventure she offered, but Anna grew attached and demanded that he commit to her. After years of sexual experimentation and wild experiences, she was ready to settle down, and she'd decided Ethan was the one. Ethan refused, but she persisted. Two days after Ethan met Gina, Anna showed up unexpectedly at his office at Morgan Stanley, demanding they have dinner to work things out. That was when he agreed to accompany her to Connecticut. But at the time, he hadn't met Gina, after which his interest shifted. Anna wasn't the right one for him. Gina, however, was.

Gina wasn't excited that Ethan was spending the weekend with another woman. She reminded herself that that was his past. Ethan told her he liked that she cared enough already to feel jealous, and promised he would fight hard against Anna's sexual advances. Gina was not convinced: "She's gonna attack you," she said. "Tell her you have your period."

They corresponded as usual as the trip kicked off. "Nice house, nice view. We're arguing a lot though," he said, giving her an update. She was comforted by his persistent messaging, despite being with Anna, who continued to pressure him to commit. But when Ethan disappeared for eight hours—a rarity in the weeks they'd been corresponding—she figured something sexual had transpired between the two. Sure enough, the next morning, Ethan reluctantly admitted they had slept together. But now, he was through with her. He promised. Gina was *real* marriage material and the focal point of his relationship-minded intentions. Despite their intense emotional intimacy, Gina reminded herself that they'd never met in person, so she figured she was in no position to demand sexual exclusivity from him. Yet.

She put the incident with Anna out of her mind and focused on Ethan's positive qualities, like his incredible listening abilities. He remembered every word she shared with him. He never blew her off—in fact, he couldn't get enough of her, without ever seeming needy. He was a mirror, reflecting back the version of herself she so badly wanted someone to see and acknowledge. And Ethan did. He took in the details of what she shared, then processed it and repeated it back to her in his own words, eloquently demonstrating how well he knew her. It was irresistible.

*   *   *

Ethan wanted to know everything about the women he dated. No subject was taboo, and that included their sexual histories. He insisted upon knowing how many sexual partners Gina had. Like most women when confronted with that unwelcome question, she drastically underestimated, which seemed to please him. Ethan, on the other hand, proudly proclaimed his number as sixty-eight. He assured Gina that she didn't want to know the number of partners the sex sociologist had. He didn't take promiscuous women seriously (despite his own prolific sexual experience), and he most certainly would not be taking the nympho home to Mom.

But his inquiry into her sex life was about more than comparing numbers: By sharing his own intimate relationship and sexual history in raw, unapologetic detail, he convinced Gina to talk about her past relationships. Ethan obsessed over each of the men. *What did she like about them? How was the sex? Was there a connection? Why?* He became particularly fixated on one recent man: Gina went on one date with a carpenter right when she connected with Ethan on OkCupid. He was attractive and they'd hooked up, but he ghosted her afterward. Because Ethan and Gina shared endless details about their lives at this point, she felt comfortable telling him about the date and how disappointed she was that he ghosted her—he wasn't in the picture and wasn't a threat to Ethan, so why would it matter? But Ethan thought otherwise. How could he possibly take her seriously when she'd gone on a date—*with a carpenter*, no less—after they'd connected? Her standards were that low? He deemed it a huge red flag and questioned whether he even wanted to meet Gina. Subconsciously, she knew his irrational hostility was the real red flag, but she was so confused and caught up in the fight that she couldn't see it clearly.

Distressed by the misunderstanding, she frantically called his Irish phone number, because her fingers couldn't type fast enough on her phone to keep up with his rant. He wouldn't answer. She had been patient about waiting to have phone conversations until they met, but by this point, his resistance to talking on the phone was leading to huge fights. It also stoked her suspicions. *Why won't he pick up the phone and talk to me?* That weekend exploded into one long virtual fight. And just when things seemed back to normal, he'd launch into another attack. She barely slept or ate.

Searching for a way to understand his sudden, irrational anger, she concluded that Ethan was looking for an excuse to call off the upcoming getaway they'd planned to the Poconos. They'd been forced to delay their meeting for so long due to their work schedules, and since they'd established such a profound connection, a regular date seemed insufficient. So they took a leap of faith and agreed to meet for a more extended get-to-know-you. She feared he was having second thoughts. As a sinking feeling settled in, she picked up the phone to call the hotel where he'd made a reservation. There was no record of an Ethan Schuman, or anything resembling that name. Her heart sank.

Reluctantly, she asked him if he'd made the reservation. Of course he had, he replied in irritation. But then why was there no reservation for Ethan Schuman? When pressed, he didn't hold back his anger.

How could she insult him like this? How dare she go over his head and check up on him? She had crossed a line.

"I really don't appreciate the implication that I was lying. I haven't lied. I have a reservation. I understand that you have baggage in that arena," he recalled, using her past against her. "But I really don't appreciate that your first port of call is to check on my story. I have not given you cause for suspicion."

Without missing a beat, he explained the nonreservation as a result of him canceling the initial booking and then eventually rebooking in order to secure a better rate—the hotel was stupidly expensive, he claimed.

"I may have hesitated in calling you, but I apologize for that. I may have been a bit fearful. You are using it as a sign of deception and that's really just not fair. I will not be bullied, though." He wouldn't back down.

They rehashed this again and again. Eventually, out of emotional and physical exhaustion, she gave up and simply apologized for the transgression. She had to believe him.

The next day, she went into her office on a Sunday to use a proper keyboard to compose an email that would hopefully put this giant misunderstanding to rest.

"I'm trembling writing this," she confessed. "Is it possible that I feel so close to someone after just 2 weeks of writing to him (however incessantly)? Yes, it's possible. I feel like I know you better than I've known many (most) of the guys I've dated for much longer. And that's so important to me. I want a lover who is my best friend, and right now you are pretty damn close! You have been my confidant. My protector (thanks for waiting up for me those nights). My wake up call and my lullabye. It's been short. It's been surreal. It's been awesome. But then there was yesterday."

She explained the situation from her perspective and reinforced her affinity for him. These other people were in their past, and now they could create something great together.

"Look, I can't go on feeling so despondent. I think we have many things to be happy about. We have to meet and see what it's like face-to-face. We will be great friends, no matter what. I'm impressed that you can express your emotions to me, too. I've never dated a man who could do that, and I'm a little caught off guard in trying to deal. It's a very rare gift you have," she said, complimenting his openness and vulnerability.

She wasn't proud of her encounter with the carpenter, but she was happy things transpired the way they did, as it led her to Ethan. "I want to head down that path with you and see where it takes us. I hope you feel the same way," she encouraged.

As they patched up their explosive fight, he called her his girlfriend, and told her for the first time that he loved her.

Later that week, a dozen red roses were delivered to her office with a card: "To my lady, the label looks great on you."

*   *   *

Ethan knew about Gina's previous engagements—details she didn't share freely with friends and family, let alone strangers. It was complicated and easily misconstrued. But her interactions with Ethan were so intense, so emotionally connected, she felt safe sharing it.

She told Ethan that Matthew lured her in with his manipulation. They fought incessantly over his lies, and the dread, confusion, and crippling anxiety she'd felt so many times with him were disturbingly familiar in many of her interactions with Ethan. And just like with Matthew, when faced with accusations of deceit, he turned their fight into an opportunity to love-bomb her. Only Ethan had a very specific avenue for that communication: formal letters.

Ethan knew how to validate her feelings and experiences with the written word. He thanked her for sharing herself with him in such intimate detail. "I can tell you don't exactly enjoy reliving that relationship," he affirmed. He expressed how grateful he was for her vulnerability; it helped paint a more complete picture of her to him, and he liked her all the more as a result of this newfound knowledge of her past. It revealed to him that she was a genuine, sweet, authentic woman. It highlighted her fallibility, but also her commitment to "make right with the world." Even how she handled the leftover drama with sex sociologist Anna endeared her to him: "The way you reacted to my hook-up with the nympho showed me a great deal about you. I'm liking this Gina person more and more," he said approvingly.

Without her ever asking him for it, he offered every reassurance she needed. He knew how to be a loyal and dependable boyfriend; loving a woman properly was something he'd desired since puberty. He'd only cheated in the past when it was clear a woman was not a fit. He was selective and judgmental, yes, but it hurt him deeply when relationships ended. Relationships mattered to Ethan; *this* relationship mattered to him. He was a monogamist at heart, and he was in love with love.

He wouldn't be like Matthew, who'd hurt her so deeply with his lies. "I can't lie, can't keep things from the people in my life, can't deceive. I don't have the face for it. If something happens with a woman, I'll come and tell you very quickly. You won't have to guess at it. You won't have to piece things together or do detective work," he assured her.

He wrote her a 495-word letter describing all of this to her (Ethan loved to formalize his correspondence with an exact word count). He could see himself completely smitten and committed to her. She deserved a healthy relationship, and he would offer her what she needed.

*   *   *

Gina and Ethan had planned to go to the Poconos the last weekend in February, but the financial crisis was still raging, and Ireland—where Ethan did some of his work—was in the thick of it. That news was making headlines in recent weeks, so Gina wasn't completely surprised that Ethan canceled due to work.

Ethan had canceled, postponed, and rescheduled reservations and date plans all month due to work and family conflicts. She was near her breaking point on several occasions, and after too many cancellations to permit, she refused to accept this final cancellation via text and demanded that he call. He promised he would, but he never did. Instead, he shamed her for being so immature and unsympathetic. Did she think he'd rather work 24/7 in a hectic office in DC dealing with the federal budget crisis instead of relaxing with her? She was selfishly fixating on this phone call and not on the fact that he was suffering.

He promised that, at the very least, he would make it to Philly for dinner on Sunday night. He'd worked all weekend in DC and would knock on her door by 7 p.m. She spent that weekend juggling work and preparations for the big day. Since her seventy-hour workweeks as an architect left her no time for housekeeping, she searched for a last-minute cleaning service and made sure she was also perfectly groomed. She made reservations at a nearby Italian place after he told her how much he loved insalata caprese. It was a BYO spot, and Ethan informed her he'd bring an excellent bottle of Barolo. She couldn't believe he would finally be in her presence, across from her at the table, and later—hopefully—in her apartment, petting her dog, and firmly situated in her everyday life.

That afternoon, nervous he wouldn't make good on his promise, she sent him an email:

a. you're coming

b. you're not coming

c. you've been abducted by space aliens

It was the only email he never replied to.
Seven p.m. came and went. He never canceled. He just didn't come.

*   *   *

February 28, after a month of correspondence and broken dates, Gina woke up and knew she was finished with Ethan Schuman.

That night, she dreamed she attended a friend's wedding in a strange location, no doubt related to the fact that Ethan had just invited her to be his date at his friend's wedding in Vermont. In the dream wedding, though, she was alone. She fell asleep in the hotel bed, and an unknown woman crawled under the sheets behind her. The woman began undressing Gina and pressing her body up against hers. She panicked and told her she wasn't into women and tried to pull away. Before she could, the woman transformed into a man and started having sex with her.

When she woke up alone that Monday morning, her passion for Ethan was gone and she began to believe there was no Ethan Schuman.

But who was this person who claimed to love her "thoroughly and comprehensively"—and what did they want from her?

Despite her canceled romantic getaway, she still took the day off from work. She left her phone at home—a first for her—and set out on a ten-mile walk through the worst part of Philadelphia, cutting through Ridge Avenue in North Philly, amid the open-air drug markets. "Fuck it. I'm so confused and so lost!" She needed to think; she needed perspective. So she just kept walking, trying to make sense of it all. It started to pour, and by the end of those four hours, staggering aimlessly through Philadelphia, she reached a conclusion: Ethan Schuman was a woman.

One question kept recurring in her mind: *Why wouldn't someone want to speak on the phone?* Clearly their voice was a secret. Some things are very difficult to hide on a call, like an accent or your gender. She initially considered the accent. Maybe Ethan was foreign? There was the Irish connection, and he did use an Irish phone number, which was certainly weird. She was not clear what the game was there, but maybe? Then there was the gender issue: Ethan's style of communication, the intensity, the level of articulation, the length of the emails, the frequency of communication—it felt like...a woman. The linguistic fluency ensured this person was almost certainly a native English speaker, but possibly Irish? Maybe an Irish woman?

She got the clarity she needed that day during her long walk through the streets of Philly. When she returned home, she confronted Ethan, but the conversation left her spinning in circles, as usual:

"YOU'RE the sex sociologist," she said, referencing Anna in New York. "You're a WOMAN. Oh, and IRISH of course," she accused him. She'd given up on any sort of relationship with Ethan, but she still wanted the truth.

"That's one way of passive aggressively talking to me," Ethan replied, unaffected by her accusations. "I apologize if you were hurt and are confused. Never meant for it to end this way. Don't start composing stories."

She demanded that he tell her one nugget of truth. "I've told you loads of truths, Gina," he replied, reverting to riddles. "Okay, I will offer you proof. I can scan my license."

She demanded a phone call and his motivation for the lies. She sent him proof that he did not attend Columbia the years he stated: She asked her coworker, a Columbia alumnus, to check the name Ethan Schuman on their alumni network. Unsurprisingly, there was no Ethan Schuman.

"Don't be ridiculous. This isn't a way to verify a man's story," he scolded her.

"Don't think I don't notice how you always sidestep questions and turn the blame on me. Classic move," she noted. Her romantic interest in Ethan was over, and now her primary focus was on solving the mystery of who this person was—all of which allowed her to boldly address him for the first time.

Ethan insisted he never gave her his accurate name. He'd had "bad experiences" that left him "particularly careful."

"You've been a fantastic waste of time. But you amuse me at this point," she replied.

He reiterated his promise to scan his license after he called her. "I don't appreciate being a source of amusement," he said, turning it back on her again.

"Ok John Doe. Jane Doe? You have my number."

"John Doe, thanks," he clarified.

Needless to say, Ethan did not call.

The day after her extended wandering, Gina went back to work. She told herself she'd take a day to continue to ponder the possibilities of Ethan's identity. Her therapist echoed in her ear: *This person seems fake. Move on. Don't play detective.* Gina wasn't about to obsess over it forever. She didn't want it to take over her life, but her curiosity was killing her. She *really* wanted to know. She *needed* to know: *Who was Ethan Schuman?* She had to try to figure it out. That was when she found Matt.

PART 3:

THE UNRAVELING

CHAPTER 12

There Is No Ethan

March 3, 2011

Twenty-two days had passed since I broke things off with Ethan. He remained on my mind, but I knew I needed to cut him off. I had a feeling he might never materialize, and he was a toxic, disruptive presence in my life.

Then I received a text from my friend Matt. Some girl named Gina was searching for Stuyvesant and Columbia alumni around Ethan's age, and—completely by chance—stumbled upon Matt. She wanted to know if he knew Ethan and included a photograph: Ethan sent many photographs, but we both happened to send Matt the exact same picture.

I contacted her immediately.

March 4, 2011, 4:38 p.m. EST

"Seems we have some mutual 'friends.' NYC is a small world. Care to tell me your real name and how much of what you've told me is a lie?" I messaged Ethan, breaking the two-week silence between us.

My life was back in full swing. I was applying for several tech accelerator programs, launching a new venture with some friends, and trying to pick up consulting clients on the side, all while teaching a full load at NYU. I was also back to dating guys who actually materialized. Reconnecting with Ethan was not at the top of my to-do list.

"What? No. I have not lied to you," he replied a minute later, obstinate in his righteousness.

"I have proof that says otherwise. At least about your name."

"What difference does it make? Either way…we're not talking anymore, right?"

Ah, how I hadn't missed Ethan's clever rhetorical tactics. "It makes a huge difference. In one scenario, you're simply not willing to meet up with me (for god-knows-why), and in the other, you're lying to people about your identity, which is a very unethical thing to do," I explained, knowing very well he did not need an explanation.

"Whatever lies you think I said to you were never meant to hurt you. Whatever lies you think there were would have been quickly elucidated in person," he replied, reverting to the old Ethan Schuman riddle game.

I played along. "Perhaps. But you conveniently refuse to meet in person, so I am left to wonder: What's his real name? (and more importantly, why would he give me a fake one?) Is that what he really looks like, or are those random pictures he found? Is he still married? Does he really have cancer? (Because you would truly be a sick individual if you lied about that.) But since you refuse to reveal the truth either in person or even via video chat, I can't be certain. You have not acted ethically."

Ethan ignored my lecture. "Who's your friend?"

"I will not reveal their identity. I'm sure you, of all people, can understand the need to protect one's identity."

"Sure. Is it someone who knows me or what?"

"That is not really the concern here. Suffice it to say, I very serendipitously found out that you've been lying about your name. I'd love to know why and what your real name is," I said, trying to steer him back to the real issue.

"I'd like to get together this month," he informed me, completely ignoring everything I'd just said.

I burst into laughter. *Of course you would, Ethan.*

5:52 p.m. EST

When we spoke, Gina was adamant that we should assume everything Ethan told us was a lie. She explained that her ex-fiancé was a very convincing pathological liar, and it wasn't until that horrific experience that she understood how conceivable it was for someone to lie so elaborately for so long.

My heart went out to her that she had been duped not once but twice by deceitful men. I'd dated some unsavory characters over the years, but nothing like this. This was new territory for me. And yet, I saw a lot of myself in Gina. Our backgrounds, our headfirst approach to dating, our communication styles, even physically—we didn't look that dissimilar. If this could happen to her, is it any wonder I also found myself prey to someone like Ethan?

Gina also planted a seed that had not previously occurred to me: her conviction that Ethan was a woman. This shocked me. Sure, Ethan was chatty and hypercommunicative, but I'd dated overly articulate guys before. Plus, Ethan's masculinity was so strong in our correspondence that among the many things I questioned about his identity, his gender was not one of them.

But Gina insisted. She told me about her dream, the one where Ethan morphed into a woman and slid into bed next to her. Gina's dreams often revealed a lot to her about what was happening in her life—things her conscious brain hadn't yet realized. That dream further nudged her toward her ultimate conclusion that Ethan was a woman. Possibly a foreign one, but definitely a woman.

Finally, after our long phone conversation, I agreed with Gina that this was a very real possibility. But I wasn't completely convinced. Had we both fallen in love with a woman masquerading as a man? Maybe. But why would she do that? What did she possibly have to gain? It made no sense.

There was only one way to find out.

6:57 p.m. EST

While we'd both reached out separately to Ethan prior to our conversation
to tell him we were on to him, we decided to team up in our confrontation
strategy, wanting to serve him a dose of his own medicine: After months of
leaving each of us in a state of emotional turmoil, Ethan received some of
the same.

I sent an email to Ethan, CC'ing Gina, with the subject: "Anna + Ethan
+ Gina = ?"

"Gina and I met via a mutual friend," I informed him. "We had some
very, very interesting conversations. Would you be willing to clear up some
discrepancies for us?"

"It's not a mutual friend. I know how you met," Ethan wrote back an
hour later, despite definitely *not* knowing how we met. "I won't be in contact with either one of you."

Four minutes later, Ethan betrayed his own words. He could never
resist communicating, even in the face of being exposed. In a string of
four emails, stretched out over an hour, Ethan wrote again (and again and
again…). He apologized for the lies we "felt" we'd received. He was just
trying to make a few life decisions, you see, and it all went terribly wrong.
It was his inability to deal with personal issues that led him to do this. He
apologized for putting us through it and assured us we were both "wonderful women." He then wrapped it up: "And of course, you will never see me
on any dating site again."

We both knew how conciliatory Ethan could be when he knew he was
trapped, so we were not convinced. "Honestly, sounds like a guy looking
to get some thrills while not completely cheating on his girlfriend," Gina
concluded in an email to me, reconsidering her hunch that Ethan was a
woman. "What a lonely, pathetic soul he seems to be."

I still wanted answers. This was not just some silly fake email he'd sent.
This was months and hundreds of hours spent forging a real, intimate connection, while presenting us with dramatic events and life-threatening

illnesses, interspersed with very real verbal and emotional abuse—*all based on lies*.

"You may be the most pathetic person I've ever (not) met. Who lies about having cancer? That takes it all to a really disturbing level. Especially after I just lost someone dear to me to cancer. Come clean. For you and for us. We deserve that much," I wrote to him.

"I did not lie about everything," he countered, as if some half-truths absolved him from his sins.

It was true, though. Some of what he said was real, including bits and pieces he told us about each other. Gina knew about me (or rather, a fictionalized version of me that Ethan created; I am neither a sex sociologist nor a nymphomaniac), though I had never heard of her. However, Ethan did speak to both of us—at length—about the other Anna, his long-term ex in the UK. We decided she was the key to unraveling the mystery that was Ethan Schuman.

But how would we find her? We didn't have a last name, and Anna was a reasonably common name. So we combed through the embarrassingly long archives of correspondence we'd accumulated with Ethan Schuman over the previous months, looking for any other identifying details about British Anna, never certain if any of those details were accurate or if she even existed.

At one point, Ethan sent me a photo of British Anna, as well as a YouTube clip of her singing with a band (though no band name was listed). We also knew she was training to be a psychologist. So, using that limited information, I did some creative googling—a trial-and-error mix of "Anna," "London," "psychology," and some references to her musical performances—fairly broad search categories. But I managed to find the Facebook page of a woman I believed was very likely British Anna, potential ex-girlfriend of Ethan Schuman.

I wanted to reach out, but how would she respond? *Would* she respond? I couldn't even send her a Facebook message—only a friend request, from a random person also named Anna. Would she know who I was? Would she be jealous? Angry? Suspicious? Was it even her? I had to try.

March 5, 2011, 2:47 a.m. EST

After two and a half years of relentless pursuit by Ethan, British Anna finally felt like she was free from Ethan's virtual grasp. Just three weeks earlier, she'd met a guy (who would later become her husband), and she was happy to be moving forward with her life in a healthy and sustainable way.

Then she received my Facebook request.

Her heart stopped. She recognized me immediately: Anna in New York. The "sex sociologist." Ethan had told her tales of the wild sexual romp he'd taken through New York City with me. (*I am so sorry I missed it!*) He'd dangled those escapades in front of her to make her jealous and hopefully make her regret her decision to move on with her life. So she wasn't exactly thrilled to receive my friend request. And yet she, too, longed to solve the mystery that was Ethan. Maybe this connection was the key to making that happen?

Reluctantly, she accepted and sent me a message. "You sent me a friend request. I'm curious as to what it's about. Is it to do with somebody we both know?"

"Yes, it is to do with someone we both know," I responded, equally cryptically. I was thrilled to hear from her, but still apprehensive about who or what to believe. "I'd love to talk to you sometime this weekend, if you're open to it."

The name Ethan Schuman had not yet been spoken, and yet we both knew exactly who was bringing us together.

3:20 a.m. EST

We exchanged email addresses and phone numbers, and I added her to an email chain with Gina. It was morning in the UK and the middle of the night on the East Coast, but Gina and I were wide-awake. We coordinated a Skype chat, and we all logged on. We still didn't know who Ethan was, but we'd solved one piece of the puzzle: Ethan Schuman's jilted girlfriends had found one another. The game had changed.

There was some natural initial apprehension when we logged on to that call. Ethan made sure to plant the seeds of jealousy and competition to exploit our individual insecurities, exacerbated by the confusing and maddening mixture of fact and fiction he'd interwoven about each of us. I hoped we would be able to overcome whatever territorial defenses he'd built up between us and come together, unified in our objective to take down Ethan.

Gina, Anna, and I talked at length on Skype, relieved to know that others had been equally sucked in and mystified by him. And despite her initial hesitation, British Anna felt particularly grateful. Her private nightmare was over. Finally, she had support.

None of us had actually talked on the phone with Ethan or met him in person, and yet we all felt emotionally tied to him. Over the previous few weeks, he had been communicating with all three of us simultaneously—a realization that left us all marveling: *Where did he find the time?*

In many ways, the three of us were so...similar. We quickly realized Ethan had a type. None of us were easy or obvious victims. How had he manipulated us so profoundly? Whoever he was, we knew he must be outed and stopped before he did this to anyone else.

Gina returned to her conviction that Ethan was a woman. British Anna mentioned the Emily Slutsky incident, but she'd decided that was too much of a stretch. We both agreed that Ethan's communication just felt...manly. It was too real to be completely fake. No one was that good. Were they?

3:33 a.m. EST

I emailed Ethan again. "I'm on the phone with Gina and the other Anna now. Fascinating. This is your official invitation to be honest and come clean."

He replied with another limp apology, this time with an explanation: "I wanted the other Anna and fucked up, majorly. I'm done." He confessed that he was in love with British Anna and "freaked out and did stupid things."

"I'll relay that to her," I assured him. "I'm sure she'll be touched." I gave him a deadline of that weekend to reveal himself to us in some traceable way, or we would find a way to coax it out of him publicly.

"Oh, and how's the chemo going?" I added, unable to resist. "From London is it? So hard to keep track of your geolocation."

"Please just stop," he said, which felt like less of a request and more of a command.

"We'll stop when you own up to the truth and reveal your true identity. You have until Sunday to tell us the full story," I told him. "You should choose stupid women. We're not a crew to mess with."

"I can't, Anna. I just can't." He wanted to know my aim in learning his identity.

"We all just want to know the truth—and to make sure you never do this to another woman ever again. We are all honorable women (you chose wisely in that respect). We will not believe that you won't do this again unless you make yourself as vulnerable to us as we have made ourselves to you. You owe it to us. If you want to come close to rectifying this situation—if you are truly sorry—you'll reveal the entire truth to us now."

He swore he would stay away from dating sites in the future. "Please. I can't afford to do this. Please," he pleaded, still clearly desperate to keep his identity hidden.

Ethan was scared. He sent a series of emails, each giving vague explanations to justify his actions, all while continuing to conceal his identity. His motivation was "self-fulfillment," he explained. "I was miserable and needed an outlet." Communicating with us gave him a "kick," then it escalated, and he didn't know how to stop. Connecting with us made him feel something, whereas he didn't feel anything in his everyday life. "I'm just a normal person who spends too much time in my head. I never meant to take any victims," he assured me, as if that explanation dismissed his actions.

By this point, I was immune to Ethan's way with words, his eloquence in minimizing even the greatest offense and his brilliant ability to invoke empathy for his abuse. Not this time, I told myself. I would not back down.

"I'm sorry your life was/is that bleak," I responded. "It should go without saying that an unfulfilling life is never an excuse for duping others into thinking you have a terminal illness. That is simply sick and wrong. Period. You need to answer some personal questions, starting with: What's your real name? Nothing short of that will suffice. You know who we are, along with other very intimate details. You answer in kind or we seek other public means of uncovering that truth. Stop skirting the issue. This will not quietly go away, we promise."

He pleaded for more time. One more week, and then he would come clean.

"More time for what exactly?" I asked, perplexed by what he planned to do during that week. "Why should we give you more time to simply tell us the truth? You screwed yourself in so many ways. You need to make this right. Now—not next weekend."

Ethan swore the esophageal issue was real, and that—at some point in his life—he lost someone to cancer. So he conflated the two as a way of working out his issues. He tried to convince me it wasn't purposely sadistic. "I became the actor playing the role—getting jealous over you for the sake of the role, not for the sake of manipulating you," he explained, referring to his jealous fits of rage. How that abusive behavior somehow linked to these medical issues, I wasn't sure. "It was a subconscious role," he wrote to me multiple times in separate emails, as if that explained and excused everything. "I didn't really think it would affect you," he added.

How could it not affect us? He knew how emotionally distraught I'd been on multiple occasions, he knew he left Gina trembling with his vicious words, and he terrorized British Anna for two and a half years! His efforts to downplay his actions were not working.

"There's not much to say," he offered, minimizing the significance of uncovering his identity. "I'm in my 20s. I'm a student."

Whatever his biographical details, I wanted proof. "How do you want me to prove it?" he asked, suddenly naive and innocent, in stark contrast to the whip-smart, resourceful, cunning person we'd all been communicating with.

"You're smart. You figure it out."

He promised he would tell me. "Everything about me is public. I'm not as fucked up as you think I am." A debatable categorization, indeed.

All of this was classic Ethan. Endless excuses, pleas for empathy, drawn-out negotiations. Enough!

"Stop justifying yourself and wasting our time. What is your f-ing name?" I started to feel like I was in some twisted modern version of "Rumpelstiltskin." Asking him to pick up the phone didn't even occur to me— if he wouldn't do it when he "loved" me, I was certain this was not the moment I'd finally hear his voice.

5:20 a.m. EST

British Anna dropped offline for a while, and Gina and I continued to bombard Ethan with demands for transparency in separate email threads, keeping each other up-to-date on what the other was saying via a third email thread.

Ethan switched from email to texting with Gina. "He's scared of you," she reported back. "He would tell me everything, but he thinks you'll brutalize him anyway." Good to know I'd left an impression.

6:58 a.m. EST

After hours of emailing privately back and forth—with Ethan minimizing the situation and me making repeated demands he come clean—he promised to email me in a few hours when he was home, at his apartment in Ireland. Why did he need to be home to reveal his name? I had no idea, but it didn't matter. There was no reason. It was just another classic Ethan Schuman attempt to stall.

And that man had managed to keep me up all night. Again.

British Anna rejoined our correspondence. I told her Ethan wanted us to keep his name private and never reveal to anyone who was behind the torture he'd unleashed on us. "Tell him anything you need to," British Anna encouraged. "He has to be stopped. Seriously. It's not about being vindictive. I can't even tell you the emotional hell he has put me through, how he's made me doubt my own sanity and myself on levels I have never experienced. He must never ever be allowed to do this to another woman."

She was right. We would say whatever needed to be said to learn the truth and stop him from repeating his actions. At this point we also knew that his word was worthless. This was a chess match in pursuit of answers, not a negotiation built on trust. So we proceeded with that in mind.

8:48 a.m. EST

Two hours later, Gina and I received a long-winded email from Ethan. Yet another attempt to explain away his actions without revealing his identity. "I'm glad this all imploded," he told us unconvincingly. He hadn't had the guts to extricate himself from the situation, but now he could, thanks to our sleuthing.

"I was in a horrible place years ago and got involved in this charade, with the sole motive of finding an outlet through which to vent my frustrations," he explained, as if tricking women online is a normal therapeutic outlet. Then, over time, his life improved. But by then, he was genuinely invested in British Anna's life. He needed the instant gratification of connecting and sharing with her. "I began to feel a responsibility to care about her." He admitted how twisted that sounded. He was addicted to the lie and to the connection. It was his escape from reality; *we* were his escape from reality. He detailed how great his life was: He had a good family, a quality education, people who loved him, friends, opportunities—Ethan had it all! And yet, he was unfulfilled.

"The realities of everyday life somehow depress me," he confided. "I'm obsessed with the lives of others when, really, my life is just as interesting to comment on."

He explained that his relationships with Gina and me were meant to wean him off of British Anna. We were his "smoking cessation program." (Lovely.) He was merely "trading in the pack a day to only a few cigarettes a day" until he was ready to "quit." (A flawed analogy given his incessant communication with us, but OK.) We were the "buffer," the gateway back to reality, and he was just "an addict who relapsed on several occasions."

Perhaps most significant, Ethan (or the person writing us as Ethan) wanted us to know that he was not really the one inflicting pain on us: He was just playing a role! "It was playing out a movie for me," he waxed on. "ES was present, but I was only in the audience during the performance. In convoluted ways that could take a book or two to explore, I was handling my own personal issues via the vehicle of ES." Deep.

But, lest we think he didn't feel our pain, he assured us he knew the harm was real. "You are real people and I have invaded your real, personal lives. I know that's cruel, and if I were in your shoes, I would experience the same emotions you are. I've done 'real' internet dating before, and I could have been you three." Now, though, after years of spending every waking moment pretending to be another person, emotionally manipulating, picking fights, and refusing to materialize with god knew how many women online, Ethan was reformed—all because we'd caught him. He could now go back to living a "normal, fulfilling life again." And should we dare to doubt it, he was "relieved" that the three of us could do the same.

If we'd only allow him a few hours to "find the guts" to reveal his true identity, he would meet our Sunday deadline.

Oh, what exquisite, compelling, thought-provoking BULLSHIT! And so very on-brand.

I forwarded it to British Anna, whom he'd strategically omitted from the email. He hadn't sent her a comparable explanation, *but* he had once again professed his love to her in a separate message, promising they would be together in four days. I knew Gina and I were a united front, angry and out for blood when it came to Ethan, but I worried British Anna might get sucked in again. He'd played her masterfully, relentlessly, for years. He knew her so well: her vulnerabilities, the deeper points of their connection. She was in a much more fragile place in that moment. His insistence on communicating with her separately made me nervous.

British Anna knew this empathy-inducing explain-and-stall tactic all too well. It was the same story he'd given her when he was trying to "extricate" himself from his Navy ex: He just needed "an escape" from his life, despite his life being totally fine, he told her at the time. As for the "smoking cessation program," she assured us that he hadn't minimized his communication with her during the months he'd been contacting Gina and me. He had been in touch repeatedly, angry that she had pulled back and wasn't available, desperately promising she was the only woman.

"We're supposed to pity him that he was 'addicted'? That he couldn't quit? This is another act. Do not be fooled," she warned, perhaps equally concerned Gina and I might waver in our conviction. "And is he fucking serious that it only took him being found out to sort out his mental fucking health issues and 'live a normal life' again? If that were true, I'd be out of a job!"

Ethan began texting British Anna rapid-fire on the side. He was sorry. She just needed to "let it go" and move on. And yet, he reminded her that he was "addicted" to her. He knew he'd hurt her the most, but insisted he couldn't come clean, couldn't appear to her and reveal himself. That confirmed to her that Ethan didn't look like his photos (either version of them). They were of his friend, he confessed. (Except for the nudes he'd sent her—of which there were many. Those he'd found online.) Inexplicably, Ethan started offering her money—$1,000, then he quickly upped it to $2,000, then made an offer to pay all her horse-related expenses for the next two years. (Why? Maybe compensation for emotional damages? In exchange for what? Her silence? We weren't sure.)

She asked him repeatedly if he was a woman. No response, but he did concede one key point:

"Ethan Schuman does not exist."

That did not surprise us. But we would not rest until we learned who the person was behind the name.

*   *   *

We knew we needed to be strategic in getting what we wanted from Ethan, so we developed a plan: The three of us took on specific roles as we tried to convince "Ethan" to give himself up.

British Anna was the sweet one, the golden girl, the person Ethan couldn't bear to hurt. We wanted to exploit that image he had of her as much as possible, so she would lean into her vulnerability in her exchanges with him in an effort to guilt him into coming clean, or at least to reveal more details that might help us solve the mystery.

I was the bad cop, the attack dog, the bitch. According to what he told the other women, he was already most afraid of me (thank you very much), so it didn't take much acting. What he feared or why, I wasn't sure, but perhaps Ethan really had read me correctly and understood there is little that will stand in my way when it comes to correcting an injustice. Plus, I was pissed: He'd faked medical emergencies, he'd verbally and emotionally abused me for months, and now I came to learn he was doing equally unthinkable things to other women I barely knew but already cared about. So I was more than happy to step into the role of Protector Who Demanded Truth and Justice.

Gina, while someone he regarded fondly, was the girl with the scary Italian family and a brother Ethan feared. Ethan often joked that her family was straight out of *The Sopranos*: Angelina Dallago, the Italian princess; and her brother, Dominic, the Italian stallion thug. (Never mind that he was actually a mild-mannered veterinarian.) We knew we could call in the Dallago mafia if and when it came to that.

1:27 p.m. EST

With our roles set, I replied to his flowery explanatory email, adding British Anna to the thread. "As pretty as this is, we're unaffected by your narcissistic explanations at this point." I told him to join us on Skype at noon the next day. We wanted to see his face and learn his name and biographical details at that time. "We'll find out who you are one way or another," I threatened. "It's your choice how that's going to unfold."

Ethan flipped the switch again. No longer the conciliatory, wounded creature, he became cold and ruthless, just like he had so many times in our correspondence.

"As unaffected as you are, I will not be going on Skype tomorrow. I will give you all my biographical information and contact information. You can verify it all."

I informed him that the noon deadline still stood, and we'd need real photos if he refused to meet on Skype.

"Stop negotiating," he demanded, removing Gina and Anna from the email chain—as if *I* were somehow the one who'd crossed a line. "I apologize that I've hurt you, but relax."

It's generally not a good idea to tell a woman you've pissed off to just "relax." That was especially true in this instance.

"Stop being so casual about your hideous actions!" I hit back. "Just out of curiosity, why exactly are you waiting until tomorrow? Going to twist the plot a bit more in the meantime? The truth will be the truth today or tomorrow."

Ethan emailed Gina to say he would reveal himself to her and her only, because British Anna and I would go apeshit on him, and she had the ability to keep our responses under control. Once again, Ethan was attempting to pit us against one another. You had to give him credit for effort and consistency.

Unfortunately for him, his attempts to make us hate each other didn't work. He wanted us to feel threatened by one another, jealous and territorial. He painted a picture of his ex-girlfriends that depicted us as enemies, not would-be allies. That plan backfired. Not only did we not hate each other, we really, really liked each other. We bonded instantly. He chose women who would naturally become friends in real life. Yes, we had the shared trauma of Ethan Schuman in our lives, but in addition to that, we were kindred spirits. Ethan curated a collection of cool, like-minded women who were smart, funny, and interesting. We didn't yet know who he was, but we knew he had good taste. I couldn't have asked for better partners in crime-solving.

CHAPTER 13

E.S.

March 5, 2011, 2:20 p.m. EST

Realizing Ethan would likely stall forever, we pressed on, determined to solve the puzzle ourselves. Ethan loved mixing fact and fiction, so we'd develop a list of clues and suspects based on information he'd shared. British Anna kept an ongoing list of various Ethan-related details she'd accumulated over the years: the dates he attended each school; addresses for him, his sister, and his parents, all on the Upper West Side; the names of friends from MIT; the name of his fraternity; an ex-girlfriend's address; the names and titles of some colleagues at Morgan Stanley; the name and contact info of his uncle who was a professor at CUNY; flight confirmation codes; the names of all the women he said he'd dated—she'd documented it all. We cross-referenced her list with the names and biographical details he'd told Gina and me—some to all of us, some to just one of us—and compiled a list of potential suspects. It was clear Ethan had been operating on an interesting combination of biographical truths and lies, mixed with active storytelling of his other women. Gina, for instance, knew about the very real house swap I'd planned in Connecticut, but according to Ethan we actually took that trip—and he allegedly refused to sleep with me on it. Determining which details were real and which were fake was going to be a challenge. We decided the only way to solve the mystery of Ethan was to pursue every lead equally, hoping something he'd mentioned would lead to the person who constructed the man we'd all fallen for.

*   *   *

2:40 p.m. EST

As we ran through our list of suspects and accomplices—roommates, family members, coworkers, ex-girlfriends—trying to eliminate each one, we sent each other links associated with each person on our list: Joseph Malinsky's teaching profile and research, the suspected Facebook and LinkedIn profiles of Ethan's ex-girlfriends, and so on—scrutinizing each bit of information for something that might indicate some sort of relevance to Ethan.

British Anna was persistent in her stealth searches over the years, doing multiple reverse IP searches, and investigating addresses and every possible biographical detail Ethan threw her way. She recalled that at one point in the years of their correspondence, Ethan had his cousin, Emily Slutsky, who had been his roommate at MIT, set up a Morgan Stanley domain for him. He described her as very cool and relaxed: Whenever he had "women over," he would hang something on the door and she wouldn't disturb him. She was chill like that. They had a lot of biographical overlaps—like Ethan, Emily majored in math and physics at Columbia and MIT—but at the time, the idea of Ethan being a woman seemed so ridiculous to her that she assumed he'd been lying about certain aspects of his life by using characters and story elements from Emily's life. She added Emily to her list of human breadcrumbs in the Ethan Schuman mystery. Now that Gina was convinced Ethan might be a woman, we explored both the men and the women, not only as potential leads but as potential suspects.

British Anna forwarded me Emily's Goodreads profile. "Has Ethan talked about any of these books recently?" I asked. Ethan was an avid reader. "He talks about Joseph Malinksy," she replied. Emily had one of Joseph's books on her Goodreads list, but Anna recalled that Ethan said Joseph was her mentor.

Thinking it was just another name that might somehow lead to the man behind Ethan, I started investigating this Emily person. We already knew they were related and went to the same schools. From what I could find online, Emily was from New Jersey, like Ethan (though he'd told British Anna he was from New York). She was an editor of a publication, so clearly she could write. Her LinkedIn profile revealed she went to medical school in Ireland—and was enrolled there now...*the Irish connection*. Plus, Emily's age aligned more closely with the revised, younger age that Ethan later told British Anna. Her LinkedIn profile listed her location as the "Greater New York City Area," so she operated between New York and Ireland, just like Ethan.

Holy crap, this could be Ethan! I thought. Or at least someone who knew Ethan. The biographical overlaps were mounting. Had Ethan stolen many aspects of Emily's identity, as British Anna originally thought, or were they the same person?

"And the initials work...E.S.," British Anna pointed out.

"That just gave me chills!" I replied. "I want to connect with Emily!"

British Anna was more cautious. She suggested we wait until Ethan revealed himself. What if he was in cahoots with Emily? After all, she had created a fake domain on his behalf. Was Ethan working with Emily in this elaborate game? Even if she didn't know what he was up to, she might be sympathetic to him. They were family. We didn't want to tip him off.

But what about the photos? If we were going to entertain the possibility that Ethan didn't exist, then who was in all the pictures? He sent all three of us many of the same photos (though British Anna had many, many more). Ethan *loved* these photos and expected us to adore them appropriately when we received them. But who was in them and why was he so attached to them? And if, as Gina had suggested, Ethan was not a man at all but actually a woman, then the abundance of photos we'd all received was even more confusing.

"Maybe he's the man she wants to be?" Anna theorized.

"I really think this Slutsky person is the missing link," I concluded.

We continued digging for Emily-Ethan overlaps. Ethan mentioned to British Anna that he ran the Cork marathon, and when she looked him up and didn't find his name, he became irate. We searched for Emily's name on the list, but she wasn't there, either. A dead end.

Anna had two numbers for Ethan: One was a 917 number (New York), which was answered by a woman's voicemail when she called, but later the number was dead. The other was the Irish number we all texted him at. Maybe the 917 number was a clue? We'd all googled the Irish number separately before meeting, but it didn't lead to any names. Once British Anna shared the 917 number, I tried to pay $1.99 to some shady online service to get access to the owner's name, but there were no results.

3:01 p.m. EST

We pressed on. I hadn't slept in days, but like Ethan, I was "beyondsleeping" at this point. Gina, who'd sensibly taken a nap, rejoined the conversation. "What did I miss? Same old shit? Apologies? Is anyone talking to him now?" British Anna and I were on G-chat together and Ethan was still texting her. We explained our new working theory to Gina: We suspected that Ethan was either the woman he claimed was his cousin, or that she was somehow involved. "Has anyone confronted him about being Emily Slutsky?" she asked. Not yet.

Gina suggested we contact Emily's friends on Facebook before she could make them private. If Emily and Ethan were working in tandem, it was very likely that Ethan had already communicated to her that the three of us had teamed up. We rushed to the page—too late. They were already private. That confirmed there was some sort of Ethan-Emily connection. We were on the right path but still needed more info. British Anna said she remembered three of the Facebook friends' names from when she'd previously investigated the cousin and knew how to contact them.

3:18 p.m. EST

Gina rejoined our chat: "I just talked to Emily's dad."

What? How? WHEN?!

Gina searched for Emily's father online, which led her to a Spokeo list-ing with his personal information. Once she knew his name, she also found his Twitter account. Ethan told Gina that his father possibly had an affair with a noted architect. That information meant nothing at first, but in an attempt to confirm his identity, she googled his name with the architect's on the off chance the two were actually linked. Sure enough, they'd worked on a project together. Emily's father also followed the architect on Twitter. She didn't know if there was an actual affair or if that was just another one of Ethan's lies, but it did verify more Ethan-Emily overlaps.

The Spokeo listing also confirmed another detail: Emily's mother—like Ethan's—was named Anna.

Gina had just spoken with her friend who was coordinating their class reunion, which she knew involved calling people, so she used that as her excuse for calling Emily's parents' house. She'd read a story a couple of years before meeting Ethan about a woman named Janna who pretended to be a man to trick a woman into falling for her. In one of her emails to Ethan, a few days prior to connecting with me, she sent him the link to the story: "This is the B.S. I think you're up to," she accused him. ("People should write shorter articles," Ethan responded glibly.) So it seemed fitting to present herself as Janna when she called Emily's dad.

Gina called the number listed on Spokeo, and Emily's dad answered. She introduced herself as Janna, and said she was a classmate from MIT who was coordinating a reunion and was looking for Emily. "Don't you know she's in Ireland in medical school?" he asked in a thick Russian accent. She admitted that she wasn't aware, and he explained that she'd been back and forth between Ireland and New Jersey for the last two years. He gave her Emily's email address and phone number and they hung up.

Gina checked. *The phone numbers were the same!*

BUSTED.

Emily was Ethan and Ethan was Emily.

Within twenty-two hours of joining forces with Gina and twelve hours of finding British Anna, we found the woman who'd been posing as Ethan Schuman. Emily Slutsky was a twenty-five-year-old medical student who, according to her CV and LinkedIn profile, was as accomplished as Ethan.

In New Jersey, where she grew up, she was the editor in chief of her school's literary and artistic magazine and won the nonfiction writing prize. She also received a Governor's Award in Arts Education in 2003 in New Jersey for her writing. She was one of twenty-seven girls selected to compete in MIT's summer Women's Technology Program. She was the president of the Organization of Student Tutors, the "warden of leadership" in the National Honor Society, a student advisor to the Culture Arts Club, a member of the French Honor Society, a member of the biology and physics competition teams, a participant in the Columbia University science honors program, a participant in the premed honors program at New Jersey Medical School, a pianist in a musical ensemble, and a student at a local music school. She volunteered at a nursing home and was a teacher's assistant at a preschool. She was also a black belt in Tae Kwon Do.

After high school, Emily attended MIT, where she majored in nuclear engineering and served as the editor in chief of MIT's *Rune* journal and as the vice president of operations for the Alpha Epsilon Phi sorority. (According to MIT's newspaper, the *Tech*, Emily ruffled some feathers when she crafted a plan to "return to AEPhi's national identity" by making it a Jewish sorority. Seven of the eight new members depledged, as that was not the sorority committed to diversity and inclusion that they thought they were joining.) She then did a master's in applied physics at Columbia University and, as of 2009, was enrolled in medical school at University College Cork in Ireland.

Ethan was born July 10, within days of Emily.

So we knew who was hiding behind Ethan Schuman, but we still didn't understand why. Why would this accomplished woman torture other women?

*　　*　　*

3:28 p.m. EST

It was time to share the good news with Ethan.

Gina sent an email to Emily's Columbia email address with the subject, "Dear Ethan": "Today was a great day. I'm going out to celebrate the death of Ethan Schuman!"

"Received," Emily replied an hour later.

Unable to completely separate herself from Ethan, Emily reverted back to communicating with us via Ethan's email address: "Yes, this is Emily Slutsky. I am studying medicine in Ireland. I went to MIT and Columbia."

As we relished our victory, Gina said it best: We were both triumphant and sad. Ethan Schuman didn't exist, but this other very disturbing person did.

And then it sank in: *This woman who harassed and lied to us was soon going to be a doctor.* That fact terrified us.

We still had a lot of questions. Emily called British Anna and they talked for hours—she seemed eager to speak with her, almost desperate to win Anna over as a friend.

Emily made a series of confessions to Anna:

- She met her first victim—a woman named Kimberly—in an AOL chat room eight years ago, when she was seventeen.
- She figured I'd disappear after she revealed the cancer diagnosis and that I'd forget about Ethan in a month. I was the "quit plan" to try to forget about British Anna. Besides,

she noted: I wasn't Jewish, and therefore not to be taken
seriously.

+   She lost her grandmother to cancer a few years ago, a fact she
     revealed as a way of justifying her fake diagnosis.

+   She swore she had a boyfriend, a lawyer in New York she met
     on JDate back in December. (So they were also communi-
     cating long-distance? Her chat-management skills seriously
     impressed me.)

Gina also spoke on the phone with Emily for around ninety minutes.
Emily explained that we were merely characters in the novel she was writing in her head—not dissimilar to the novel Ethan told me he was writing.
Was that why she was creating such dramatic twists and turns in Ethan's
life? To evoke an emotional response from us and get better writing material? It felt dirty. We felt used. We were all just caricatures of ourselves in
Ethan's world, fodder for Emily's future novel.

"Why did you choose me?" Gina asked Emily.

"Bad luck, I guess," she replied nonchalantly.

"Bad luck for you?" Gina clarified.

"No, for you."

Emily told us that the photos she used were of a friend from high school,
a writer named Tim. We looked him up and the photos matched, so we
knew it was the right guy. She started using his image when they were still
in high school, completely unbeknownst to him. We gave her a Sunday
deadline to inform Tim of her actions, confess to her family, and seek medical assistance with a licensed mental health professional.

We had many questions we tried to get Emily to answer, but the validity
of any of her responses was as questionable as everything else Ethan said.
Yes, we'd learned that Ethan was Emily, but that also meant that Emily
was Ethan.

Her commentary straddled a contradictory line between the insistence
that her life was wonderful and a sort of melancholic misanthropy. In one

of several phone conversations with British Anna, Emily lamented that people often disappoint her by "not living up to her expectations."

Same, Emily. Same.

By this point I was beginning to feel a bit jealous that I didn't have the pleasure of a phone call with Ms. Slutsky. I had some choice words I wanted to share with her, questions to ask, and an equal need for closure as the other women. But Emily's hostility toward me persisted, even as she tried to win over and defend herself to Gina and British Anna. She did not regard me as one of her victims; I was the enemy.

*   *   *

We discussed at length how to proceed. Was an apology enough? How should this be handled? We felt strongly that she had crossed medical ethics lines and that her medical school should be notified. We also felt her family should be notified, and we decided her sister was the most appropriate point of contact. How would we explain this to these people? We needed some time to strategize that communication. In the meantime, we felt she clearly needed therapy; it would be hard to verify if she was actively in therapy, but we could try. We'd start there and see how things unfolded.

Gina went to dinner with her parents and her brother, Dominic—the same brother who intervened with her lyin', cheatin' French fiancé several years earlier. He knew she'd met someone online and that Ethan existed, but he didn't know everything. When they met up, Gina was in a frenzy, as she'd just gotten off the phone with British Anna and me, and she was still reeling from the revelation that Ethan was Emily. Gina and her brother have been known to feed off of each other, so once he witnessed her heightened state, he matched her energy.

After dinner, Dominic and Gina went back to Dominic's apartment. They had a few drinks, which only amped him up more. Dominic encouraged Gina to call Emily. He was irate and wanted to confront her. Dominic is a protective older brother, and he wanted to speak with the woman who played this sick trick on his sister. So Gina texted Emily, demanding that she call her (as Gina didn't want to pay the international charges for the call). Emily still refused to do it. They upped the stakes: If she didn't call, they would reach out to her family again and inform them of her behavior. That was the only leverage they had.

It was around 11 p.m. EST and early morning in Ireland. It was clear Emily hadn't gone to bed. When they finally got her on the phone, thanks to their threats to contact her family again, Gina was no longer speaking to the man she fell in love with. She was confronting the woman who violated her trust. Gone was witty, cute, flirtatious Gina. This was Gina unleashed. She was sleep-deprived, running on adrenaline, slightly tipsy, and bouncing off the walls. She had no filter. But Emily refused to show any emotion. She approached their discussion as a sort of intellectual exercise, coolly rationalizing her behavior. "What's wrong with you?! You need help!" Gina yelled at her. Gina and Dominic's priority was to ensure she stopped, got help, and never did this to anyone else.

Emily protested: They were being unfair. It would be impossible for her to find a therapist in the middle of Ireland. Besides, she insisted, there was nothing wrong with her. She had a very fulfilling social life. She even had a boyfriend.

Gina's brother stepped in and grabbed the phone. He was scared for his sister. No one knew who this person was or what she was capable of. He feared she might come after Gina. "You're sick!" he screamed. "How do I know you're not going to show up and break into my sister's apartment and try to kill her?"

"Of course I'm not going to hurt anybody," she replied calmly. She insisted everything was fine. She would just stop. She didn't need therapy.

Dominic was not convinced. "I don't trust that's the case!" he yelled. "You need help! You must get help or Gina's going to be in contact with your parents!"

He gave her three days to place herself under the regular care of a licensed psychiatrist. Otherwise, he would go to her parents and report her to the police. "This would be done in hopes of allowing a loved one in your family to seek the appropriate type of care for you while also being sure that you are under the watchful eye of authority," he explained. The laws around this sort of thing are tricky, especially given it was all digital across multiple states and countries, so we weren't sure if there was any viable legal action to take. Threats of involving her family and community seemed to be the best leverage we had.

Dominic set a deadline of Friday at 5 p.m. EST to provide proof. He asked that she give the physician permission to contact Gina to confirm, followed by a fax that proved their credentials.

Gina thought about her ex, Matthew, and the damage he'd done. Something needed to be done to ensure Emily would stop harming people. She targeted people who would not be a physical threat, but eventually she was going to piss off the wrong person.

*   *   *

Emily called British Anna again. Emily's voice was quiet and calm on the phone, and Anna oscillated between emotionally charged yelling and moments of wounded silence. Anna entertained these calls primarily because she wanted answers, but there was more to it for her. She knew there was no Ethan, but this other person—Emily—was the person she'd connected with, the person who knew her so well. It was a surreal feeling, trying to let go of that connection, even once the facade of Ethan no longer existed.

Emily told British Anna she was scared of Gina and her brother, and finally agreed to go to therapy—though she continued to insist she did not need it. Perhaps, she suggested, British Anna could serve as her therapist? Through tears, Anna explained why that was not professionally appropriate. She needed Emily to understand just how severely her actions had hurt her. Anna served as Emily's fantasy plaything for years, and she was still grappling with the trauma of it all. *She* needed therapy as a result of Emily's actions. "I feel like I've been run over by a truck," she wrote to us.

Me, too. My god, was I tired.

March 6, 2011

Emily emailed the three of us (from Ethan's email address—*still*) to apologize and confirm that she would send Tim an email. She assured us that nothing like this would ever happen again. Moving forward, she would find healthy ways of dealing with her emotions. She promised not to contact any of us—unless we needed something from her. "If there is anything else you need from me, please say so," she offered.

It was not a tempting offer.

She G-chatted with British Anna on the side.

"It's traumatic for me to think that that guy isn't the person I cared about," Anna said, referring to Tim's photos. "That the person I loved doesn't exist."

"I know, it's difficult for me to accept, too," Emily said. "Well, that he doesn't exist for you. I denied it, because the moment I was talking to you, he did exist for you."

"Don't you see how manipulative that sounds?" Anna was not feeling consoled by Emily's explanation.

"Manipulative? No . . . I wasn't manipulating you. I wanted him to exist for you. I didn't find any part of this enjoyable. I was tortured, too. Every emotion that you felt, I felt on this end, too. Probably in a very similar way, because I'm a woman, too."

*   *   *

In compliance with our demands, Emily confessed to Tim that she'd used his photos to deceive women online for years. She forwarded us the email she sent to him as proof, and BCC'd British Anna.

In typical Ethan fashion, she took the opportunity to explain everything to Tim via long, eloquent prose. At the time, we had no way of verifying she'd actually sent the email to Tim, and operated on blind faith that what she sent us was real. She revealed to him what she did, then tried to justify it as a much-needed "escape from reality."

"As a writer, you must understand this need to spill your guts/frustrations/inner-workings through the conduit of fictional characters, words, dialogue," she said, attempting to form a creative connection with him that might justify her actions. "I didn't feel like I had the fodder to write a novel, so instead, I found my subconscious pulling me toward creating a new reality on the Internet. I wanted the new persona to be as different from me as possible, so as to not crossover into my reality in the slightest. These were two disparate worlds that I in no way wanted to intertwine. Posing as a fake woman served me no purpose, because I already experience the world as a woman. I needed something entirely different."

Emily told Tim that she first found photos of a random guy online to send to women, but when she realized she needed to produce a larger quantity of pictures to substantiate her online identity, she made Tim the face of Ethan Schuman.

She assured him that the deceptions had all been revealed and uncovered and that she would never engage in "anything as traumatic as this again." She added, "They now know that I am behind the fairy-tale spinning and are very keenly aware that the man in the photos had nothing to do with it and was, in fact, a victim, as well."

"If you ever want to discuss this, we can meet in person the next time we are in town or have a phone conversation," she offered.

Wouldn't that be something, I thought, imagining them discussing her years of lies over a latte. I found it fascinating how eager she was to discuss these matters with her victims (except for me) but was so resistant to speaking with a mental health professional. She loved philosophizing about it all. The trickery had been her therapy, and therefore she thought she no longer needed formal therapy.

She signed off: "In earnest, Emily." But what captured my attention was the quote in her Gmail signature. It was from Marie Curie (though Emily

Anna Akbari

referred to her as "Madame Curie"), the two-time Nobel Prize winner in physics and chemistry:

> Life is not easy for any of us. But, what of that? We must have perseverance and above all confidence in ourselves. We must believe that we are gifted for something and that this thing, at whatever cost, must be attained.

Perseverance. Confidence. A belief you are gifted. Emily and Ethan certainly shared those traits. But what was "this thing" she hoped to attain "at whatever cost"? For Emily, the likely cost of her actions seemed huge. To what end?

* * *

Throughout the day, fragments of memories popped into our heads and we pieced together disparate Ethan-Emily threads, all of which led to ongoing revelations:

- I recalled that Ethan's OkCupid profile received a "great date" award from another profile. (This was an OkCupid invention meant to reassure future dates that this was a real, normal person you were sure to enjoy!) That would mean Emily created the other woman's profile to issue the award to Ethan.
- British Anna realized she'd actually spoken on the phone with Emily before—*for an hour*—when she'd posed as Ethan's sister, Riva, with whom she'd corresponded at length. The emails she'd received from Katie, Ethan's ex-wife, were also from Emily. And, quite elaborately, it was very possible that the weird Ben-Ava–British Anna JDate love triangle in London was manufactured by Emily—though we were still making sense of what was and wasn't real there. It was exhausting just to contemplate it all.

- Gina remembered that Ethan told her he asked Janeane Garofalo out on a date in a restaurant, and she turned him down. *Who makes this shit up?*

- Ethan's age and location changed over the years, which made sense, but she also changed strange details, like telling Gina that Ethan was the oldest of three kids and telling me he was the youngest. What was the point? Wasn't it impossible to remember all the stories? Did she keep a spreadsheet as a cheat sheet?

- A friend of a friend of mine went to MIT; Emily lived in his dorm, though they overlapped for only a year and she didn't make much of an impression. That guy's friend knew of Emily's sister, who was still a student at MIT. He also knew only the face and name, but nothing more about her. It creeped me out to think how closely Emily was orbiting in my social circle.

- Tim launched a fundraiser for one of his projects; Emily contributed to it—while still using his photographs.

- Ethan's father was a lawyer. Emily's father is not a lawyer, but Tim's father is a lawyer. Oh, how Emily loved to mix her realities.

- Ethan was always invisible on G-chat, or he would change his status from the little green dot of "available" to invisible midconversation. Gina asked him why he did that, and he said, "My ex just signed on. Don't want to talk to her." We deduced it must've been one of us (or maybe another victim).

- As far as we could tell, she only ever targeted women. Never men. We didn't know why.

The fact that we pieced all of this together in a single day is surreal. We made a great team, and our anger was incredibly motivating. It didn't hurt that Ethan had also trained all of us to operate with extreme sleep deprivation.

Emily confirmed several other women we suspected were her victims from names she casually mentioned and emails she'd forwarded to the three of us. She'd used them as a means to verify Ethan's existence (if they were real, Ethan must be real). We started to ponder the number of other victims there might be. There had been several of us in a matter of months, and she'd been doing this for nearly a decade. How many more of us were there? And how would we find them?

*   *   *

Understandably, both Gina and British Anna struggled with their emotions after we learned the truth. Gina booked an emergency session with her therapist, and Anna realized she had a lot of trauma to process in the wake of Emily's years of lies and manipulations. The fact that Emily kept contacting her after we outed her further exacerbated her stress and stalled her healing process.

And yet, despite those struggles, a weight had also been lifted—from all of us, but especially from British Anna. After learning that Ethan was Emily, she slept better than she had in a long time. She realized that the level of anxiety Emily created in her was like living with a poison in her system. The very existence of Ethan was an emotional burden on her every day. But now, she was free from him after two and a half years.

In one of their postreveal phone conversations, Emily told British Anna that she really wanted the perfect love story for her. That was what she was trying to provide her through their fake digital courtship. *Never mind that it was all fiction. Or that Ethan would never actually materialize. Or that Ethan treated us horribly.* As if dissecting literary characters with the author, British Anna asked Emily why Ethan constantly talked about the other women he'd slept with if he loved her so much. "Because the way to make a man attractive is to make women jealous," Emily reasoned. But while he tortured her by making her jealous and perpetually standing her up, Emily made sure Ethan always reassured Anna that he loved her the most.

As for me, whether I wanted to admit it or not, beneath the tough "bad cop" exterior, I felt a double pang of rejection. Not only was I grappling with the surreal heartbreak and embarrassment that the man I'd been most hopeful about in years didn't exist, but I also had to reconcile the cruelty of Ethan's puppeteering and the fact that it was another woman who'd tortured me. After revealing myself in every way imaginable in our months of intimate correspondence, never shying away from the vulnerability that was requested of me, while also demonstrating my willingness to support a stranger through a serious illness, Emily treated me with zero remorse. I'll never know exactly why she put me in a different category than the other women, but I've always felt that she blamed me for the fact that she was eventually caught. Outing her was a team effort in every way, and yet, all her ire was directed toward me. It's not that I wanted to be friends with Emily—far from it—but any acknowledgment of the pain she caused me would have been some small comfort.

March 8, 2011

Emily continued to reach out to British Anna, trying to appeal to her to show loyalty to her, not Gina and me, which was affecting her greatly. Anna emailed her in an attempt to make her stop.

"I need you to try to understand that we have a complicated relationship, you and I," she wrote, stating the obvious.

She admitted feeling connected to Emily on one level, but that connection, and any loyalty it was breeding, disturbed her, because it was the direct result of the abuse she suffered. She was trying to assess her emotions and recover from what she was realizing was significant trauma. That was her first priority, and she begged Emily to please respect and understand that.

Anna would not keep things from us, despite Emily's pleas. "They were deceived about reality, too," she reminded Emily. "I need to be honest about how I am processing this, with all parties, or I will not heal as effectively. When you lie, you lose control of the outcome. Please do not ask me, as the main victim of the lie, to help with damage limitation. The repercussions on me have been huge, and I simply can't be the one to control them for you. Ugh this is all awful."

March 10, 2011

Our demands to Emily were clear: Get a therapist, stop harassing women, and delete all of our personal information. While she said she would comply with all of this, she still hadn't sent proof that she was in therapy. Given her repeated insistence that she was "fine," we weren't confident she would follow through.

It was time to summon the Italians again.

Gina sent Emily an email reminding her of her promise to secure a therapist. She "might" be able to convince her brother to extend the deadline until Monday.

Speaking of her brother—hold on, he's right here! Gina pasted a message from Dominic into the email.

"I remain unsettled with my feelings concerning your deplorable actions of maliciously lying to innocent people," he chimed in digitally. "Your lies are over and they must remain that way! If you are a good person, then you will stand by your actions, seek proper help, and realize that only a mentally sick individual would act in such a disgusting nature." He closed with a dramatic flourish: "If you are not a good person, you will experience the 'outing' of your evil soul by those who brought your 'reality' to an end."

"We are not negotiating or bargaining. Please do not try to come to any one of us individually to gain more leniency. We stand united in our purpose to make sure you cannot do this to anyone ever again," Gina informed her.

The Dallagos had spoken!

However, apparently Emily's fear of them had waned and she pushed back. She would meet with a licensed psychologist the following week, but "like any professional, she respects patient-doctor confidentiality, and I do not see the benefit of involving any outside party in that relationship."

*   *   *

That day, Emily initiated a G-chat with British Anna to reiterate her plan to go to therapy, as promised. But she also reiterated her belief that there was "nothing to help." Her thoughts and emotional burdens were akin to everyone else's. She agreed to talk to a therapist, however, because it "could be fun to force someone to listen."

Anna was in shock. *There's nothing to help?*

While she stated that she regretted the consequences, Emily remained steadfast in her belief that her motivations were not wrong.

Anna struggled with Emily's nonchalant attitude toward her behavior. "You put me through things that would lead many people to a nervous breakdown. You let me buy gifts for your family, pack to come see you, tell my family about you. You let these things happen many times. Can you see this destroys someone? You seem to think it was a dalliance." Anna was beside herself.

"You're misunderstanding," Emily told her.

"Those actions are never ok, under any circumstances," Anna went on.

"You're misunderstanding," Emily repeated.

"The layers of lies, the stuff you concocted, talking me through being in court, you gave me moment by moment updates," Anna said, referring to Emily's extensive account of Ethan's alleged divorce.

"You're misunderstanding," Emily said a third time.

"Pretending Ava came to Pittsburgh—you took me through detailed scenarios."

"Oh they weren't details," Emily corrected her. "I mean, how would I know what court is like? It was part of the story."

Anna's outrage exploded. "Ava being in Pittsburgh and trying to get into bed with you, having a fight, driving her to the airport..."

"It was part of the story," Emily reiterated.

"It being part of the story doesn't make it ok—it makes it twisted, to go to such lengths," Anna corrected her.

"I'M NOT SAYING IT'S OKAY!" Emily typed in all caps.

Emily seemed maniacal to Anna. Communicating with Emily allowed her to finally understand Ethan: His volatile pattern of linguistic manipu-lation was perfectly mirrored in how Emily spoke to Anna.

Anna asked why she chose to use Tim's photos. "Did you have a crush on him at some point or something?" she suggested.

"Um, no. He's good looking and has many photos, that's all. You're add-ing layers to this that aren't accurate," Emily said.

"What were you doing on the other end all those times when I was hav-ing sex with him?" she asked, in reference to Tim's photos. Over the two and a half years that Ethan had been in Anna's life, there were moments where things got sexual. Anna had asked her this question before, and Emily had refused to answer. She once again deflected the question.

"I think we shouldn't talk about this through text," Emily suggested. "I think you're misunderstanding a lot of what I'm trying to say."

So NOW Emily found text-only communication to be too limiting and prone to misunderstanding? Emily's words sucked Anna back into the state of mental abuse where Ethan had held her hostage for years.

"That's what I told Ethan was the problem with typing for a long time—and of course he argued with me," Anna rebutted, acknowledging the irony.

"Well, yes, because I couldn't talk to you," Emily replied rationally.

"You made me doubt my sanity, as if nothing I said was rational."

"Okay, but if it was rational, which of course it was, how would I respond to it? You can't argue with something when you agree that it's rational," Emily explained, clearly putting the matter to rest.

"Okay, can we have a new rule?" Emily then asked, changing course. "That if we want to talk about this stuff, we do it audibly? You're misun-derstanding me, and it's just feeding the villainization." She assured Anna that there were many complex layers to what led her to lie, and that therapy would be "fine," though she believed she would be able to fix it herself over an extended period of time.

"How the hell?" Anna marveled at everything she was hearing. "The whole reason we're here is because your unhealthy way ruined my life for 2.5 years."

"WHY DOES IT MATTER? I said I'll get therapy tomorrow!" Emily was no longer calm.

Emily informed Anna that her friend thought therapy was a good idea.

"Is your friend not horrified?" Anna asked genuinely. "You don't seem to understand that what you did is outside the realm of what most people could do."

"I never said it wasn't."

"That is not just a few emotions that need fixing," Anna clarified.

"I KNOW IT IS," Emily said. "Okay, Anna, I am a sick individual who needs medical attention." It seemed from her flippant attitude that she viewed therapy as beneath her. This had all just been a fun game—what was the big deal?

"Well clearly you don't think that," Anna replied.

"You're not really in a position to judge, you don't have context, you don't know who I am in my life," Emily said.

"I don't need to know your context. It's not normal."

"Okay," Emily replied glibly.

"Is your friend not horrified?" Anna reiterated.

"No, because she has context."

Anna's physical and mental discomfort increased as Emily engaged in this extended wordplay—always vague and indignant, just like Ethan.

"Context or no context, there is nothing that makes it anything less than horrific to put someone through what you put me through," Anna told her, appalled. "Every time you had me up all night, making up women you'd slept with, getting me thinking I was going to New York to meet your family...it should be intolerable for you to do that to me. Standing someone up for a coffee is pretty horrible, never mind allowing them to humiliate themselves 100 different ways."

"Alright, Anna, do you realize that wasn't to torture you? That was my way of trying to get out of this," Emily said.

"What the hell were you doing while I was online having sex with someone I thought was a man?" Anna asked yet again.

"I think we should not be talking about this through text," Emily replied, deflecting once more.

But Anna wasn't finished. "I cannot believe you're saying your friend isn't horrified because of the context. Everyone has context. Serial killers have contexts. It doesn't bloody well change the horror of what they do."

"Ok Anna. I conceded."

"So your friend should be horrified."

"I'll pass that onto her," Emily replied.

"Don't mock me. Don't you dare."

"I will talk to a therapist, the therapist will correct my incorrect perceptions," Emily said.

"Incorrect perceptions? You probably won't tell the therapist the full story anyway."

"I will tell her the full story," Emily assured her.

"All the times you attacked me, the layers of lies, making me change my life for you. That's not a fucking joke," Anna emphasized.

"You

Did

Not

Change

Your

Life

For

Me," Emily typed dramatically.

"Oh really?"

"Yeah really. How did you change your life?"

"Not getting any sleep, not having a boyfriend, being put through emotional hell that left me depressed, changing things to accommodate coming to see you, then hiding it from people because I was ashamed, humiliating myself in front of my family, booking time off work—by being conned. I didn't change my life?" Anna asked again, indignant.

"You always had the option of leaving," Emily replied dryly.

"Unfortunately, I didn't know we weren't playing the same game. So I'm sorry, but don't you dare say I had the option of leaving. You made a lot of effort to make sure I couldn't bear to."

"I was in a similar situation, by the way," Emily informed her.

"What?" Anna said, once again stunned. "I didn't torture you, I didn't let you down. I didn't lie to you."

"No, I mean, I was talking to a guy online for an extended length of time—"

"Who was a woman?" Anna interjected.

"No. Who kept not showing up. Not calling."

"Great, even better, so you thought, having experienced it, that you should put me through the same times 10000?"

"No, but eventually, when he didn't call for the 1000th time, I told him to fuck off," she said, as if to note the proper way of dealing with someone like that.

"I'm sure he didn't have such sophisticated emotional manipulation tactics," Anna countered.

"You're totally misunderstanding me," she said again.

"You're denying it? You're denying that creating an email account from Ethan's sister to write to Ava wasn't that? You're saying that talking to me as Riva wasn't that?"

"You're really misunderstanding me," she repeated for the seventh time.

Anna's rage mounted. "You're saying getting me to pack to come and fucking see you and go to Fortnum & Mason to buy your MOTHER TEA wasn't that? Really? REALLY? To fake having a heart attack to Ava? Pretending to be mugged? Pretending to be stabbed?"

"Alright, Anna," Emily replied. "We can make a list of everything you think I should mention to my therapist, and I'll do that."

"You're saying that's not emotional manipulation?"

"It's manipulation," Emily conceded unapologetically.

"I'm not saying I had no choice. I chose to have faith in Ethan because I couldn't countenance that he would be here, for many reasons that you made sure looked viable, unless he was genuinely emotionally invested. And yes I should have told him to fuck off really. But what chance did I have when the decisions I was making weren't according to real information but information designed to manipulate me? So believe me, I take responsibility for being a fucking idiot. But I never had a chance." Anna felt defeated.

"That's really an unhealthy way of looking at it," Emily said, though whether it was meant to criticize or comfort was unclear.

But she assured Anna, "Anyway, like I said, we'll make a list of things that I should mention, and I'll mention each one of them so you don't feel like I'm skirting the issue. I'm actually looking forward to it, because I think it will be nice to explore this situation with someone objective."

"You're actually hoping for her to tell you it was ok," Anna said, envisioning the therapy session.

"See, you're completely misunderstanding," she said for the eighth time. "She'll objectively help me interpret my actions/motivations."

"What will an objective person say? 'OH, EMILY, IT WAS HER CHOICE'?"

"NO,

no,

no," Emily typed emphatically. There was always so much digital drama with her. "Anna, really, we need to stop talking about this because you're not understanding me at all."

"All I can say is you don't seem to be that bothered or think it's that worthy of an endeavor," Anna said.

"Not bothered? CALLING HER IS FINE. I'M NOT DREADING CALLING HER. THERAPY IS FINE, I'M NOT DREADING THERAPY. I just feel like you want me to be tortured by the idea of therapy. I've accepted it, I've 'manipulated' myself into looking forward to it," she said in a clever callback to earlier in the chat—in true Ethan Schuman fashion.

"You really don't know what I've been experiencing the past week, or especially the past 2 days, so please take a step back away from me," Emily added.

"Oh you want me to have compassion and empathy? Let me tell you that whatever you've been experiencing is nothing in comparison to what I've experienced for the time I've known Ethan. You made this. Not me. I'm going through hell because of what you made."

"Don't be so quick to attack," Emily said, as if this entire situation were over one missed phone call or a minor misunderstanding.

Then she asked, "Do you think it would be better if we stopped being in contact?"

"I'd appreciate answers," Anna pushed. "This whole shite has made me feel like a child feels when they have an abusive parent. They are so angry at them, but they also still love them, and it's a twisted up way to have to deal with feelings. It's unforgivable that you've fucked with my sanity. I'm going to go. I need to sleep and I am practically having palpitations." Emily's endless verbal retorts tore Anna's sanity to shreds once more. This was Ethan *all over again.*

"I think we should stop talking, because I'm a reminder of him."

"You're not a reminder," Anna clarified. "You *are* him."

"The distance will make it easier on you I think," Emily rationalized. "That's why I'm sure the other girls are finding it easier than you are."

March 12, 2011

Emily continued her relentless pursuit of befriending British Anna. Perhaps she was still addicted to their communication and her ability to control and manipulate her, or maybe she just wanted to cover herself by ensuring that British Anna was on Team Emily and not aligned with Gina and me. She emailed Anna, pleading with her to sign on to G-chat.

"ANNA, COME ON! PLEASEEEEEEEEEE," Emily begged.

"I don't think friendship involves one person abusing the other," Anna told her, standing her ground.

"This is a twisted situation where all our emotions are mingled and confusing. Your definition of abuse is inaccurate because we're both surviving trauma of one type or another," Emily explained. "SIGN ON."

So accustomed to dutifully acquiescing to Ethan, Anna followed Emily's orders and signed into G-chat.

Emily got right down to business: She was hurt that Anna was standing behind the "ridiculous emails" we were sending her. She didn't think any of us were vindictive bitches, but she did think Gina and I were "a bit crazy," and she questioned why British Anna would align herself so closely with us. Cooperating with Gina and me to punish her was beneath British Anna; Emily expected more from her. She expected Anna to "deal with this to the beat of [her] own drum," not join our "support group." For Emily, it was Gina and me against them.

"Well I'm clearly an empathetic idiot," Anna responded. "Which is why I sat here for 2.5 years."

"I'm glad you have such a passionate spokesman then," Emily said sarcastically, referring to Gina's brother. "I just think he's a bit of an idiot. And worse than that, he's a bit of an idiot who thinks he has the 'upperhand.'"

This was still a game to Emily, and it was clear where Ethan's persistent air of superiority came from.

*   *   *

British Anna sent Emily her bank details, as requested, so she could wire her some money: £500. How she arrived at that number and what exactly it was paying for, we never understood (though it was a significant downgrade from the $2,000 Ethan originally offered before being outed). Yes, there were years of international phone bills. But was there more to it? Emotional damages? Hush money? Anna wasn't sure, but she did know that Emily owed her a great debt and she would take whatever was offered.

Emily told British Anna that she wanted to transfer the money, but that she also wanted to draw up a contract that "elucidates exactly what the money is for." Anna was confused. Emily explained that she'd "watched as many heist films as the Dallagos," and knew that transferring money into Anna's account could be misconstrued.

"Is this to protect you or me?" Anna asked. "You mean it would look like you're paying me to go away?"

"Protect me—yup," Emily clarified.

Emily wanted to ensure that no one mistook the transfer of money as an admission of guilt or a bribe or a way of "seeking leniency" with Anna. She didn't know what Anna might say to Gina and me to explain the money.

"Well, I am not going to lie to them," Anna said.

"Truth has many versions," Emily replied.

The contract would also make it clear that only Anna was entitled to money—not Gina or me. "Who's to say they won't email me tomorrow and say, well, you paid Anna's bill, so you have to pay mine, too? And I have no desire to pay anyone else's." Never mind that Emily knew my phone bills were a financial burden as a result of her, or that she had Ethan promise repeatedly that he'd pay them. That was in the past. These were the new terms.

"So this is about you not admitting guilt?? As in, you did nothing wrong?" Anna was still confused.

Emily explained that she was separating the two things: Yes, she was apologizing to Anna, but she wanted nothing that could potentially haunt her legally—and for whatever reason, she thought her proposed contract would be her protection.

Anna continued to try to make sense of the logic. "What could they do? Put you in prison?"

"No, they obviously can't," Emily responded. "The 'funny' part is that at this point I have more of a legal complaint against them than they have against me."

Really?

Emily transferred the money. She never sent Anna the contract.

March 13, 2011

A week after Emily was outed, Ethan was still active on G-chat. "I hope Slutsky is talking to one of you," I said to Gina and Anna. "Otherwise, why on earth is she still communicating as him?!" Emily was still in contact with British Anna, and she informed her it was merely to delete all of our messages.

We still didn't believe most of what she said.

Gina and I met up in New York for dinner that night. It was our first time meeting in person; we only wished Anna could join from across the pond. We talked and hung out for nearly four hours, lingering at the table the way one does when catching up with an old friend. We celebrated the death of Ethan Schuman and the start of a new friendship.

Two tasks remained: We needed to inform Emily's sister and her medical school of her actions. First we wanted to deal with everything Emily-related—getting as many details as possible and trying to confirm she was in therapy—and then we could shift focus to using that information to craft a message that would hopefully resonate with the people in her life. We knew this would be shocking for them to hear.

We sent them each slight variations on the same message, detailing the extent of her offenses: faking life-threatening illnesses, a mugging, divorce proceedings, stealing photographs, and forging documents, not to mention emotionally manipulating and traumatizing each of us.

"We are professionals with nothing to gain by coming forward. We share this information with you for Emily's sake, for the sake of past and future victims, and for the well-being of her potential future patients."

March 24, 2011

Emily continued to reach out to British Anna. She wanted to be friends. She was sad. She felt like she had broken up with someone. So did Anna, only with an added layer of anger and outrage, combined with a form of digital Stockholm syndrome. She couldn't break free.

"Emily, I'm just reminded of Ethan everywhere I go and it really hurts. I have something you wrote me as him saved on my desktop because it was so sexy and he so got me. I keep having to remember he doesn't exist and it didn't exist and everything I thought was so real wasn't even real. Ever. What am I supposed to do with that?"

"I got you because we're very much alike," Emily said in a strange attempt to comfort her. "I do miss 'him,' too…Or rather, I miss what he was like with you."

My heart hurt for Anna and my resentment toward Emily grew. What Emily did to me for two and a half months, she did to British Anna for two and a half years. It was unthinkable. She knew her continued openness to communicating with Emily was her yearning for some sort of misplaced attachment. I checked in on Anna regularly and made it clear I was available to talk and would continue to support her. This was not something she would get over in a few days or weeks.

Emily refused to answer our continued laundry list of questions, especially anything related to her motivation or what pleasure she derived from this twisted game we'd all been lured into. So we gave up on getting any further closure from her. We handled the situation the best that we could. There were many "truths" we'd have to be content not knowing.

April 4, 2011

My father, whom I'd never met, called me for the first time. I also spoke with my half brother (whom I didn't know existed). It was all surreal. People I thought existed suddenly didn't, and ones I didn't know existed suddenly did. My mind was so confused; 2011 was getting wild.

April 19, 2011

We finally received a reply from Emily's Irish medical school. Their lawyer, Dr. Kieran Doran, a senior health care ethics lecturer, asked us to send evidence of our allegations. He informed us that upon receipt of this evidence, he would arrange a meeting with Emily to present it to her.

This, of course, left us wondering if Kieran and his colleagues were interested in reading thousands of pages of correspondence, all riddled with lies, misrepresentation, and fake medical diagnoses, not to mention hundreds of hours of flirtatious G-chats.

So we compiled a PDF of some of the "greatest hits" from our collective correspondence with Ethan-Emily, including and emphasizing the medical lies and her admission of guilt.

This back-and-forth dragged on for nearly four months. Finally, Kieran confirmed that he and Professor Mary Horgan met with Emily, discussed the allegations, and that "all necessary steps have been taken to prioritize and safeguard Ms. Slutsky's health and welfare."

"This matter is now closed," he informed us curtly. Though he was sure to thank us for our concerns about "Ms. Slutsky's health and welfare." *Her* health and welfare? What we would've given to be in the room where she cleverly explained away all those years of deception.

To our knowledge, Emily was never disciplined in any way for her actions—at least not to the extent that it had any significant bearing on her career. We know she went on to become an ObGyn physician. ObGyns have possibly the most intimate doctor-patient relationship with women of any medical specialist. I'll let that sink in.

This was a disappointing outcome, to say the least, but we felt that we did our best to ring the alarm bells before she was granted a medical license. The rest was out of our hands.

We never heard back from her sister.

June 19, 2011

British Anna and Gina's birthday! When I emailed them well-wishes, British Anna informed us that Emily had also reached out to her, still desperate for them to be buddies, or something like that. It disturbed me that Emily was still pestering her, making it impossible for her to truly break free. At the time, I didn't understand the frequency with which Emily was contacting her. I considered reaching out to Emily to scold her, but decided against it. It wasn't emotionally healthy for me to reengage.

June 24, 2011

Emily had an eventful week: Her sister finally told her about the email we'd sent, and the dean's office at her medical school called her in to discuss what we'd reported. She was not pleased about either, and initiated a G-chat with British Anna to inform her.

She was particularly perturbed that we'd reached out to her sister, rather than her parents. "It was highly inappropriate," she informed British Anna. Our thought process had been that as a sibling, she might be in a better position to speak with Emily about the issue. But as Emily saw it, we avoided her father because we "didn't have the balls" to call him.

The email to her sister was sent from Gina and CC'd each of us, signing our names. Emily expected such things from Gina and me, but—once again—she expected better from British Anna. She informed her that her father would be reaching out to Gina and me to let us know how inappropriate we were to email his daughter. (Neither of us ever heard from him.)

"It caused a 19-year-old a lot of emotional stress—and you, personally, know that she has a medical condition," Emily scolded, referring to the issues Ethan's sister experienced.

"That was the made-up sister. I had a bloody nervous breakdown and failed a year, too," British Anna reminded Emily, lest she forget who the victim was in this scenario.

"I'd like you to admit that it was inappropriate," Emily instructed. "This has nothing to do with Ethan. This is real."

"You created this situation," Anna reminded her.

But Emily told her to remind Gina and me that we'd crossed a line by contacting her sister.

"You want to talk about your sister? Well this has really been damaging for me. ME. Out of everyone, I'm the one left struggling with it STILL, trying to detach myself and STILL feeling like a fuck up because of the attachment that is still there."

"You could've told me that you contacted the school," Emily said, moving on to her second grievance.

The school waited until after she finished her exams to call her into their office, at which time she saw a thick folder with copies of some of the emails we'd forwarded them.

"You must've forwarded him 100 emails," Emily told her. Anna reminded her that it was only a tiny sampling.

"Did you at least think about giving me a head's up? I mean, really, I would think that £500 could at least buy me a 'Head's up, you're going to get professionally screwed soon.'" Wow. So much for the money not being a bribe.

Emily insisted on giving Anna a play-by-play of what happened when she was called by her medical ethics professor and asked to meet with him and the dean.

"This is making me feel very uncomfortable," Anna informed her. "I can't handle this right now. I'm feeling horrible and like I'm going to cry. If you want to tell me the rest, send me an email, ok?"

But Emily was manipulating Anna the way that Ethan did. "No, no emails," she said, rejecting Anna's plea. "I want to share the experience with you. I did a horrible thing to you, I know, but I also listened to two years' worth of your problems. Now I have a problem you can listen to." As if Ethan had been a lighthearted, problem-free breeze to communicate with for two and a half years.

"Are you serious? Is that what you're honestly saying?" Anna couldn't take any more.

According to Emily, contacting her parents would have been the better, more acceptable choice. Scolding us for how we dealt with her indiscretions in a way that was not to her liking might have been the most Ethan thing she could have done.

"Look—really, you are the aggressor in all this, so don't tell me that as the victim I could have managed caring for your well-being better," Anna pushed back and tried to exit the chat once more.

"Let me finish the story," Emily insisted.

She told Anna that the punishment was "more than a slap on the wrist," but she wanted Anna's word that she wouldn't tell Gina and me if she shared more details. Anna said she would tell us if we asked. This displeased Emily greatly, and she accused Anna of being "split" in her loyalty. Was she with Emily? Or was she with Gina and me? She needed to pick a side.

"This is fucked up," Anna concluded in exhaustion. "What do you want from me?"

Emily didn't see any reason that the connection they'd created as Ethan and Anna couldn't transfer seamlessly into an Emily-Anna friendship. Why was that so hard? Yes, Anna had suffered, but, as Emily reminded her, so had she. They were equal.

Emily worried that she would be deemed psychologically unfit to get a job as a result of us contacting her school. (This, of course, was why we had contacted her school in the first place—to ensure that assessment was done properly using all available data points.)

"Something in you allowed you to cause suffering to other people (i.e. me) and not have the empathy to stop it, and that's what upsets me," Anna explained in an effort to justify why we contacted her school. "This conversation has upset me a lot."

"I've had a rough two days, too," Emily reminded her, again trying to equate their suffering.

"I'm so upset with you for not being Ethan," Anna lamented. "Although he was also fucking abusive."

"Well I'm pretty angry for not being him, either," Emily agreed. "It was a lot easier to be him than to be myself—mostly because he wasn't real."

"Right, but I thought he was real, and all this is a real connection that now I have to get my head around. And I'm right back there in an instant."

"But it's obviously different now," Emily assured her. "It sucks, you lost your best friend, but I'm trying to give you a substitute; different, but similar in some ways."

What Emily failed to acknowledge was that Ethan wasn't a sweet, loving boyfriend. He was incredibly sadistic—a character trait she had chosen and fully committed to, like some sort of method actor.

"How can I be friends with someone who did that to me?" Anna asked. And yet she still found herself stuck there, chatting with Emily, finding it difficult to draw a hard line between her and her abuser. Anna told Emily that she made her feel crazy.

"I think sanity is overrated," Emily told her. "Take it from me, insanity is a lot more interesting. I could have chosen the sane route and just been Emily in Emilyworld. But insanity was a lot more fun."

Emily told her she'd recently seen a Paul Simon concert in Ireland. "It was nice to see a Jewish boy from Brooklyn in Cork," she reflected.

Anna loved Paul Simon and had gotten Ethan into him. She started to cry.

September 14, 2011

Emily reached out to British Anna to ask how her job search was going and complain about her mounting student loan debt.

"Are you as angry about stuff as you were before?" Emily asked, pivoting abruptly.

"I don't think about it as much," Anna shared, angry with herself for even continuing to engage with the person who caused her so much pain. She continued to contemplate the torture Emily had inflicted and still did not understand it. Why did she do it?

Emily tried to explain that she was torn. She knew she should get out of it, but wasn't sure how, and she didn't want to. Then she ultimately concluded, "Honestly, I was just bored with my life."

PART 4:

THE RETURN OF ETHAN SCHUMAN

CHAPTER 14

Fool Me Twice

January 13, 2013

After we'd tried and failed to get anyone in Emily's orbit to hold her accountable by the summer of 2011, we'd loosely kept in touch with one another over the following year and a half—forwarding links to things that reminded us of the Ethan-Emily saga, or checking in to see how everyone was holding up and what new, more favorable life events we were each experiencing. The sting of E.S. never fully disappeared, and we remained suspicious of her movements, skeptical that she could truly reform overnight. But we all tried to get back to living and dating as usual.

By 2013, I was back on OkCupid. I received two messages from someone with a blank profile and the username Ethan212nyc:

"Hi"

I did not reply.

"Into wild parties? ;)"

I did not reply.

Yes, I was traumatized by the name Ethan, but that username and message just felt…off. It reeked of a very particular Ethan: Ethan Schuman.

January 16, 2013

The sports blog *Deadspin* published an article exposing a hoax involving Notre Dame football player Manti Te'o and his "girlfriend" who didn't exist. The story dominated headlines. I half expected to see Emily's name at the end of the story.

January 29, 2013

In the years after the Ethan-Emily drama, I started an anonymous blog where I occasionally posted stories about my life. It wasn't listed anywhere and I didn't promote it. Only a handful of close friends knew it existed and read it, mostly for a laugh. In late January 2013, I uploaded a draft of the account I'd written about my experience with Ethan Schuman nearly two years prior. While it mentioned Ethan's name, it did not reveal Emily's.

That same week, a girl named Rachel got "back together" with Ethan.

As with British Anna, Rachel's relationship with Ethan lasted more than two years. Her family was aware of Ethan, and when she told her sister, Samantha, about the renewed status of her relationship, Samantha was less than pleased. She hadn't met Ethan, and she didn't like the effect he was having on her sister's life. Samantha immediately regoogled Ethan's name (something she'd done multiple times over the years, to no avail), hoping that something new about the man who kept torturing her sister might pop up. This time, it did: my anonymous blog. She began reading my latest post—which had been up for less than a week—and knew immediately that it was the same Ethan Schuman. The details aligned so perfectly that she initially thought it was her sister's blog, only to realize it was written by another victim.

Samantha left an anonymous message on my anonymous blog:

"Please contact me. I think this 'guy' is back."

I received an email notification of the comment.

Chills rippled through my body. My stomach sank and my entire body clenched. *Noooo. It can't be. Is she still operating as Ethan? Or is this actually Emily and she is just trying to mess with me again?* Writing about that time for my blog felt therapeutic. But this felt traumatic. I realized I had some sort of PTSD related to all things Ethan-Emily. Given the strange Ethan212nyc messages I'd recently received, my suspicions were high.

Nonetheless, I replied to the email address associated with the comment immediately.

Subject: Ethan Schuman?

Did you leave a comment on my blog?

Samantha replied, but didn't yet offer her name, and the email address was just a collection of letters and numbers. She said she left the comment and was concerned about a "very close friend" of hers who was involved with Ethan.

I asked for her name and number and offered to help.

Her name was Samantha and she was a lawyer in California. She suggested multiple ways for me to verify her identity: the California bar website, her law firm website (which she lamented showed a "rather unflattering" photo of her), and her Facebook and LinkedIn profiles, as well as various links from her college years.

She understood why I was hesitant and also appreciated my discretion. "This is one of the most bizarre situations I have ever found myself in," she confided. She was hopeful I could offer insights and advice on how to help her sister—"or at the very least, confirm that I'm not crazy to think there was/is something weird going on."

The distrust, the self-doubt. Ethan's signature moves. My heart ached for her and her sister.

I was in shock. Ethan Schuman was back in my life. That ghost of a man had been resurrected—or rather, never really died. And once again, uncanny timing and serendipity outed him. The universe was not in Ethan's corner.

January 30, 2013

I emailed Gina and British Anna to update them on the latest developments. I knew they would not be happy to hear from me under these new circumstances.

Subject: Ethan Schuman—still alive...

Hi ladies,

I have some news: I think Slutsky is still at it.

I am slightly scared that she might get pissed if she knows I'm "outing" her (again). Do we think she might be dangerous? Cause if not, I think her name now needs to be made public.

Also, I'm sure you both heard the mistaken identity story surrounding the Notre Dame football player. If so, I'm sure it hit a little too close to home for you, too...

I forwarded the email from Samantha and informed Gina and Anna that I would be speaking to her, should they care to join.

Aside from the shock and horror we felt in knowing that Emily was still inflicting the same emotional pain and drama on other women, the stakes somehow felt higher this time. It felt clear to me she wasn't going to stop.

British Anna replied immediately. She had a similarly traumatized, visceral reaction when she read my email. Anna agreed that we needed to do whatever was necessary to stop Emily this time. Emily was about to graduate, so we'd need to contact her school—again—and it might be time to reach out to Tim. (Had she actually messaged him, or was that also fake?) British Anna wanted to join the call, but she didn't know how she would explain the 5:30 a.m. phone conversation to her boyfriend—whom she'd never told about Ethan Schuman. Anna confessed that she still couldn't hear the name Ethan without shivering.

Moments later, Gina replied. Same soul-sucking feeling for her, too. Ethan-Emily certainly did make an impact.

We hated that she still had the power to affect us so deeply. But we were also angry. Really, *really* angry. She'd gone to great lengths to sell her apologies and explanations, acting innocent, trying to position herself as a quiet, studious girl who did a bit of harmless pretending for a mere eight years but had gotten that all out of her system. Her promises to never do this to anyone again rang hollow. Everything she'd said felt like yet another Ethan Schuman–style manipulation. Had we been too easy on her? We were livid that another innocent woman was suffering.

The gloves were off this time. But Emily was smart, and we trusted her even less than we did two years earlier.

* * *

Gina and I spoke with Samantha on the phone for two hours. She feared Ethan was ruining her sister's life.

Ethan met Rachel—a thirty-two-year-old Ivy-educated Jewish New York lawyer—on OkCupid a couple of months prior to when we unraveled the Ethan Schuman mystery. Despite our appeals and threats, and despite Emily's promises to seek help and never do this to another woman again, she instead continued to court, confuse, lie to, and torture Rachel over the next two years. Rachel fell hard for Ethan, and her professional and mental well-being suffered greatly as a result of his persistent advances.

Ethan also had a "best friend," Paul, an Irish guy who was interested in dating a cousin of Rachel and Samantha. They emailed for a while, but like Ethan, Paul never materialized. The cousin was suspicious that it was Ethan emailing her.

Meanwhile, I deleted the blog post. I didn't want Emily to google Ethan's name for some reason and be tipped off before we spoke with Rachel. (Did Emily google her fake persona's name? I had no idea, but I wouldn't put it past her.)

Samantha was worried about how Rachel would take the news that Ethan was Emily. She worried Rachel might not believe her (Emily was *that* good). So she waited two weeks until she would be visiting New York and could tell her in person.

February 16, 2013

Samantha broke the news to Rachel and, thankfully, she believed all of it. It was devastating and humiliating, but she was grateful to finally know the truth. Rachel then confronted Emily (without mentioning our names). She denied nothing.

Rachel wanted to meet me, but she wasn't quite ready. She needed a day to process it all.

February 17, 2013

I met Rachel in Chelsea at La Maison du Macaron. She was sweet and timid, and she struck me as an intelligent, accomplished woman who was both mortified and heartbroken, mourning the boyfriend who never existed. Their relationship mimicked Ethan's relationship with British Anna in many ways: It was long-term, with family and friends aware of Ethan's existence. He'd broken plans that took time and resources to put together. He let her buy expensive gifts for him and other people in his life; she even custom-knit a baby sweater for his relative. Rachel found herself lying to many people in her life about details of her relationship with Ethan to keep them from thinking she was crazy. But she wasn't. Emily had just preyed on her vulnerabilities and sympathies the same way she did with us.

*   *   *

On March 4, 2011, the same day I reached out to Ethan to inform him the jig was up, he emailed Rachel to reschedule their Sunday date. It had been an "insane week," and he needed to fly to Ireland to tighten up all his "loose ends."

They'd been communicating incessantly for months already, and Rachel was over the moon about this promising new connection, so she was naturally extremely disappointed by the postponement of their date.

To ensure she'd stay hooked on him, despite the postponement, he simultaneously sent a separate, detailed, line-by-line reply to Rachel's responses to the get-to-know-you quiz he'd sent her. In one of the questions, she revealed she'd wanted to be a doctor as a child; Ethan said he, too, wanted to be a doctor, only to later realize that "studying medicine was mind-numbing." He also mentioned house swapping (a concept he first heard about from me). She closed by saying that he now knew more about her than most people.

In the days that followed, Ethan's communication dwindled and Rachel was hurt and confused. This wasn't just another guy she'd met online. This was *the* guy. Their connection was instant and extraordinary, and their communication had been extensive, even before meeting.

So, on March 21, 2011, Rachel reached out to ask what had happened. She knew she might not get a response, but she had to try. She just wanted to know where things went wrong.

"Dear person who may or may not be named Ethan Schuman," she started her email. She wasn't making a bid to get together, she just merely wanted an explanation. His last communication was "heya" via G-chat a couple of weeks earlier. She considered the various things that might have turned him off. "My photo essay? A new love interest in Ireland? A secret CIA mission?" Or, more seriously, she wondered if Ethan had just been screwing with her this whole time. But she wanted an explanation.

Ethan responded, but not to tell Rachel the truth and reveal himself as Emily, since we'd already outed her. Rather, he offered more lies and promises, which continued for nearly two years, until Samantha found my blog.

Rachel forwarded us some of their correspondence, including lengthy

G-chats that mimicked our own experiences with Ethan-Emily. The jealousy, the mentions of other women, the fights, the plausible excuses not to meet up. At one point, Rachel mentioned a friend of hers who was in medical school in Israel. She noted that foreign medical graduates often had a harder time matching for residencies in the United States. Ethan pushed back: "I knew some American I met who was studying in Ireland and they did fine." He suggested that he and Rachel should both quit their careers and go to medical school.

Like the rest of us, they fought about his masculinity—any questions around it tipped Ethan off into a mean-spirited tirade. But mostly, they fought about other women in his life. He mentioned his ex, British "Anne" (not Anna), revealing she'd practically put child sensors on his computers to monitor him. There was also another Anne (not Anna)—Anne Heaton, a singer, like his "main" Anne. British "Anne" was a psychologist and horse whisperer, and Rachel was jealous of her. The other Anne was just a one-night thing because "she was a lesbian." Ethan sent Rachel a YouTube video of the other Anne, along with a detailed biography. I surmised that after Emily was outed by using too many real names and biographical details about her victims, she started changing things up slightly in an effort to avoid a repeat of what happened when Gina, British Anna, and I teamed up. But, evidently, she loved the name Anna so much she could only bear to change one letter.

He also dangled the Navy ex in front of her repeatedly, copy and pasting her love letters to him into his chats with Rachel. In one conversation, Rachel broke down in tears, sobbing uncontrollably. "How can I keep fighting for you?" she asked, unable to justify her continued tolerance of his behavior, but equally devastated by the thought of losing him. She suggested they take a break for a few weeks to think. Ethan refused. "I'm losing faith. Are we really on the same page?" she asked, desperate for answers. "Yes," he said, assuring her she was his only relationship and the only woman he wanted.

Rachel had neck issues, and the stress of their relationship exacerbated them, eventually putting her in a state of chronic pain, which led to significant out-of-pocket medical expenses, not to mention time lost from work. Ethan acknowledged on several occasions that he was the source of not only her emotional pain but also her very real physical anguish. But Rachel wanted children and was ready to settle down. They talked about marriage and building a life together. They were already nearly two years into their "relationship," so, despite her concerns, she told herself Ethan was worth the trouble and hung in there just a little bit longer.

February 19, 2013

Not long after Rachel learned the truth, Emily deactivated her Facebook account, but not before Rachel took screenshots of her friends. She noted that Emily had been using the photos of one woman's children to support one of Ethan's plotlines.

Like Gina and British Anna, Rachel had a phone conversation with Emily after she confessed, in an effort to get some answers and closure. (*Seriously, where was my call?*) Like them, Rachel found Emily to be emotionally detached from the situation, but she reiterated an apology. Her calm, zen-like state remained intact, even when Rachel escalated to screaming and crying.

Ethan had mentioned a neurologist in his correspondence with Rachel, and when Rachel asked Emily about her, she confirmed she was another victim. At the time, Emily was in the process of "matching" for her medical residency program. Rachel jabbed at her by deriding her medical school, and Emily punched back by assuring her that multiple Ivies were courting her. She was hoping for New York, which angered Rachel. Both of them cautiously fished for information, but Rachel was careful to keep quiet. Emily told Rachel she was smart (a seeming attempt to butter her up), then later said her capacity for self-loathing was endless—a typical Ethan-like jab, particularly when contradicted with a compliment. Ethan's and Emily's personalities were eerily similar.

As Rachel pressed Emily for answers as to why she'd done this, Emily once again articulated that she was operating as Ethan to fight some deep personal loneliness, while also suggesting that Emily was in love with Ethan.

Desperate to make Emily understand the damage she'd done, Rachel described the horror and misery she experienced as a result of the perpetual fights Ethan initiated. Emily replied, "Well, I think I'd get along with him better than you do." Rachel had heard enough and hung up.

Emily referred to British Anna, Gina, and me as "the Baby-Sitters Club" (a categorization I took pride in, despite the amateurish implications; big fan of that series). She told Rachel that she was sure we were saying all sorts of horrible things about her and that Rachel should let her know what we were up to, as if they were allies. Emily also said that she was terrified of me—a recurring theme. I had no idea what I said or did to trigger it, but I had no problem playing Bad Babysitter in the charade that was the Slutsky Chronicles.

Whether we were the Baby-Sitters Club, Charlie's Angels, or an overly educated coven of Nancy Drews, we were angry and united. Emily played us the first time, but now we saw things clearer: We worried that she couldn't—or wouldn't—stop. Her pursuit of women online was an addiction, as she herself had articulated in her initial confession letter. When functioning in addiction, addicts are prone to lying, often quite convincingly, to cover their behavior. It seemed Emily was no exception.

And so, the psychologist, the sociologist, the architect, and the lawyer decided it was time to take more serious measures.

First up: finding more victims.

Rachel forwarded us an email that Ethan sent her on January 25, 2011. The subject was "Yet another site to get addicted to," and in it, he said, "Friend of mine is trying to get a movement started. Check it out," followed by a link to a website. But not just any website: MY website. It was the site I'd started to tell anonymous, funny, true stories from teaching—the same site Ethan obsessed over during our correspondence. He'd told me he shared it with some friends, and for once he hadn't lied. As Ethan, Emily forwarded it to six women, all openly CC'd. Rachel was one of them. But who were the others? Had she boldly CC'd several of her victims? No doubt another attempt to legitimize her web of lies with real, googleable people, as well as an attempt to make them jealous. And yet, perhaps like the other women CC'd on that email, Rachel remained silent, fearful she might look crazy or pathetic if she reached out to any of them—the same fear British Anna had once she learned about me. That was exactly what Emily had banked on. And it worked.

We noted and googled their names, verifying they were real, and started a spreadsheet of potential victims, adding several other names British Anna had accumulated over the years, bringing it to a total of twelve. We knew it likely wasn't a complete list, but it was a starting place. We wanted to reach out to the suspected victims, but we still needed to figure out how best to approach them. If they were as traumatized as we were, they might be sensitive to receiving our message out of the blue and be as distrusting of all things Ethan-related as we were. We wanted to handle it with care. I thought that something public, like a published article with Ethan's name in it, would be most convincing, so I started contemplating how to make that happen.

An article would also ensure that Ethan Schuman was forever googleable—and always linked to Emily. We wanted to cover all our bases. Two years earlier, we gave Emily the benefit of the doubt. British Anna, in particular, found it hard to be cold to her back then, but that kindness had now turned to rage upon learning she was still up to her old antics. We would not make that same mistake again.

We knew there must be more victims—how many, we weren't sure. If Ethan was in a "relationship" with Rachel, it was unlikely Ethan's profile was still online. So we had no idea just how many aliases she was using.

We assumed that moving forward, she would swap out Tim's photos and the name Ethan Schuman (and likely choose a name that did not have the same initials as her own). Maybe she'd also change our names, instead of giving real names to her other real victims.

Or maybe she'd continue to live on the edge and see how much longer she could get away with it all again.

* * *

British Anna upgraded to an iPhone 5 and was now able to send and receive free international iMessages to us. Technology was advancing rapidly, which I'm sure pleased Emily, who also upgraded her phone, as it allowed her to graduate from email and pester Rachel incessantly.

Admittedly, Rachel was finding it hard to resist replying. She, too, felt the same digital Stockholm syndrome that British Anna experienced, which was prolonged by Emily taking the same "we can be friends and allies" approach as she had with British Anna. She reiterated to Rachel that she was scared of what I would do now that Rachel was part of the equation and I knew the harassment continued for years. She knew I was the path through which Rachel's sister had learned the truth and that I likely wasn't pleased. (Oh, Emily, you know me so well.) Emily asked Rachel to keep her informed of my plans and offered to "sign a paper" saying she would not do this to anyone else. (No papers were ever signed.)

February 22, 2013

Emily texted Rachel: "Happy Friday!"

February 26, 2013

Emily emailed Rachel and British Anna from her personal email account to report back about the "immensely rewarding psychological session" she'd had with a professional. She assured them she was sorry and was actively reflecting on why she did this. Rachel was a regrettable relapse— one that lasted two years. She professed to have confided in a friend who would serve as her "sponsor," and of course, this would never, ever happen again. Since she wouldn't verify any of it, we had to take her at her word, which at this point was worthless to us.

(Ah, and there was the "Madame Curie" signature quote again. Good to see Emily still confident in her belief she was gifted for something that—at any cost—must be attained.)

She also offered to "help" her victims: "As always, please feel free to reach out to me for any answers or reassurances. I wish you only the best and I want to thank you for the amazing kindness and warmth you have shared with me." It was as if she regarded her elaborate charade as a fun, mutually agreed-upon game. It was over now, but she was happy to unpack and analyze it upon request.

British Anna was furious after reading the email. "Never again is she going to manipulate me, that's for sure." I breathed a sigh of relief. The spell had finally broken. Finally, her outrage toward Emily was stronger than the pull Emily once had over her. Anna was free.

Rachel felt numb. The letter was all about Emily and not at all about her or the other victims. She wanted Emily to put herself in our shoes, to truly understand what it was like to let your guard down, despite your many doubts. "I can't explain how much I gave of myself to Ethan. To know that what I got back was a game feels like such a violation," she reflected, wounded and still adjusting to a life without Ethan.

"It's one thing to be constantly disappointing someone in a one-sided way (like if I had been begging Ethan to meet my family, but he'd never mentioned me meeting his)," Rachel said. "But she was also constantly hurting me in situations completely of her own creation." That was the E.S. playbook: creating expectations and setting plans, accepting nothing less than full commitment about those expectations and plans, only to then strategically, purposefully, fail to deliver. Rinse and repeat.

Rachel envied the two years the rest of us had to get some distance from him. "I wish I'd pushed harder and gotten out sooner," she confessed regretfully. We sympathized and urged her to try to put any lingering shame to rest. She wasn't alone.

Emily's apologies and reassurances would almost be convincing if it hadn't played out exactly the same way two years prior. It felt like déjà vu. *Fool me once, shame on you. Fool me twice…* If she were truly sorry, why weren't Gina and I also CC'd? Was she only sorry for some of it? Maybe we "deserved" it? And what of the other victims? Would they get a similarly reassuring and conciliatory email?

Emily's message felt like the kind of stock response one receives from a large corporation after filing a customer service complaint: *We're sorry, we promise to do better, thanks for sticking with us.*

*   *   *

I remained steadfast in my belief that we needed to publish something to connect with past victims and hopefully stop Emily from doing this in the future. But Rachel continued to struggle in the immediate aftermath of her discovery that there was no Ethan, posing a problem: So many of her friends and colleagues knew about him that the painful personal loss was coupled with social humiliation, should they find out he never existed. And since everyone in Rachel's life knew the name Ethan Schuman, she asked us to wait awhile before we went public and published anything that included his name.

April 19, 2013

I received another message from OkCupid user Ethan212nyc.
   "Have a few mins to talk?"
   I did not reply.

CHAPTER 15

Aftershocks

October 2014

Despite Emily's best attempts to keep her all to herself, British Anna got married! It was the guy she'd met just as I reached out to her. Learning the truth about Ethan allowed her to open her heart again and reconnect with herself and real men. I was thrilled.

November 4, 2014

Nearly two years after Rachel learned the truth about Ethan, I published an article in the *New York Observer*, telling an abbreviated version of our story. (It took much longer than we'd hoped to publish it, because the *Atlantic* backed out at the last minute when they couldn't get a statement on the record from Emily—but it did seem fitting that it eventually landed at the *Observer*, which was owned by Jared Kushner, who hailed from the same town in New Jersey as Emily.) That article ensured that whenever anyone googled the names "Ethan Schuman" or "Emily Slutsky," they would learn the truth. It was her digital Scarlet Letter, and all the degrees in the world weren't going to cover it up.

The day that it ran, we sent all of the suspected victims an email with the subject, "Ethan Schuman is Emily Slutsky," along with a link to the article:

If you're receiving this email, it's because I believe you know "Ethan Schuman" and were one of Emily's victims—and therefore would be interested in hearing the truth about that person's real identity.

After reading the article, feel free to reach out to us with any questions.

Five of the women on our list came forward. I've changed all of their names to protect their identities:

Stephanie: Stephanie never offered much detail about her life, but she reached out to thank us for uncovering the truth. She was beyond grateful and felt validated in her hunch that Ethan was lying, but she never would have guessed he was a woman.

Naomi: Naomi met Ethan at the same time I did, and their correspondence lasted for around six weeks. (Which means Emily was communicating with Naomi, British Anna, Gina, and me incessantly and simultaneously.) At the time, Naomi was in her midthirties, had a busy career, and wanted a family. She forwarded some of their emails and lengthy G-chats. Ethan's bio was identical to the one presented to Gina and me.

In one of their first exchanges, Ethan requested more photos of her. Using them, he offered a detailed characterization of her, which she found impressive. "I have a feeling you would be a fantastic FBI profiler," she told him. Ethan replied, "Heard of the book, 'Reading People'? Well, I wrote it. Not really, but I could have." His "trick" was paying attention to facial cues, which he believed revealed a lot, and which he excelled at, despite her face still being two-dimensional.

They bonded over their mutual love of sharks and dogs, and Ethan explained how he taught his dog, Harvey, to win women's affection ("I think he learns from my tactics") and hide women's bras as a hobby.

His constant request for more photos made her self-conscious about being critiqued. Eventually, Ethan started picking fights, accusing her of not seeming flirtatious enough. Their courtship fizzled right around the time he met Gina.

Ava: Ava was the infamous "Navy ex," who communicated with Ethan for many years. (We knew it was at least six years and suspected it started even earlier.) Ethan pretended to have a heart attack as an excuse not to meet Ava at one point when he left her sitting somewhere waiting alone. Emily also emailed Ava as Ethan's sister, using a fake email address, to corroborate Ethan's lies. Ava reached out to us, expressing her gratitude for the email and for the article, and indicated that she wanted to speak with us on the phone. Unfortunately, we never heard back from her after that.

Kimberly: Forever stirring the pot, Ethan mentioned Kimberly in his correspondence with British Anna, insisting she was just a girl who had a crush on him. Emily even went so far as to have Ethan's sister mention Kimberly fondly in an email that Ethan forwarded to British Anna.

Kimberly was Emily's first victim that we were able to find, the one she'd met in an AOL chat room when Emily was only seventeen and Kimberly was twenty-one. When we emailed her, she had been communicating with Emily for nine years. Emily used a biography similar to the one we encountered, accompanied by the same photos of Tim, but there was one significant difference: Kimberly communicated with someone named Stryder Piore, not Ethan Schuman. We deduced that Stryder must've been one of the early names Emily tested out, back in her chat-room days, before settling on Ethan. (I have to hand it to Emily on this one. "Stryder Piore" was a pretty epic fake name, if we're judging aliases. I imagined he would be friends with someone like "Carlos Danger," the online alias of disgraced politician Anthony Weiner. Worth noting: Stryder also had a Facebook account, still active as of 2023.)

When Kimberly met Stryder, she was in a particularly vulnerable place: She had just been assaulted. Communicating virtually with Stryder felt safe, as it eliminated the risk of physical danger. Over time, she healed from that trauma and wanted desperately to meet Stryder, the man she'd grown so close to. On multiple occasions, he stood her up. She felt wildly embarrassed, as her friends all knew.

At times, months and even years would pass between messages. She blocked his email multiple times, but it never worked: Stryder would simply create a new email address to bypass her digital gates, manufacturing a new opportunity to convince her to allow him back into her life. While Stryder's initial email address was myownblackalbum@..., he also used stryder.piore, stryderpiore, stryderpiore.esq, stryderpiorejd—among others—all in a desperate attempt to lure Kimberly back in. As with all of us, their deep, emotional connection was strong, which made it easier for her to open herself to communicating with him once more during vulnerable moments.

She always knew something wasn't quite right about Stryder, but what was his endgame? Eventually, nine years in, she resigned herself to being casual friends (who also loved each other), and hoped that one day he might materialize. She assured us she was a professional, independent woman dedicated to making the world a better place. Her interactions with Stryder in no way reflected her real-life experiences.

Upon reading our article, her feelings of violation resurfaced. No, Stryder hadn't physically assaulted her, but she still felt abused. She was horrified knowing she'd shared intimate details with a woman and future doctor named Emily Slutsky.

The day before Kimberly received our email, she received yet another email from Stryder, wanting to chat about the election coverage. In their chat, he mentioned a dream he'd had where all his ex-girlfriends were mad at him. (I guess Gina isn't the only one with eerily accurate dreams.)

The next day, upon receiving my message, Kimberley emailed Stryder in a fit of rage: "Don't contact me again. Ever."

Sarah: Sarah was the doctor whom Ethan mentioned to Rachel—the same doctor he'd gone out with to get back at me after I went out with Speeddater. She was living in New York at the time, and she'd communicated with Ethan for a few months after a bad breakup, just prior to meeting her now husband. The timeline of their correspondence overlapped exactly with mine (which, again, if you're keeping track, means Emily was *very* busy during that time). Sarah is an Ivy-educated physician, and she was particularly appalled that Emily was also a doctor.

Everything aligned perfectly with our stories—the extensive communication, the canceled dates, the refusal to speak on the phone, the defensiveness and verbal abuse unleashed if she dared to question anything, the obsession with British Anna, the endless medical drama: His sister had severe hypoglycemia, his grandfather had late-stage Parkinson's, and Ethan's esophageal issues were landing him in the ER and tying up his schedule with GI specialists. As a doctor, she had great compassion for him over these issues. As always, Ethan substantiated all his claims with copious amounts of detail, and since he wasn't trying to scam her for money or sex, she assumed he must be telling the truth.

That Valentine's Day, Ethan stood her up and never replied to any of her messages that day. Several days later, she texted him, "What is going on? Are you ok?" Ethan replied with an angry email asking what took her so long to inquire. *What kind of person would wait that long?* Indeed, something horrible had happened: There was a plane crash, and one of his high-ranking professional associates in the Irish banking world was killed.

She was understandably dubious about the claim, so she googled the information: It was all true. A plane from Cork to Dublin had crashed, killing a prominent Irish banker.

By June 2011 (months after we'd outed and confronted Emily and she'd promised to stop), Ethan still had not materialized, but he became increasingly more psychologically manipulative. (Which aligned with all the other contemporaneous drama that was unfolding for Emily during that period.) She cut him off, but he continued to reach out to her for several more months. She finally ceased all contact in September 2011, when he claimed to move back to New York—but still refused to meet.

Sarah told us she now had the life she'd dreamed of, the life Ethan tried to convince her she would never have because she was "too messed up" and "didn't know how to have a real relationship."

Sarah insisted that we report Emily's behavior to the National Institutes of Health, where Emily was employed at the time. She intended to send her own letter to Emily's workplace via email, but became fearful that she might face some sort of blowback from Emily. So, she instead opted to physically mail an anonymous letter to Emily's department head in the Medical Informatics division of the NIH. Sarah worried that someone like Emily had access to the government's secure internet systems, and she shuddered to think about Emily eventually having patient contact, particularly with other women, and gaining access to their personal information. Like us, she held a strong conviction that future offenses must be stopped and that justice must be served for all existing victims, whether or not they came forward publicly.

*   *   *

Nine victims and counting. It was remarkable to see how impressive, articulate, professional, and kind all of her victims were. None of them were deserving of the type of psychological abuse and manipulation they endured. They were guilty of nothing but seeking love and companionship.

Nearly a year after the article ran, another victim, Abigail, reached out. (I assume she had googled "Ethan Schuman.") Ethan picked up Abigail on JDate in 2008, just as things were heating up with British Anna—Ethan mentioned her frequently to Abigail, and he also mentioned Abigail to British Anna. When Ethan and Abigail were scheduled to meet, Ethan disappeared, reemerging a few days later with a tale of spending days in the hospital with aspiration pneumonia after choking on some steak. She cut him off, but he returned months later and they occasionally corresponded.

All of that sounded incredibly familiar, including the fact that she was also a PhD. But when Ethan resurfaced and started messaging her on G-chat, Abigail and Ethan were no longer in courtship mode, as she'd recently started dating the man who would later become her husband.

Abigail and Ethan advised each other on their respective dating lives. She was pretty sure Ethan didn't exist, but she found the advice useful. The fact that it came from a man who wasn't real and had lied to her for months didn't seem to bother her too much.

That made one woman in ten who hadn't been traumatized and horrified by Ethan. Not a great percentage.

December 15, 2015

I received a Facebook message from a woman whose male best friend had recently met Emily—as Emily Slutsky, dating as herself—on JDate. At the time, they'd been on three dates. Her photo matched the photo in the article, so she was sure it was the same Emily Slutsky. She wanted to share this information with her friend before their next date. They'd seemed to hit it off, and she imagined he'd want to confront her personally about it.

Unfortunately, the message she sent went into my "filtered" messages on Facebook. So while she sent it in March 2015, I didn't see it until December. When I finally replied, I never heard back.

July 5, 2016

I received an anonymous message via my website from someone who knew Emily from her ObGyn residency at the University of Toledo in Toledo, Ohio, where she'd enrolled sometime in the previous two years after leaving the NIH. Emily was currently a resident, caring for women, managing patient care, and educating medical students. This person doubted that the school was aware of her offenses, and she was concerned about Emily's interactions with patients, given what she had done to all of us. She encouraged me to reach out to her school to notify them.

After consulting with British Anna and Gina, I decided to alert her program. Not knowing whom the appropriate point of contact might be, I reached out to two physicians there who I believed were the program directors. I shared the anonymous message I'd received, as well as the article. I informed them that my only goal was to forward the concerned message I'd received. I told them we knew of at least ten victims, one of whom she was still duping the day the article came out.

They never replied.

August 18, 2016

We became concerned that Emily would continue to troll us forever—sending anonymous messages, creating fake accounts, or any other number of things intended to always keep us suspicious and on guard—as revenge for blowing her cover. I'd also received those weird messages from Ethan212nyc a couple of years earlier. So when I received an email from a woman named Emily Slutsky, claiming to be a *different* Emily Slutsky, I was mildly suspicious.

She informed me that she'd read my article after googling herself and was horrified to read about this other Emily Slutsky. She hoped she would never be confused with her, but wanted to know more about the story: Was it a blog? A work of fiction?

British Anna and I discussed how to reply. Were we sure this was just another "Emily Slutsky" and not *the* Emily Slutsky? We opted for brevity: "It was not fiction—everything was very true, unfortunately!"

The Gmail address did not reveal a name, but rather some random letters that appeared to be some sort of abbreviation: nwindf. When I searched those letters, it led me to a user profile with the same collection of letters on the now-defunct dating site How About We. Two days later, a Twitter user named "Emily S.," whose user handle used the same collection of letters, started following me on Twitter. The profile was created in 2012, and as of 2023 they follow only sixteen people and have zero followers. There is no profile photo or bio.

Maybe it really was just another Emily Slutsky. But something felt...off. Again.

I blocked the account.

August 29, 2016

Salima, a medical student (now physician) who had recently worked with Emily, messaged me. She asked that I protect her identity, as she was applying for residency in the next month and didn't want any repercussions. But she was concerned: Emily was an ObGyn caring for vulnerable women. She wanted to know if Emily was still duping women online and if anything was being done about it. She knew many people who lied about their identity online were not prosecuted, but she felt that a physician should be held to a higher standard. She reasoned that physicians should conduct themselves outside of the hospital the same way they would inside it. And since deceiving a patient is considered unethical, and therefore grounds for losing your license, she believed this level of deception outside of the hospital should be considered a comparable offense.

She informed me that word of Emily's behavior had spread at the Ohio hospital, and several people approached her about the article. Even beyond the accusations in the article, Emily's behavior among her peers gave them pause: Emily told one of Salima's friends that she had a boyfriend in Ann Arbor, told another friend that she had a boyfriend named Ethan in New York, and told Salima directly that she had a boyfriend there in Ohio who waited for her to make him dinner when she got home.

Salima offered me her phone number and said she would keep me updated, but told me she could not risk personally getting involved at this stage in her career.

I told her I'd heard from another person affiliated with the program the previous month and reached out to the program directors, but never heard back.

There was nothing more I could do.

December 13, 2018

Laura's sister worked at Toledo Hospital and had just shared the article with her when she reached out to me. She informed me that many people at the hospital had read it. Emily was now treating female patients as an

ObGyn. "This is pure craziness. I am worried for these women and their babies!" she proclaimed.

*   *   *

While none of us had been in touch with Emily for years, I'd heard from Ethan212nyc and the "other" Emily Slutsky, but the message that grabbed my attention the most was from "Kyle." (It's worth noting that Gina and British Anna never received any such messages.)

Immediately after the article ran, the user handle "exstanforddude" created a Twitter account just to tweet a response to me. Kyle (which he acknowledged was a pseudonym) wanted to tell me about his own similar story. So I DM'd him my email address.

The minute he started reading my article, he told me, he knew how it would end—because he was part of a similar story.

Kyle began his email to me by expressing his sympathy to me and all of the victims. He knew people could be inclined to victim-blame and wonder why they didn't know better.

But Kyle knew better.

"What they fail to understand is that emotions are immensely complex," he explained. "And no matter our level of intelligence, we can always rationalize these emotions to fit into this box that holds all things we believe to be/can be true because we've performed an acceptable level of analysis. The box becomes bigger when an emotion such as hope becomes part of the equation, because we want so much for things to be true. We give ourselves some leeway when our analyses don't add up."

His convoluted philosophical diatribe reminded me a little too much of someone else's preferred communication style.

"That's not the reason why I'm writing you," he went on, regaining focus. "I'm the last person on Earth who will defend the actions of this lady, but that email she wrote you?" (He was referring to Emily's confessional email.) "It was an email to state that, 'hey, I'm not the Internet loser that you think I am.' And that would make you feel one of two things: a) less awful about the fact that you fell for a trap engineered by an MIT graduate, b) less awful about her, period. It didn't even sound like she was remotely sorry for her actions."

Thanks, Kyle. Now get to the point.

"I know all this because I was once an 'Ethan,'—only I was 'Kyle.'"

He told me his story was "eerily similar" to that of "the real Emily." He described himself as an educated, social, "normal," good person, despite what he was about to confess. He got a "highly sought-after" finance job and his life spiraled, so he looked for an escape.

"Instead of turning to drugs, or alcohol, or sex, or anything of that sort, I decided to assume an identity that was different from mine. I simply woke up on a gorgeous Saturday morning and created a profile on a social media platform, and put a picture of a relatively attractive guy from stock photos on the Internet. 'Kyle' would be my name, and he would be everything that I wish I was. It was almost an experiment."

Kyle went on to explain that a celebrity took notice of him and slid into his DMs. He assured me that if I knew the celebrity's name, my jaw would drop, because "you wouldn't think someone with her intelligence would fall for such an act."

The two communicated for two and a half years. He emphasized that— unlike Emily—those two and a half years were devastating for him. He truly cared about his victim and was fully invested. He was in love with her, addicted to her. She was his drug, and he needed her to get through the day.

Kyle once again pointed out how he was different from and better than Emily because, unlike her, he eventually voluntarily confessed to the celebrity. Just as Hurricane Irene (which he referred to as "Typhoon" Irene) was about to hit New York in 2011, he told her everything. He couldn't bear the thought of something happening to her without her knowing the truth. He told her over the phone, and she sobbed.

It took Kyle years of therapy to recover from the trauma he experienced from his own lies. But he was no Emily: He could never put himself through that again.

"I don't know. Maybe I'm just an Emily Lite," he said dramatically with what seemed like fake humility. He never meant to hurt anyone, he assured me. "And I hope, I HOPE, that sets me apart from her."

He wanted me to know that his relationship with the celebrity didn't end after his confession. How could it? They were kindred spirits. They connected intellectually and emotionally. She knew that he, too, lost something when the truth was revealed. They were *both* victims, both broken.

Eventually (mercifully), he brought his elaborate confessional to a close: "When I think of what I had done, almost innocently, on that gorgeous Saturday morning, I'm nearly brought to my knees," he lamented. The pain, the suffering—"How do you give back someone several years of their life?" ("... Forgetting is so long," he added, quoting Pablo Neruda.)

"I carry that burden with me every day, Anna, and maybe that—in itself—is justice."

Well. That was ... *something*. The long-winded writing style, the flair for the dramatic, the literary reference, the self-victimization, and the creepy way he unnecessarily inserted my name reminded me a little too much of someone else. Was it actually a woman? But something specific made me question whether this was Emily: He referred to the hurricane as a "typhoon." Was this person American? Was I being played—*again*?

And yet, I decided to play along. I had questions for Kyle.

Did he ever do this with anyone else? Does he "miss" Kyle? How had he filled that void? How did he manage to find excuses not to meet up with her for so long? Did he talk on the phone with her during that time? Was he still in touch with the woman?

He happily answered my questions:

- There had been another woman briefly, but duping multiple people as Kyle overwhelmed him.
- He suggested that perhaps the celebrity was his "British Anna." She was his One.
- His excuses not to get together centered mostly on needing more time to heal from a breakup. If she'd only be patient

with him, he would eventually be ready. Other excuses
involved travel, work, and, in what he described as his low
point, his sister died.

+   He changed his voice via GarageBand and got a New York
    number via Skype, which allowed them to speak on the phone
    frequently. She pressed him to video-chat, but he resisted, giv-
    ing in only once and then making it seem he had connection
    issues, which made her suspicious.

+   She wanted proof of all of his claims, so he Photoshopped
    his driver's license and created multiple people to support his
    claims—he became his own friend, coworker, and personal
    assistant. All of which sounded very familiar.

+   He was no longer in touch with the celebrity. He was from
    Toronto, and they met twice in New York and spent consid-
    erable time together. Then one day he woke up to find she
    was gone from his BlackBerry BBM chat, and she wouldn't
    answer his calls or emails. It destroyed him. And he knew he
    deserved it.

+   He sometimes missed Kyle—mostly because Kyle was every-
    thing he wanted to be. He wondered if the celebrity also
    missed the persona.

I wondered why a man would need to change his voice to speak to the
celebrity as Kyle, deepening my suspicion that Kyle, like Ethan, was actually a woman.

There was one way to find out: I suggested that we meet in person if
he found himself in New York, and he said he planned to be there over
Thanksgiving.

I shared this exchange with British Anna and Gina, and we all shivered
at the similarities in communication style and tactics. We were not fans of
Kyle.

Four days later, Kyle emailed me again. He would, in fact, be in New
York over Thanksgiving and would like to meet for coffee.

272   *Anna Akbari*

Anticipating my potential questions, he posed them to himself: What did he hope to gain from this? Reparations, along with stopping the victimization of other women. (How sharing his story with me would do that was beyond me.) He wanted other "Emilys" to seek help, "because life is and can be better when it's real." He came to this profound realization after his "ongoing journey to healing."

I told him I'd be happy to meet him, and we discussed specific dates and times, settling on Pop Pub on University Place on December 1 at 4 p.m. He was curious if our conversation would be informal or on the record for publication. I told him it was just an informal chat.

Several days later, he emailed me again: He'd reread my article and wanted to be sure I was ready to meet him. *Might this be too traumatizing for me?*

And then he said something weird (as if everything else had been perfectly normal): "I won't lie: part of me is thinking I should let bygones be bygones, but another (if not greater) part of me feels like you deserve some answers. It comes from a place of remorse, I suppose. But I'm not Emily, and while there may have been similarities in our patterns of behavior, there are also stark differences."

What a truly odd thing to say. *I deserve answers. He is remorseful. But he's definitely not Emily. Huh?*

"You know the phrase, 'speak the truth even if your voice shakes'?" he asked, reverting to linguistic drama. "I'm ready to do that—if it will do you good."

What the actual hell is he talking about?

"You've been through a lot, Anna."

UGH. My whole body cringed when he invoked my name like that.

The last thing he wanted to do was retraumatize me, so he suggested I reconsider whether I was ready to meet and let him know.

Anna, Gina, and I gave him a 75 percent chance of bailing. We also felt it was 100 percent Ethan.

I assured him I would not be traumatized and confirmed my desire to meet.

"I'll be there," he replied.

I'll believe it when I see it! I thought.

Much to no one's surprise, the day before we were set to meet, I received an email from Kyle: "I've changed my mind about this. I apologize."

I did not reply.

*   *   *

Six weeks later, in true Ethan fashion, Kyle resurfaced. He sent me a new email with the subject, "A Big Question."

He apologized for not meeting up and wondered if I could "help" him by answering a simple yes/no question: Did I ever miss Ethan? If I could just tell him that, he would not bother me again.

The verbosity. The writing rhythm. The attempts to seem familiar and unnaturally intimate. Using displays of vulnerability to draw me in. Periodic attempts at overly confident humor. We couldn't prove it, but we became convinced it was Emily—so I replied saying as much.

Even if it wasn't her, we were done with Kyle.

I replied to Kyle, BCC'ing British Anna and Gina: "Emily. Please. You're a sick, pathetic, crazy person. Get a hobby."

This pushed Kyle over the edge. He was *not* Emily, he insisted. But he needed to know if I missed Ethan, if it was as difficult for the person he hurt to forget about him as it was for him to forget about her. It was imperative that I tell him so he could move on. "You can answer with a yes or no," he reiterated.

When I didn't reply for thirty minutes, he wrote again: "You know what, forget about it. Your reply to 'Emily' says it all."

That was the last I heard from "Kyle."

CHAPTER 16

The Fake Ethan Schuman

July 27, 2014

While we'd confronted Emily, we never gained any clarity or resolution around the mystery man who posed as Ethan in the photos. Back in 2014, when I decided it was time to write an article that publicly linked Ethan and Emily, I knew I needed to contact Tim, the floppy-brown-haired, hazel-eyed, slightly scruffed man whose photos she'd been using. We'd been hesitant to do so in 2011, and again in 2013, unsure if the email Emily forwarded us actually went to him, or if she'd fooled us yet again. (She was a master at faking emails.) Reaching out to him made us nervous: If a group of women email you, telling you they all fell in love with your photograph due to elaborately crafted stories made up by a woman you went to high school with—you might need a minute to process.

Also, this was Ethan Schuman, a man we'd all corresponded with at great length. He knew *so* much about us, *too* much about us. And yet, Tim was not Ethan. We needed to loop this in our brains: *Tim is not Ethan; Ethan is not Tim.*

I started referring to Tim as "the fake Ethan Schuman" and entertained the idea of reaching out to the email address in the message that Emily forwarded us (we had no idea if it was real) with a message like, "Hi, you don't know me, but I had a fake online love affair with you a few years ago…"

But that seemed weird. So, instead, I wrote something only slightly more normal:

> You don't know me, or the two women CC'd on this email, but we are very familiar with your image. I'm curious if the email exchange below looks familiar to you and if that is, in fact, your response?
>
> If it does not look familiar, then you are probably extremely confused right now!

Thankfully, Tim replied (and not Emily), confirming that he did receive Emily's confession back in 2011, and that was his reply. He was sickened to learn she continued to use his image with Rachel. We'd assumed they were rather friendly in high school, but he said he barely knew her. They both wrote for the school paper, but he never had a conversation with her. He recalled that his friend had a class with her, and they joked about something she said in their sociology class: "Marriage is a futile institution." *Oh, how strongly Ethan Schuman would disagree with high school Emily!*

Their sophomore year of college, Emily friended him on Facebook. She wrote him private "fan" messages every time he shared an accomplishment, explaining how much she admired him, but that she was too shy to say it to his face. After Emily revealed to him that she'd been using his photos, he deleted his Facebook account and all the photos on his personal website, afraid she would still use them—which, of course, she did.

Tim wanted to avoid communicating directly with her, as he worried any interaction might provoke an unpleasant response. He did, however, want us to notify Emily's parents before our article ran, which we thought was a strange request. Nonetheless, we agreed to do it, but Tim preemptively reached out to them himself. Her father told Tim they knew these things were happening back in 2011, but that he was confident it then stopped. Rachel's experiences—and Emily's subsequent admission of guilt—begged to differ.

We sent him the photos and videos of him that she'd sent us, along with the colorful descriptions Emily used to contextualize some of the images.

He marveled at the sheer volume of photos she'd managed to obtain of him, many of which he did not even remember posting online. He corrected the lies attached to each photograph: Ethan's ex-wife was actually Tim's sister. Ethan's brother was Tim's best friend. Ethan's New York driver's license used a formal portrait of Tim. One of the girls in the photos was Tim's girlfriend—who was also named…Anna. *Because of course.*

In an attempt to make sense of what she'd done with his photos and this fake identity, he characterized her as "a DJ, sampling images from my life, but making them her own." Knowing that he unwittingly contributed to deceiving so many women was difficult for Tim to grapple with. In a moment of humility, as he reflected on the absurdity of it all, he said what many of us might feel upon learning our image was used to make people fall in love with someone: "It's hard to believe anyone would want to be me. It's just me, for Christ's sake."

November 5, 2014

When more victims resurfaced after the article was published, we had proof Emily was still using his image. Tim was beyond fed up by this point. He hired a lawyer and emailed Emily, demanding that she destroy all images she had of him and stop circulating them under the name Ethan or Stryder or any other alias. She replied, saying she would do so—but she'd said the same thing (in more elaborate prose) two and a half years earlier. So we were not hopeful.

Why was she so attached to Tim's photos all those years? None of us knew.

March 6, 2018

Several years later, Tim emailed me to see how I was doing, and I caught him up on everything.

"Nice to hear from you under non-psychotic circumstances :)," I replied. "It's hard to believe it's been 7 years since we first cracked the case of Ethan/ Emily."

We were both in LA, so he suggested we meet for dinner that Saturday.
He texted me to coordinate:

"Hey Anna, It's Ethan . . .

". . . I mean Tim."

Perfection.

We met in Venice at Baby Blues BBQ on Lincoln Boulevard at 8 p.m.
I asked him why he reached out after so many years (unlike Ethan, Tim
was not much for prolonged digital communication). But his response was
vague. He said it popped into his head and he went back and read everything. He was also recently out of a long relationship.

Between bites of brisket, it was hard not to stare at him. I'd studied his
photos in great detail during my virtual courtship with Ethan Schuman.
They were the only visual connection I had to the persona I came to care
for so deeply. I'd longed to hear his voice, to smell him, to watch the way his
face moved when he smiled and talked. Then, once I realized the images
and the person behind the words were two different people, the person in
the photographs transformed: Who was this mysterious man? I wanted to
scrutinize every curve and crevice of his body to compare, to finally see how
that now-infamous image looked when animated in 3D form. Many of the
photos Emily used were from when Tim was in his twenties, and he was
now in his thirties. His appearance naturally evolved over the years, but it
was still, unmistakably, Ethan Schuman.

I sensed he had equal curiosity about me—about all the women who
had fallen for the fake persona created around his real image. After all,
how flattering to know that an army of women had fallen—and fallen
HARD—for "him," or some version of him.

We're both creatives, and our circles and interests overlapped, so the
conversation flowed effortlessly. Tim was convinced the various sketchy
messages I'd received over the years were from Emily, though we couldn't
prove it. I feared neither of us would ever fully rid ourselves of her. What
was never articulated by either of us, however, was how strange it was to
meet each other in person, given our history.

By all accounts, Tim and I had a great IRL dinner. We had a certain bond;

we were both E.S. survivors, tethered together by the trauma inflicted by the utter strangeness of our shared circumstances. We'd emailed several times in 2014 and had a phone call back then, but it was all very perfunctory—two people taking care of unwanted business. And yet, when we met in person, we instantly felt incredibly familiar to each other. It was far more like a reunion than a first meeting.

As Tim and I sat there eating BBQ, laughing and sharing life stories, it felt, for lack of a better word, like a date. It was flirty and filled with the kind of nervous tension one has on a first date. But if it was a date, it was the weirdest one I've ever been on.

Though... *was* it a date? To experience what both of us went through at the hands of Emily, only, in Tim's case, to date the person who fell for a fictional version of him, or, in my case, to date the "real" version of a fictional love interest? *Could he ever live up to that facade, the desirability of Ethan?* It was like fan fiction come to life. Even if we were attracted to each other, I think mentally, emotionally, it was just too confusing.

Telling British Anna and Gina that I was meeting the fake Ethan Schuman also felt weird. We'd all "dated" the same "guy," but now I was the only one to meet him in the flesh. We couldn't separate the man behind the photos from the persona of Ethan.

It was pouring rain as we left Baby Blues, and Tim offered to give me a ride home. When we arrived at my apartment, we sat in his car chatting for an extended period of time. It felt—inappropriate? presumptuous? too soon?—to invite him in. So, instead, we just sat there, disparate threads of conversation interspersed with long pauses.

The pockets of silence suggested this was the point in the date(?) where words get in the way. And yet, the undefined nature of the evening exaggerated the stillness. Everything hung in the balance.

The forced heat from the car vents clashed with the cool rain pounding on the windshield. The windows steamed. My seat heater radiated on high, warming my body and flushing my cheeks. The air was as heavy as the unspoken expectations.

This was the meet-cute I'd imagined so many years ago with Ethan. The easy conversation, the sexual tension, the lingering goodbye that promised to lead to another hello sometime soon. It was seven years in the making, preceded by thousands of words exchanged over hundreds of hours. Ethan knew my deepest fears and my strongest desires. He knew how to make me laugh and hurt me with equal precision. He knew the life I envisioned, made more complete with him in it.

But this man, this Ethan Schuman look-alike, knew none of this. He was just a guy with whom I'd exchanged a few rather sober emails and shared one enjoyable meal. He was Tim, a man whose life looked nothing like the fictional adventures projected on him by Emily, a woman he barely knew.

I don't know how long we sat in that car. Maybe it was minutes, but it felt like hours. I eventually leaned over to embrace him and tell him good-bye. I dreaded that awkward moment of every first date, where both people wonder if their bodies and intentions will mutually align. A hug? A kiss on the cheek? Something more amorous on the lips? Brief or lingering? It's brutal under more ordinary circumstances, but this was not ordinary. It was extraordinary. This was *Ethan Schuman.*

Only, it wasn't.

I inhaled his scent as we hugged, and I ran from the car to my door. The rain soaked me as I sprinted those twenty feet. I closed the door, dropped my bag, and collapsed on my couch, water dripping down my face.

"*What* was *that?*" I asked myself, stunned. I sat there in stillness, just staring into space, unable to move or make sense of the previous few hours.

What happens when real life becomes fiction, only to eventually manifest into some same-but-different reality years later? I had just experienced it, and it was a real mind fuck.

The next day, Tim texted me the name of a friend he thought might be professionally relevant for me. I thanked him. "So nice to meet you in person," I typed, knowing the layered complexity of those innocuous words.

And that was it.

Tim and I never spoke or saw each other again. We didn't need to. That relationship was complete. It ended before it could ever begin.

PART 5:

AFTERWORD

I'm a sociologist, which means examining human behavior is my occupational obsession. I taught university courses for six years before I broke out of academia and committed to applying sociology in the public sphere. Everything I do—from academic research to corporate consulting to dating—I approach through a sociological lens.

Sociologists engage in what is called "participant observation," a type of fieldwork in which we immerse ourselves in the lives and realities of our subjects. Participant observation is something I grew up doing, unofficially. As a precocious half-Persian child who grew up in poverty with an Irish Catholic single mother in an industrial Midwestern town, I always looked and acted differently and never felt at home. The examination of "the other" and the study of how to fit in was my survival mechanism. My mom said the nurses called me "Bright Eyes" in the hospital after I was born because, unlike the other babies, I never slept and preferred to watch everything 24/7. I guess you can say I've been in the business of looking at and studying people from birth. Subconsciously, I think I knew that skill was my ticket out of my immediate surroundings: If I could understand the game and its players, I could be a contender.

While psychologists dive into the *why*, sociologists focus on the *how* of human behavior. *What is the formula for "success" in a particular context? Which words, actions, and nonverbal visual cues will tip the outcome in an exchange? What are the official and unofficial rules of engagement? What are the societal consequences?* In any given moment, we respond to an infinite number of these signifiers—a phrase, a specific hairstyle, a subtle gesture—all of which inform the endless string of decisions we make every day, from whom to approach for instructions, to whom to hire, to whose profile earns a swipe right.

My academic research and the courses I taught at NYU focused on identity and how we construct and perform it. Specifically, the relativity of it: The ways in which we manipulate our self-presentation affect how we're perceived and inform our subsequent claim to power in social contexts. This manipulation happens in both real-world and virtual spaces, though the degree to which we can stretch those manipulations extends even further in virtual worlds. In other words, changing your "appearance" can change your reality.

The thesis of my doctoral dissertation zeroed in on one particular aspect of identity: "aspirational identity." I argued that we are no longer locked in the circumstances and biographies into which we are born. Instead, we are given a chance to dream beyond those limiting realities. What you are born into and what you become can largely diverge. Perception, particularly in the age of technology, is the marker of reality. A prospect that is as liberating as it is terrifying.

But what are the ethical boundaries of those aspirational dreams, particularly on digital platforms?

Meeting Ethan-Emily was like encountering a real-world case of this thesis—one that challenged the possibilities of identity hacking in ways I could not have imagined or designed. In this person whose real and fictional identities commingle so fluidly, it's difficult to know where Emily ends and Ethan begins. There is no distinction. They are E.S.

The best liars hide their lies in truths. Ethan and Emily are both Ivy educated and from New Jersey, the children of Russian Jewish immigrants, and Emily used the real names and biographical details of her other female victims, as well as her mother's name, to substantiate stories and associations for Ethan's fictional reality. Thus, Ethan was very real and completely manufactured, all at once. His projected identity was that combination of biography and aspirations, facilitated largely by technology, that I wrote and taught about. Only E.S. represented the dark side of that theory. A sort of lab experiment gone terribly wrong.

In a world of millions of virtual connections and increasingly fewer real-world interactions, we will go to great lengths to form connections, find happiness, establish trust, and bond deeply. Often, that demands presenting different aspects of our identities. Who I am with you may be slightly (or significantly) different from who I am with another. Is one false? When does it cross a line?

The internet provided Emily with an endless collection of would-be victims and new challenges for deceit—but perhaps most of all, it offered new outlets for reinvention, for creative storytelling. We all aim to create and project our preferred version of ourselves online. Is anyone ever fully honest in how they portray themselves? Where do we draw the line? What qualifies as "authentic" in a mediated world? And when does it become evil?

Manufactured identities—be it on Instagram or a dating site—work. We not only believe them, we reward them—as long as that person never has to materialize.

Emily was already a decade into this serial deception when we cracked the case and identified ten victims—and those were only the ones we could find via the virtual Easter eggs she left in our collective correspondence. I have no idea what the total number of victims might be. I would not be surprised if there are those who would never come forward because of the stigma, the embarrassment.

Emily wasn't some guy scamming for sex or money. She was a woman studying to be a medical professional. We were all duped by an atypical predator, for an atypical outcome. Without our permission, our lives were made into a work of fiction. We were cast in a role for which we never auditioned.

Nothing about Ethan's elite collection of victims screamed "easy mark." We were the "women who knew better." And yet, Ethan Schuman, animated by now-Dr. Emily Slutsky, knew how to play the persuasion game and win. There is no Ethan Schuman. But real or fake, E.S. is no amateur. Like so many others before and after us, E.S. conned us.

*   *   *

As of early 2023, Emily's biography on X (formerly Twitter) read, "Physician who believes in making common decency infinitely more common."

But can we divide our lives in two? Can we be an ethical physician while also having a history of deceiving innocent people online? Does the latter cancel out the former? Are our online actions divorced from our real lives?

Dr. Emily Slutsky is a highly educated overachiever. According to her own websites and LinkedIn profile, from 2003 to 2007 she attended MIT, where she received a degree in nuclear engineering with a minor in biomedical engineering and published a thesis called "Modeling of $[^{18}F]$-FHBG in Tumor and Normal Tissues."[1] From 2007 to 2009, she attended Columbia University, graduating with an MS in applied physics, during which time she was also a clinical research associate at the Cardiovascular Research Foundation. From 2009 to 2013, she attended medical school in Ireland at University College Cork, and upon her return to New York, she completed her clinical informatics postgraduate training at Cornell Weill Medical College's Center for Health Informatics and Policy in 2014. She also worked as a clinical research fellow at the National Institutes of Health (NIH) during that time. From 2014 to 2019, she did an ObGyn residency at the University of Toledo Medical Center in Toledo, Ohio, where she was the academic chief resident. From 2019 to 2021, she did a fellowship in clinical genetics at the Medical College of Wisconsin, while also completing a postgraduate degree in genetics at Stanford University School of Medicine. As of 2023, she is the director of women's health and medical genetics at a major health facility.

She's published multiple scholarly papers, including "Home Birth: The Case Against,"[2] "Atrial Fibrillation as a Rare Complication of the Use of

---

1   http://dspace.mit.edu/handle/1721.1/41693.
2   https://www.obstetrics-gynaecology-journal.com/article/S1751-7214(11)00187-4/fulltext.

Nifedipine as a Tocolytic Agent: A Case Report and Review of the Literature,"[3] and "The Rising Triad of Cesarean Scar Pregnancy, Placenta Percreta, and Uterine Rupture: A Case Report and Comprehensive Review of the Literature."[4]

A list of credentials like that is rare. It's even rarer to learn that an academic superstar and practicing physician has also led a double life as a cyberharasser.

Like Ethan, Emily's biggest alibi is her continued achievement. Ethan isn't some wannabe influencer fuckboy; he's a Serious Adult with a Serious Adult job and all its accoutrements. Equally, Emily's degrees and accomplishments shield her from suspicion and, it seems, from facing any real consequences for her actions. She couldn't really have done those things, right? It couldn't be that bad.

*   *   *

In the immediate wake of learning that Ethan was Emily, a part of British Anna was comforted by the idea of speaking with Emily. She was repulsed by her, eager to hold Emily accountable for all she'd done, and like all of us, she wanted answers. But she also had to grapple with the reality that Ethan, this extraordinarily-flawed-yet-irresistible man who had occupied so much of her life the previous years, simply did not exist. Or rather, at least not in the form he'd presented. Intellectually, she understood Ethan was fake. But the emotional reality was only beginning to settle in. It left a void. Learning the truth about E.S. was like experiencing the death of someone with whom you have a very complicated relationship. Yes, there is some relief, but you continue to wrestle with the complexities of those emotions long after the funeral.

And then there's the added twist: Not only did Ethan never exist, but all those emotions and intimacies were shared not with a man, but with a *woman who was becoming a doctor.* It's not easy to reconcile all of that. These

---

3   https://pubmed.ncbi.nlm.nih.gov/29862104/.
4   https://pubmed.ncbi.nlm.nih.gov/29984018/.

weren't simple flirtations or the casual exchange of information. These were extensive encounters that spanned everything from a discussion of past traumas to personal sexual details. We fully shared our lives with E.S. The reason these manipulations stung quite so much is because they were done with the level of trust one encounters in romantic relationships.

Emily knew this and exploited it. She didn't trick us into taking our clothes off, but she did take advantage of us. None of us consented to these experiences with Emily. Lying to create intimacy is a violation, whether it's virtual or embodied. For Emily's victims who also experienced physical assault or psychological abuse in past relationships, her actions retraumatized them.

Emily's actions provoke many larger questions:

Where is consent in all of this?

What does it mean to be violated in a digital world? Is physical touch necessary?

What does it mean to steal from someone? Must it include money? What of trust and time?

These are not easy questions to answer, and they're worthy of debate that extends beyond the pages of this book.

Using medical excuses to create empathy and connection is equally detestable. I have been confronted with and survived life-threatening ovarian cancer twice since my encounters with E.S. Those were some of the darkest, worst moments of my life. Gina also survived breast cancer, and each of us has been pained from watching loved ones suffer from serious illness. For an aspiring doctor to trivialize these conditions by faking them in an effort to buy more time or to dramatize the plot—or whatever her motivations—is unconscionable.

Emotional blackmail without financial or physical sexual gain is animated by a special sort of insidiousness. While Emily's actions didn't empty bank accounts or inflict visible scars, she trampled hearts and emotionally and psychologically terrorized. Her self-defense, when we questioned her later, was that we all just could've walked away at any moment. But anyone who's ever been in an abusive relationship knows it is almost never that simple. And when the abuser goes to great lengths to ensure you *can't* virtually leave, that option becomes nearly impossible.

But Emily was right about one thing: The solution to ending the pain and torture was to walk away. *She* had the power to walk. If she had been truly sorry for her actions at any point over the years, she could've simply made Ethan disappear. She didn't even have to come clean and tell all of us the truth. Once she realized this little charade she'd created in high school was having serious effects on the health and well-being of kind, trusting, well-intentioned women, she could've stopped. With a single click, Ethan would never pursue another woman again. Sure, we might all wonder: *What happened to Ethan Schuman?* But that would have been a more honorable end for a man who never existed.

This wasn't an isolated incident or a crime of passion. It was a calculated, slow-burning game. E.S.'s pattern was consistent across all of the victims. There was a signature style, a strategy, a playbook. Even the victim selection felt deliberate. Our lives resembled one another's, because they resembled Emily's to some degree. As with many perpetrators, Emily's prey fit a type. Every master predator knows their victims' weak spots, and who better understands the profound need for emotional connection than another professional woman? Emily brokered in connection—or the illusion of it. She embraced language as her weapon of choice, persuading and emotionally manipulating women with attention, affection, and the promise of love and companionship because the thing many women, especially high-achieving women, lack most in this digital age—far more than access to money or sex—is meaningful romantic companionship. Regardless of how she self-presented, Emily *was* her victims. "We're very much alike," Emily told British Anna. Emily was in sync with her victims in a way few traditional con men ever are. Getting inside our heads wasn't a challenge; she already lived there.

For victims like Gina, this wasn't the first time she'd encountered egregious duplicity. When Gina broke up with Matthew, she sent out an email to people in her life, informing them that this person they'd gotten to know through her simply was not a good person; they should be cautious of his lies. She wasn't concerned about victim blaming or being called dumb or gullible. She knew he was a master manipulator, and her money was on him succeeding again. She felt the same about Emily.

While I did initially wonder how this could happen to me—what I'd missed, where I went wrong—I ultimately look back on this horrible betrayal not as a cautionary tale but as an instructive one. Healing, for me, was not about avoiding online relationships or exercising greater suspicion in new encounters. Instead, I vowed to live my life with equal openness and trust as I did with E.S., repairing the damage by creating new proof points that the rewards of calculated vulnerability with strangers are worth the risk. Emily's actions might have left me doubting myself and feeling angry, but I refuse to allow her to dampen the enthusiasm I bring to my relationships, even when they form in unconventional circumstances.

*   *   *

We are drawn to these stories like moths to a flame—not so much due to schadenfreude (though that certainly plays a role), but because, if we're honest with ourselves, we know we might be one swipe or one wrong click away from it happening to us.

The stories of scammers we hear about most frequently make it difficult to remember that life is not brokered in cash and sex alone. Emotion, intimacy, trust, *connection* are the real glue of any healthy, functioning society. And yet, when money and sex are *not* on the table, it becomes difficult to understand or fault someone's actions and motivations—and even more difficult to measure the damages.

To date, the law is still catching up on how to handle people who engage in nonfinancially motivated virtual offenses. There is a lot of gray area around what is and isn't legal online. When it comes to damage done, emotional distress rises to the top. But regardless of legality, shouldn't we hold our physicians to an even higher standard?

You may wonder if Emily persists in these deceptions, perhaps under a different name, with different stolen photos. I can't answer that. As this book was going to print, Emily's lawyer sent a letter stating that the events were in the past and that the publication of this book would "carry a very real human cost." (Apparently she thinks that her human cost matters, not ours.) I currently have no way to know or prove if her actions are in the past. I know that she told us she'd stopped when we outed her in March 2011, but she didn't. Two years later, she said she stopped after we discovered Rachel, but she didn't. She was still using Tim's photos and still communicating with at least one victim using an alias when my article came out in November 2014. She then said—again—she would stop. Nothing new has come to my attention since then, but I don't trust her.

What did she want? What was the goal?

By her own admission, Emily wanted to escape her life, and Ethan was her vehicle for actualizing that fantasy. She was writer, actor, director, producer, and audience member in this cyber-psycho thriller. We still don't know if she derived any erotic pleasure from her encounters with us. But it certainly seemed she couldn't get enough of it. To feel desirable is an addictive drug. And women like us became her endless supplier. So perhaps Emily's ultimate motivation is not dissimilar to what those other con artists want, the thing that motivates them even beyond the financial gain: Power. Influence. And the exhilarating thrill of getting away with it.

The promise of the modern, technologically mediated age is the chance at an alternative existence. The internet feeds on the art of reinvention—the ability to write and rewrite our stories in a way that feels more like us or better serves our goals. Aren't we all just cashing in on that promise? Does the person who creates the best illusion win? When life is a long parade of smoke and mirrors, how do you differentiate between scamming and enviable success?

Emily used this virtual superpower as justification for her acts:

"I found my subconscious pulling me toward creating a new reality on the Internet," she explained. "These were two disparate worlds that I in no way wanted to intertwine...I needed something entirely different." That "something different" manifested in the form of radical self-reinvention, an

American value we revere and that the internet promotes—only this time, it happened at the expense of other women...just like her.

Committing crimes and deceptions in broad daylight is sometimes the most stealthy approach. *Who would have the audacity? There must be an explanation.* The art of the con thrives in a posttruth world where illusions are reality and deceptions are rewarded at every turn. Emily casually dismisses her actions as a combination of creative expression and personal catharsis. Artists regularly push boundaries and challenge the status quo with their creations, and technology democratizes many aspects of reality—leveling the playing field by privileging imagination over pedigree.

So is Emily merely the Banksy of the online dating world? A creative genius who purposefully obfuscates her identity to avoid negative repercussions, giving a virtual finger to societal norms? Or is she someone darker and more sinister who—to date—has cleverly evaded being brought to justice for the damage she caused?

That's for you to judge.

ACKNOWLEDGMENTS

This book was a long time in the making.

I'm so incredibly grateful to my agent, Liz Parker, and everyone at Verve, for their enthusiasm and for believing this was the moment to tell this story.

I'm indebted to my meticulous editor, Suzanne O'Neill, for working tirelessly with me to sharpen the text, as well as Jen McArdle and everyone at Grand Central / Hachette. Thank you for your confidence in me and this project—and for being such a joy to work with.

I spoke about Ethan, and later this project, to numerous friends over the years. Some provided expert counsel, some helped me connect the dots, and others served as sounding boards as I tried to make sense of it all. Thanks to each of you for lending an ear and sharing your insights.

This book would not have been possible without "the other women," my brilliant co-sleuths, Anna and Gina. I love our weird, wonderful, forever bond. Your friendship has been a gift, and our extended correspondence and digital chats perpetually delight me. Thank you for allowing me to share your stories. I love you both.

To all of the other victims who came forward and any who have not: I hope this book contributes to your healing, provides clarity, and helps to close that chapter of your lives.

ABOUT THE AUTHOR

Anna Akbari, PhD, is a sociologist and the author of multiple books, including collaborations with more than a dozen authors and public figures. She is a former professor at New York University and Parsons School of Design. She speaks internationally, makes regular media appearances, and has written for or been featured by many top media outlets, including the *New York Times*, CNN, *Forbes*, the *Atlantic, Time*, the *Financial Times*, TED, Bulletproof Executive, *Psychology Today*, Google Talks, SiriusXM, and many more. She is the creator of the Substack "The Sociology of... Everything." Learn more at annaakbari.com; follow her on Instagram / Threads: @annaakbari.